Voice of Protest

VOICE OF PROTEST

*A History of Civil Unrest
in Great Britain*

Harold Priestley

LESLIE FREWIN : LONDON

First Published in 1968
by Leslie Frewin Publishers Limited
15 Hay's Mews, Berkeley Square, London W1

This book is set in Plantin
Printed by Anchor Press
and Bound by William Brendon
both of Tiptree, Essex

09 089110 4

Contents

Author's Preface

ON 30TH OCTOBER 1967, five hundred villagers of Redbourn in Hertfordshire walked backwards and forwards over the two zebra crossings in the High Street, while traffic piled up for miles on both sides of the village. The centre of Redbourn, on the main A5 road, is in a dip, down one slope of which cars and lorries, to get up the opposite slope, often exceed the speed limit to the peril of pedestrians, especially children. The by-pass which had been planned was not likely to be constructed for some time, and the villagers wanted a controlled crossing with lights that could be worked from the kerb.

This, in its simplest form, is what this book is about. Here we have a body of people, made conscious of some disturbing factor in the conditions under which they live, moved by a sense of frustration to do something about it. Reaction may take a number of different forms. It may consist in the voicing or publishing of objections and it is sometimes accompanied by more direct actions such as throwing impediments into the normal functioning of society, principally to make authority and the public conscious of the protest. Most often it leads to the formation of *ad hoc* groups which remain in existence as long as the grievances complained of persist; or the for-mation of permanent associations which hold a watching brief over certain sectors of public life, reserving to themselves the right to protest as soon as their interests are threatened.

Associations capable of exerting pressure on authority are a common feature of modern life, and have their origin in pro-test. They have been defined as pressure groups, having specific purposes and seeking to influence government policy. In one or two instances these have grown strong enough not only to influence, but to attempt to control governmental policy, and have thus become political parties.

The line between one and the other is not always easy to draw. In the story of the complex relationship between monarchs and people between 1580 and 1630, for instance, it is easy to see that the actions of Peter Wentworth and John Hampden were those of protest, whereas those of Pym were political action. In time the parliamentary leaders succeeded in their aim of controlling governmental policy and were faced by new protestors out of their own party, such as the Levellers, who sought in turn to influence them. A rough line is drawn in this book where protest ceases and political action takes over.

Occasionally protest has taken a more active, even a violent, form. In modern times techniques have been evolved by which individuals and organisations may apply measures of direct action varying, for instance, from sitting down in a crowded thoroughfare to the planting of infernal machines. By such methods it is possible to keep governments and communities on edge for long periods, either until the desired end is gained or until the movement dies for lack of further support. Up to 1685 protest occasionally flared up in revolt. While dealing with the circumstances causing such revolts, it is beyond the scope of this work to deal with the revolts themselves. Little is therefore said about the events of the Peasants' Revolt of 1381, that of Jack Cade in 1450, the Pilgrimage of Grace or of Ket's rebellion, though the causes, or the 'occasions' of protest, are dealt with.

From the fifteenth to the eighteenth centuries religious troubles had much to do with political and economic unrest. The agrarian and political disturbances of Henry VIII's reign cannot be separated from the English Reformation, nor can Elizabethan England be studied without mentioning the Catholic recusants, while in the mid-seventeenth century religious differences were so closely interwoven with politics as to be one of the causes of the Civil War. Indeed, many of the political conceptions of the nineteenth century and the pacifist theories of the twentieth originate in the ideas put forward by the dissenting preachers of the seventeenth.

'Human society is never completely static. Every society contains within itself the seeds of its own decay; it is always dissolving and re-forming in an infinite sequence; sometimes the process of change is so gradual that it creates a delusive appearance of absolute immobility; at other times it is enormously accelerated by catastrophic influences which sweep over mankind with the force of a tornado.'[1]

Civil protest is one of the factors causing this kind of change. It has been present since the days when the people, or certain groups of people, first became conscious of their disabilities and discovered ways of ventilating their grievances. For this reason, although this book is not a history of the freedom of thought and expression, these features play a great part in it, especially before the nineteenth century and in the twentieth.

No book of this length could deal with all the protest movements in Great Britain, and the problem in writing it has been mainly one of choice and stress. For this reason, emphasis has been laid on (a) those which were most fertile in the contribution of political ideas and (b) those which best illustrate the progress of organisation and the appearance of new and more ingenious methods of pressure.

Under the first heading, much has been said about the party of Common Weal in the sixteenth century, the ideas of the Levellers and the Wilkes period; under the second, the Yorkshire Association (Christopher Wyvill), the Ten Hours Movement (Richard Oastler), the Anti-Corn Law League (Richard Cobden), a model of efficient organisation, Women's Suffrage (the Pankhursts) and the various groups which advocated nuclear disarmament, all of which practised and perfected new and striking methods of protest. The story of Chartism and that of the Trade Union and Co-operative Movements begin

[1] *The Growth of English Society*, E Lipson, A & C Black, 1949.

9

in protest and later figure in English history as political movements. They have been dealt with in great detail in other works, and only their earliest stages have come within the scope of this volume.

Since the book is entitled *Voice of Protest*, the leading figures have been allowed to speak for themselves. Quotations, especially short quotations, are exceedingly risky and can, if not well chosen and taken too far out of their text, misrepresent the points of view of their originators. Every effort has been made to avoid this. Many have been taken from the original works.

Finally, I should like to put on record my thanks to Mr Frank Sainsbury, Deputy Librarian of the London Borough of Newham, for his help and interest, and to my wife for her valuable assistance at every stage in the preparation of this work.

H P

I

The Silent Commons

AT THE TIME of William the Conqueror, most of the inhabitants of England were unfree. The Domesday Book lists them as villeins, bordars, cottars, serfs, and by many other names. Their living was on the land which they held of their lords, paying dues and services in return for their holdings.

They were bondsmen, but their forefathers, the Teuton nomadic farmers and the Anglo-Saxon villagers, had enjoyed a far greater degree of freedom. The primitive communities of the Saxons, the 'ings', 'leys', 'hams', 'tons' and 'steads' were small, made up of tiny knots of people in the expanse of forest, heath and parkland that was then England. Every man was a warrior, and as such had the right to have his say in the village meeting. Arable land was common property and was in most cases redistributed from year to year, each villager getting his share of strips in the open fields. Matters of general interest were talked out in the open, and decisions were reached amid acclamation and the clashing of sword on shield, the party stronger in numbers generally overruling the weaker and thus establishing majority rule. The Anglo-Saxon fathers were thus by tradition and usage accustomed to, and even fond of, controversy, and had no fear of speaking their minds.

Between the ninth and eleventh centuries, however, this tradition of freedom was broken. The English peoples, at first crystallised into seven kingdoms, for the most part at war with each other for supremacy, had to face the Danish invasions. These brought about a great change in the pattern of English society. The old free village was no more, for its people needed protection from the invader. Men of power arose among the native populace and to these the smaller ones commended themselves, joining their bands and following them in war. Meanwhile England, previously the battleground of the seven kingdoms, achieved a more permanent unity under Wessex.

But while the country was welded into one political unit through the energies of such leaders as Alfred and Athelstan, it was at the same time divided into at least two social classes, the military aristocracy, including the leaders and king's thegns on the one hand, and on the other the humbler countrymen, tillers of the soil in peace time and soldiers in the 'fyrd' or national army in war.

The relationship between these two classes came in time to be both personal and political. In return for the protection of the leader, the followers took their share in cultivating his land for him, and in providing him with food out of their own stock at certain times of the year. From this time he was non-producing and was kept out of the surplus raised by his dependents. With power came wealth, the possibility of enlarging his own personal estates at the expense of others, the natural tendency for him to regard himself not merely as leader but as lord, and the villagers to hold their lands of him, paying him a rent in kind and in labour, doing three days' work on his estate and three on their own, and giving him extra time for ploughing and harvest, together with their tribute in kind at set times of the year.

Thus their personal relationship came to be connected with land and, though there still remained even at the time of the Norman conquest traces of the old free village, the status of most English peasants had deteriorated during later Saxon times.

The transition from freedom to bondage, of which this is a very general outline, took many generations and was brought about in different ways, but this relationship between lord and vassal came into being in England long before William I conquered the country. He did not invent it for it also existed in Europe. He simply took it for granted, adapted it to suit the

12

requirements of the day and made it universal. There is evidence from the Domesday Survey alone that in the years following the conquest the proportion of unfree to free tenants increased greatly.

There were slaves in England until the thirteenth century, and other kinds of bondsmen until much later. The countryside, on which more than ninety per cent of the people lived, was made up of small villages, connected for the most part by pathways running through the forest or over marsh, well-trodden in summer but often almost impassable during the worst seasons of the year.

The agricultural unit was in Norman times known as the manor (*manerium*). In some cases it included the whole of a village, the boundaries of the village and manor being the same. In others a village might have two or more manors within it, or a manor might consist of two or more villages possibly containing outlying lands within other manors. One lord might have many manors in different parts of the country, each managed by a bailiff and visited periodically by the lord's steward or the lord himself who would then preside over the manor court and collect the revenues. One of the greatest landowners in the country was the Church. Abbeys and priories were founded and endowed by kings and nobles, some holding estates in many counties and paying military service for them to the king, by furnishing their customary number of knights as other great landowners did.

On these manors most peasants, free or bond, held land, the only landless peasants being the serfs, though in later medieval times many of these were allowed small agricultural plots. The other bondsmen went by different names according to the quantity of land they held and the kind and amount of service they did for it. The land descended from father to son, and where there was no son to inherit the holding it reverted to the lord. Where there was more than one son, the lord usually granted to the second and successive sons holdings which had reverted to him, or if there were none the arable land of the manor was increased by taking in more land from the waste. There was thus a permanent relationship between master and man, the lordship of the manor descending from father to son and the holding of the peasant doing the same.

In 1086 William sent out his commissioners to make a survey of the whole country. He had been king for twenty years and had carried out a redistribution of land which had put most of it into Norman hands. His aims in having the survey made were severely practical; to find out who held the land, by what authority, and how much the land was worth, so that he would know whether his gifts had reached the right people, and whether anybody held land which was not rightfully his.

The survey, later called Domesday, was the means of settling thousands of disputes, and of establishing how much revenue was due to the king. The questions that were asked covered the extent, nature and value of the land in every manor, the number and status of the men who worked it, the name of the person who held it, the animal population, the natural resources, with a comparison of the manor in the Conqueror's day with its value in those of his predecessor, Edward the Confessor, and a statement as to whether it was capable of greater production. At the appointed time a chosen number of villagers, the priest, the reeve and six villeins, went from each village to meet the commissioners and there gave evidence, swearing on oath 'by the Splendour of God'. Here, at a very early stage in English history, we see the peasantry in action, humble men telling what they knew about the manors in order to settle the claims of the great.

When William died in 1087 the survey was incomplete. It was never finished, but the two volumes that existed were used as an official record of the extent of the property of lords and of monasteries, the size of estates, the boundaries of forests and the dues customarily paid.

The affairs of the kingdom were afterwards in constant flux;

14

estates changed hands, turbulent barons raised private armies and built fortifications, and the country was torn by civil strife, but the Domesday record remained, setting forth certain principles which were beyond question. One was the idea first prevalent on the Continent and later accepted in Norman England that the kingdom was royal property. Without this conception it would have been impossible to draw up the Survey in the form it took. The second was that, from the lowest to the highest, every man should have his lord, and the lord of all, people and land, was the king himself. Thus by Domesday, or rather by the system of which Domesday was the expression, the shape of English society was fixed. In it, in theory at least, all men had their places as freemen or as bondsmen. The niche of each one in society was settled according to the condition into which he was born and there was no rising out of it. The system, already fully grown on the Continent and maturing in England at the time of the Conquest, being based on the 'feod' or fief held by a man of his lord, was, by later historians, known as the Feudal System.

What was the position of all those whom we very loosely call 'the people'? Given that over ninety per cent of them were countrymen, and also that nearly half the land in England was held at the time of the Conquest by no more than about twenty great Norman families, the answer is not far to seek. At the Domesday Inquest the peasants, six by six, attended the courts with their reeves and priests. It is the last we hear of them for more than a couple of centuries. As a class, whether as individuals or as groups, they are silent. The stage is taken by the political strife of kings and barons, a long series of struggles and of experimenting during which the basis of English law, government, finance and administration was worked out. But in all this the dumb millions played no part.

Thus from generation to generation the villager went about his daily business, ploughing, harrowing and reaping his own strips in the fields, paying his dues of labour, his extra services

15

and his boons, working at harvest time under the rod of the lord's officer, rendering at each meeting his share of the special manorial tax called tallage, arbitrarily fixed by his lord. To marry he had to have his lord's permission, for he was part of the stock-in-trade of the manor as would be his children after him.

'*Ita in misericordia est*', runs the familiar phrase in the manor rolls – 'Therefore he is in mercy' – for absenting himself from the last court, for leaving his ditch unscoured, for letting his lean cattle roam on the land of others, for stealing his neighbour's seed, for assaulting the manor constable, for trespassing with cows on his lord's land, for taking timber without payment, for not keeping his tenement in repair. These and scores of other petty offences were part and parcel of his daily life. His village would normally number no more than two or three hundred people, all well known to him, and this would be his complete little world. A journey of ten miles from his birthplace would be the event of a lifetime. Of the world outside he would know nothing from his own experience, but a great deal from the stories and gossip of those who chanced to call or who picked up scraps of information from the back rooms of manor house or castle. From this life there was no escape save with the consent of his lord; should he attempt it he could be brought back to the manor and flogged.

Yet, compared with the lot of the slave in ancient Rome or the Negro slave, that of the bondsman in Norman England was happy. If a Roman slave died or was flogged to death, there was a good supply of replacements from captives taken in war; if a Negro slave was lost, there were others to be had in the slave markets. The Norman lord had no such ready supply of labour. The bondsman was born on his land and there, after a lifetime of service, he died. Apart from the moral responsibility as a Christian to attend to the wellbeing of his dependents, it was in the lord's material interest to keep his bondsmen alive and reasonably healthy, for to abuse them was to deprive himself both of labour and income. Without a full complement his ploughing would be neglected, his harvests would rot, his barns would be empty and he himself would not be able to meet the dues which his own master the king required of him.

This factor of irreplaceability had a most profound effect on the life of the English peasant. Though the lord had power of life and death over him, it was hardly in his interest to destroy those who provided his wealth, whatever crimes they had committed. It was not even good that a bondsman should be treated harshly, for his limbs were as valuable as those of his lord. For this reason the peasant was rarely separated from his wife, for it was to the lord's interest that he should breed strong, well-nourished children, and this interest was all the more keen in view of the heavy mortality of the day, especially among male infants. Thus, however noble the lord may have been, the bond between him and his vassals was personal, and the one was essential to the life of the other. They were bound together by a very necessary love-hate relationship.

Though William I made sure as far as he could that every man should have a lord, there were certain aspects of English life that were wholly or partly outside his system. The first was the Church. Though he had come to England with the blessing of Gregory VII, William had no intention of letting the Pope have his way in English church affairs. He refused to do homage to Rome, he appointed abbots and bishops without reference to the Pope and insisted on his consent being required before any papal letters or decrees could have any force in England. But during the reigns of his successors the power of the Church grew, and its influence spread into every corner of the realm. Lords of manors dotted the country with the small churches they built and staffed these with their own nominees, most of them foreigners. The twelfth century saw the building of numerous new abbeys and priories, and there was hardly a noble who did not seek to buy the salvation of his soul by putting up a religious house, inviting one of the orders of monks to occupy it, and endowing it with substantial portions of his own possessions and estates. Within little more than a hundred years of the Conquest a striking change came over the land, a goodly number of whose clerics were neither English nor gave their first allegiance to the English crown.

Henry II tried to check this growing influence of the Church. The Constitutions of Clarendon of 1164 put a stop to prelates leaving the country unless they had the king's leave, made priests who had committed crimes subject to sentence in the king's courts and made it necessary for an English peasant to have the consent of the lord of his manor if he wished to assume holy orders. Though to the lord this meant the loss of a bondsman, consent was rarely withheld. To enter the Church was one avenue by which the son of a villein or bordar could escape lifelong servitude as a labourer, and many an English peasant boy lived to carve out a distinguished career in the Church.

In whatever way the priest or monk used the liberty he had gained, the ultimate effect worked against the king. One man, an honest, painstaking labouring cleric, might be more eager to observe his vows to Rome than to London; a second, at heart still a peasant, stung by the wrongs done to his kind by arrogant nobles and grasping churchmen, might join the ranks of protesting preachers who from pulpit and market cross poured vituperation and satire on the follies of the age and in particular on the villainies of the powerful men. These were the agitators whose words inspired not only the peasants to rise against authority in 1381, but also found an echo in the sermons of the Dominican John Bromyard, Bishop Brunton and in the epic vision of William Langland, the creator of Piers Plowman. The third product of his age was the clerical libertine who valued the cope and the monk's cowl for the fatness and ease of the living, and for the access it gave him to money, luxury, wine and women. The profligate priest was the butt of endless in-

18

vective and satire from more earnest men of his own cloth. The pulpit was therefore the first source of English protest.

The second was the town. From the beginning towns were foreign to a social system based on land-holding. In the first year of his reign William I recognised the peculiar standing of the burghers of London by issuing to them a charter. This, written in Latin on a small piece of parchment no more than six by one and a half inches in size, guaranteed to the Londoners their rights:

> . . . I do you to wit that I will ye be all law-worthy that were in Edward's day. And I will that every child shall be his father's heir after his father's day, and I will not endure that any man offer any wrong to you. God keep you.

Rarely have words so pregnant with meaning been crammed into so little space. Londoners were given the privileges of free men in courts of justice, the right to appeal to their equals, and for their property, security of tenure. Henry I in a second charter gave them the farm of Middlesex for £300 a year, the right to elect their own sheriff and the privilege of hunting in Middlesex, Surrey and the Chilterns.

Towns have always been places where protest and demonstrations took place, for while the peasant, overridden by authority, was dumb, the townsman, headstrong and raised in an atmosphere of independence, was vocal. In 1139, when Geoffrey de Mandeville and Aubrey de Vere tried to persuade the Londoners to forsake Stephen for Matilda, they rioted and Aubrey was slain in the confusion. A second time, when Matilda gave Geoffrey the wardenship of the Tower of London, they flew to arms, marched out to the Palace of Westminster, put the Empress to flight and then blockaded Geoffrey in his own fortifications.

This was protest plus force. A more classic example of protest with reasoning is given in the records of the City of Leicester in the year 1253. Two cousins, quarrelling about a plot of land, were adjudged by Robert de Montfort, Lord of the Manor, to try their case by battle. One, driving the other to the verge of a ditch, called out to him to beware of falling in. The rules of the trial by battle were that no man, combatant or spectator, should raise his voice, and on this serious breach a clamour arose. The chief citizens, ashamed that actions should be tried in this way, went in protest to Earl Robert. Protest led to bargaining, and in the end he gave them the right to hold their own courts in return for a payment of three pence a year for every house which had a gable on the high street. Thus, while in the countryside the commons were silent, townmen were achieving their freedom through the granting of charters.

The town has always acted as a magnet to the countryman. Probably many a poor peasant in the Middle Ages listened avidly to the yarns of pedlar and pilgrim which set him longing to be free of the grind and drudgery of field labour, and the tyranny of taskmaster and bailiff. The town, this exciting realm he had never seen, offered him three things – variety, freedom and the prospect of making money. The streets may not have been paved with gold but we can understand the allusion in the popular Whittington fable. For these reasons the manor lost more labourers to the town than it did to the Church. Moreover it was a privilege of most towns of any importance than a bondsman who had lived there for a year and a day as a citizen, and whose lord had not claimed him, was for ever free. However few may actually have achieved citizenship, the temptation to run away to the town must have drawn many off the land.

Apart from the influence of the Church and the town there were many other factors which, as the centuries passed by, gradually ate into the old manorial system. Men were called from their work to fight in the wars at home and abroad, and some never came back. Some serfs were able to buy their freedom, others were manumitted by considerate masters for their services. But the chief factor which helped to break down the manorial structure was the increasing use of money.

In Medieval England there were two social classes, the peasant and the merchant, who created wealth, and two other classes, king and nobility, who dissipated it. The wealth of the peasants was the surplus of labour passed to the manorial lords in goods; that of the merchant was a money surplus, part of which was yielded up in taxation, part retained as capital and private wealth. It was the gradual change from a land to a money economy that made for personal freedom. The king, whose military service had been exacted in knight service, was ready to commute it for scutage or shield-money. In the same way the manorial lord found it more convenient to accept a rent from his vassal in lieu of personal service on his demesne.

This 'quit-rent', as it was called, had the ultimate effect of transferring the label of bondage from the man to the land because it made easier the sale and exchange of plots. By the thirteenth century the custom of re-allocating strips in the common fields was wearing itself out, and men were holding what their fathers had held, by old custom. Thus a villein might, by permission of his lord, transfer land in villeinage to a free-man, or vice-versa. The process of transference, which was really one of sale, was for the holder to give back the land to the lord, the lord to regrant it to the purchaser, the purchaser to pass the purchase price to the vendor and to pay a fine to the lord on transfer. From that time the purchaser held the land from the lord and paid the quit-rent annually as his predecessor had done. This process of land sale worked all the time to take from a man the stigma of personal bondage.

By the fourteenth century all these social changes were in full swing. There were serfs holding land, villeins who were themselves lords of estates, and large numbers of men who, as the property of the Church and the population of towns in-creased, had by devious ways become free of the old system. People were moving; the rough roads were alive with pilgrims,

21

hucksters, merchants, messengers and clerics. But they were moving not only in body but also in mind. News of national events was percolating through to the countryman, important national figures were becoming known to him. More than that, he was beginning to compare his own lot with that of others, to recognise the disadvantages and deprivations of which his ancestors had been largely unconscious, to lament the oppression of landlord and to fume at the corruption and venality that had crept into the Holy Church. The peasant leaders were becoming capable of forming political and social bonds, one with another. They were, in brief, becoming politically conscious.

This was the beginning of effective protest.

2

'When Adam Delf'

IT WAS NOT by chance that the fourteenth century produced
the first popular leaders, preachers and poets since before the
Norman Conquest. This was essentially an age of unrest and
transition. After the failure of Edward II to complete the conquest of Scotland, the country was plunged into the faction
fight which ended in his death (1327) and the succession of his
son, the young hero-king, Edward III. Edward's claim to the
French throne heralded a period of national pride, when
diminutive war-bands with the aid of the longbow won the
battles of Crecy and Poitiers against what seemed to be over-
whelming odds; when the captains of free companies burnt and
plundered the French countryside at will; when the Order of
the Garter was created to glorify gallantry in war; when, among
the common people, adventurous youth in tavern and tippling-
house listened openmouthed to gruesome tales of rapine and
plunder told by grisly veterans. It must have seemed, as the
captains mustered their men from field and hamlet to fight for
their king, that England had at last found a soul.

Then in the midst of national ardour came a devastating
attack of the bubonic plague. The Black Death struck down
between one-third and one-half of the population. Whole villages were almost wiped out so that, as the chronicler says, there
were hardly enough living to bury the dead. Parishes were left
without priests, monasteries without monks and manors without labourers. Some landlords, ruin facing them, refused any
longer to accept quit-rents for bond service, and began to insist on personal labour being done on their fields. Others, unable even then to keep them in cultivation, offered them on
long lease to the speculator. The hired labourer who had sur-

vived the plague was able to ask a far higher price for his work, and wages rose steeply. Lords and landowners complained, and since they were the governing class, the Ordinance and Statute of Labourers (1349 and 1351) favoured them, fixing wages at the same figure as before the pestilence, and forbidding the peasant on pain of imprisonment to quit the manor on which he served.

A mood of gloom descended on the country from which not even the victory of Poitiers (1357) and the capture of the French King could raise it. The bondsman, already half way to independence, saw with dismay and resentment his dearly won privileges torn away from him; the lord, driven by necessity, despair and sometimes by greed, tried by force to wring extra day work and increased boons from his complaining vassal. Of all landlords during this time the Church proved itself the most uncompromising and merciless. Abbots and priors, ostensibly devoted to relieving poverty and distress, sometimes seemed to be more concerned with creating it to their own profit.

Politically England sank into as deep a morass. The wars had brought nothing but a few flashes of glory. By the Peace of Bretigny (1360) northern France was lost, and Edward waived his claim to the French crown. France, ravaged by war and plague, was a land of want and misery. England, the social canker eating at its heart, was full of unrest. But while the former under Charles V and the military genius, Bertrand du Guesclin, took some steps towards recovery, the condition of the latter became steadily worse. The days of glory were gone. The Channel ports and even the Thames-side towns were attacked by marauding French. One costly expedition after another crossed the Channel to France only to meet with defeat and disaster. The poor were ground under the weight of land tax, property tax and polltax to pay for these wanton extravagances. The King, once the inspiration of a vigorous and forward-looking nation had, even at the early age of sixty, sunk into a depraved and unseemly dotage; the Black Prince, hope of the dynasty, died of a disease contracted abroad, leaving his young son helpless in face of his overbearing uncles.

This half-century of gloom was one of the most formative periods in English history because of the rise of a new force – the articulate voice of the people, heard for the first time. As a peasant movement, we see its two sides. There was manorial unrest in widely separated parts of the country; on one manor the serfs deliberately refusing to perform labour services, on another absenting themselves from ploughing and haymaking, on a third claiming to have been degraded from the status of free men. But these are not all. There is evidence of a more solid volume of protest stirred up by wandering agitators, many of them priests, fomenting discontent, and creating a mass movement of serfs, villeins and even freemen towards active resistance. This kind of thing England had never seen before.

Disputes about tenure and complaints against manorial lords must have become common, since they inspired the creation of a body of political song and satire. We read little about these disputes in official records, for as far as royal justice was concerned, the villein's case against his lord could only be pleaded in the manor court; in other words, the victim of oppression could look for redress only to the oppressor himself – a pretty hopeless matter. And, since few manor court rolls for the thirteenth century have survived, we have to look to other sources such as the Curia Regis Rolls, the calendars of Patent Rolls and Close Rolls for evidence.

In the early part of that century these land disputes were becoming frequent. Even as early as 1250, a hundred years before the Black Death, prices were already rising, landlords were becoming commercial cultivators and selling the produce of their demesne lands in the markets. Peasant farmers found additional services pressed on them, and men who had long regarded themselves as free were being treated as villeins and extra labour demanded of them. When they resisted, the lords sought to prove their servile status by quoting that of other members of their families – 'This man's cousin is a villein, therefore . . .' – or by obtaining evidence from old men who remembered the status of the litigant's grandfather.

One of the most common manœuvres of the peasants was to prove that the land which they held had at some time been crown demesne at the time of Edward the Confessor, for on such land they could still claim royal protection against increased services even though the land had been granted to other lords since the Conquest. This applied particularly to monastic lands, since the monasteries had been the greatest recipients of land gifts and were on the whole the most exacting of all landlords. This process of proof involved the searching of Domesday Book.

Time and again the weight of the law came down in favour of the lord, whether lay or spiritual. This feature had two important results. Peasants were drawn by a common cause to combine with each other. In the thirteenth century we find all the men on one manor acting together, in the fourteenth, bands of peasants on neighbouring manors joined in supporting their joint claims. The stiffening of resistance on the part of the lords often drove them to illegal and semi-legal actions. There is nothing new in go-slow and work-to-rule. From 1279 to 1311 there were 146 separate convictions on the manors of one abbey alone. At Harmondsworth manor houses were broken into and charters taken away. At Halesowen, the tenants were excommunicated for assaulting the Abbot who had proved that they were bondsmen. In 1336 the peasants of Darnall manor of the Abbey of Vale Royal went as far as Rutlandshire in pursuit of the Abbot and his retinue. Stewards and bailiffs were ambushed, there were dramatic escapes of men from escorts who were taking them to judgment. The original Robin Hood is said to have been connected with the earlier resistance of the peasants against the heartless forest laws. He had by this time already become a legendary figure, and there was no lack of men to follow his example in resisting the tyranny of manorial lords.

The stories of his merry men and their exploits, sung and recited abroad, were a sort of wish-fulfilment. There is no such light-hearted or gallant spirit about the popular political rhymes which lamented the lot of the oppressed poor. The Song of the Husbandman (*temp* Edward II) is a long reiteration of complaints, unrelieved by fantasy or even by the expectation of better days:

> *I heard my brothers make much moan*
> *How they were injured in their tilling;*
> *Good years and corn away are gone;*
> *No words they speak, no song they sing.*

> *Ill is it to lose what little we have.*
> *Full many men are that hope thereto.*
> *The hayward commands us that ours may be his.*
> *The bailiff doth smite us, and thinks well to do.*
> *For they rob the poor man who is of small price*
> *In sweat and in swink doth he waste away so.*

> *Yea, they rob the poor man and pick him full clean,*
> *And the rich men lord it without any right;*
> *Our lands and our people they lay full lean.*
> *By asking of bailiffs such harm they have hight.*
> *Thus will walks the land and misgiving is keen.*
> *False-ship grows fat and marreth with might.*[1]

A popular fable of the time is that of the lion, the wolf and the fox and the ass. One day the wolf and the fox were brought in turn before King Lion, the wolf for worrying goats and sheep, and the fox for raiding the hen-roosts. Neither saw any wrong

[1] *The Political Songs of England*, Thomas Wright, Camden Society, 1839.

in what he had done, for they had both given a good half of their gains to the Lion in tribute. 'Let them go, then,' said the Lion, 'for in doing what they have done, they were but obeying the laws of their nature.'

Then the ass was brought before him on a charge that he had nibbled the grass in the meadow. The ass pleaded that the grass was God's gift and therefore free to all. But the poor ass, because he could pay nothing, was condemned to be hanged, drawn and quartered. The moral of the story was plain to all.

Class bitterness, growing throughout the earlier part of the century, was infinitely greater after the Black Death of 1349–50. Popular hostility against the landlord increased, the protest of the preachers against the injustices of the day became more vehement. In that pestilence died Richard Rolle of Hampole, recluse and mystic. Part of a rhyme attributed to him later became one of the cries of the peasant movement:

> *When Adam delf and Eve span,*
> *Spir, if thou wil spede,*
> *Whare was then the pride of man*
> *That now merres his mede?*
> *Of erth and slame, als was Adam,*
> *Maked to noyes and nede,*
> *Ar we, als he, maked to be*
> *Whil we this lyf sal lede. . . .*

'When Adam dug and Eve span . . . where was man's pride that now mars his reward? Adam was made of earth and slime, born to sorrow and need, and we are, as he was, as long as we live.'

'Are we not all one flesh? Are we not all brothers? Why then, do landlord and Church prey upon the common people, their kin?' From the original rhyme another thought took shape:

'Who was then the gentleman?'

28

The Church had always had its aristocracy, the bishops and abbots together with the legion of smaller functionaries who profited from the wealth it acquired. It also had its commoners, the parish priests, the deacons and those priests who made a living like William Langland, by saying prayers for those richer than themselves.

I live in London and on London too,
And the limbs I labour with to earn a living
Are my 'paternoster' and my prayerbook, with 'placebo'
and 'dirige',
And I sing for the souls of such as help me,
And those that find me my food seem friendly enough
And are willing to welcome me once or twice a month.

At the time the parish churches were built, many priests had of necessity been foreigners; now they were English and for the most part of peasant stock. It was natural that these men, the 'bright boys' of the monastic schools, active in mind and critical in spirit, should be the ones who gave voice to the grievances of their brethren. The preacher in churchyard, at the market cross and in the country pulpit was steadfast in the faith, but he was nevertheless a critic, a maker of political rhymes and songs, and an inflammatory orator. In those days the authorities were not alive to the growing peril of revolt; they did not recognise the seriousness of the movement. Had they been experts in repression they would have clapped the foremost of the preachers into gaol. As it was, they were allowed to go freely about, sowing the seed of discontent, heedless as to what the harvest would be.

The wandering preacher was not a communist, nor did he propound any political doctrine. It was enough for him to draw for his hearers a clear picture of the injustices under which they lived, to ventilate their wrongs. Should they do anything about it? He was not concerned about any solution on this earth. The parable of Dives and Lazarus was enough for him. In the next

29

world divine vengeance would fall on the oppressors. Let the poor then be patient, for they would find their reward in Heaven. The Dominican friar, John Bromyard, writing his book for preachers, *Summa Predicantium*, in the early part of the century makes this, and not any political solution on earth, the constant theme of his message: Where are the evil princes, he asks, the kings and lords who lived in pride, who had wide lands and large rents? Where are the false wise men of the world, the judges, assessors, advocates who sold God for bribes? Where are the usurers, the wicked ecclesiastics, the haughty, the envious, the lustful, the gluttonous?

> Their soul shall have, instead of palace and hall and chamber, the deep lake of hell, with those that go down into the depth thereof. In place of scented baths, their body shall have a narrow pit in the earth; and there they shall have a bath more foul than any bath of pitch and sulphur. In place of a soft couch they shall have a bed more grievous and hard than all the nails and spikes in the world. . . . Instead of wives they shall have toads; instead of a great retinue and throng of followers, their body shall have a throng of worms and their soul a throng of demons. Instead of large domain, it shall be an eternal prison-house, cramped for both. Instead of riches, poverty; instead of delights, punishment; instead of honour, misery and contempt; instead of laughter, weeping; instead of gluttony and drunkenness, hunger and thirst without end; instead of excessive gaming with dice and the like, grief, and in place of the torment which for a time they inflicted on others, they shall have eternal torment.

Popular preaching and satire are part of a long heritage, dating back at least to the thirteenth century, and expressed in thousands of lost sermons. The very language and style of the English preacher is copied from these pioneers. When in 1586 Robert Wright, chaplain to the Puritan Lord Rich, later 1st Earl of Warwick, had the temerity to call the parsons, who preached little but followed blindly the Book of Common Prayer, 'Dumb Dogs', he was but repeating the words of

Thomas Brunton, Bishop of Rochester (1373–89), who applied them to the evil-living priests of his day who would not teach their people. Arthur Dent, Rector of North Shoebury, whose *Plain Man's Pathway to Heaven* (1601) inspired the writings of John Bunyan, spoke the same language and evoked the same mental pictures as his predecessor in Chaucer's Day. For all the doctrinal differences there is a direct and unmistakeable connection between the *Vision of Piers Plowman* and the *Pilgrim's Progress*.

'Blessed are the poor in spirit, for theirs is the Kingdom of Heaven' was the true Gospel of the fourteenth-century preacher. Far from wishing to stir up the peasant to rebellion, he strove to persuade him that the poor man, unspoilt by pride, free from covetousness and without all the temptations that riches bring, was nearer to heaven than the rich man who lived in luxury. 'Let the poor then be happy and rejoice that they are poor.'

As long as there were enough mendicant friars and poor brethren to give weight to this doctrine the peasant was more inclined to accept it, but with the break-up of the old land system and the corruptions creeping into the Church, the intelligent peasant was no longer willing to wait for 'pie in the sky'. He wanted at least a promise of good things on earth, and he was in a position to attempt to realise it.

We are accustomed to think of the medieval peasant as ignorant and illiterate, but as far as the leading spirits were concerned this is hardly true. They had long realised that a battle, especially a legal battle, could not be fought without knowledge, and the most far-sighted and able men had already acquired it in the hard school of manorial experience. They had learnt much from the preachers, but their practical training had come from duels with men of law. They probably knew more than their masters about the rights and wrongs of manorial tenure, and were quick to see how misrepresentation and fraud on the part of the landlord and justice contributed to their undoing.

By 1380 there was no doubt that the peasants had an organisation covering at least the south and east of England, with local leaders and organisers, and messengers to keep the various groups in touch. Some of the London aldermen and more prominent citizens had been won over and they had the general sympathy of the people in the city.

This was no longer a mere protest against oppression; it was a movement whose leaders at least knew something of what they were doing. Their object or programme was the abolition of serfdom, labour by free contract, a low rent for land, the freedom of the peasant to carry on independent trading, the restoration of usurped common rights and the division of church land among the peasants. These were six points quite as precise and definite as those the Chartists presented to Parliament nearly five centuries later. The main difference was in the method of gaining the concessions they wanted.

The language of the malcontents was as allegorical as any the preachers used, and as inspiring as any call to action.

> *John the Miller hath yground small, small, small.*
> *The King's son of heaven shall pay for all.*
> *Beware or ye be wo* [worse].
> *Know your friend from your foe.*
> *Have enough and say 'Ho!'* [stop]
> *And do well and better and flee sin*
> *And seek peace and hold therein.*
> *And so bid John Trueman and all his fellows.*

John Ball's purported message is in the same tone, but more definite.

John Schep, some time St Mary's priest of York, and now of Colchester, greeteth well John Nameless and John the Miller and John Carter, and biddeth them that they beware of guile in borough, and stand together in God's name, and biddeth Piers Plowman to his work, and chastise well Hob the Robber, and take with you John Trueman and all his fellows and no mo; and look sharp you to one-head [union] and no mo.

The confusion arises at the point where negotiation stops and violence steps in. The peasant had, even as the Russians had in the nineteenth century, a romantic but mistaken belief not only in the goodwill of their monarch but in his ability to aid and protect them. Their object was to 'flee sin and seek peace'.

Violence may or may not be implied in Ball's message to chastise Hob the Robber, their name for Robert Hales, the Treasurer, who had been principally responsible for the late poll-tax. Their aim without doubt was to negotiate through strength, but even before negotiations could start, violence had shattered any prospect there might have been of improving the lot of the peasants in that way. Before even the peasants arrived at the gates of London, manor-houses had gone up in flames and manor rolls with them.

3

Protest and Heresy

When you come to the Pope, take it as a rule, there is no place for the poor, he favours only the giver, or if there is not a bribe of some value or another forthcoming, he answers you, 'I am not able.' The Pope, if we come to the truth of the matter, has his name from the fact that, whatever others have, he will suck the pap. . . . The Pope begs, the brief begs, the gate begs, the cardinal begs, the cursor begs – all beg! and if you have not the wherewith to bribe them all, your right is wrong, and the whole cause comes to nothing. . . . O, you full purses, come to Rome! at Rome there is choice of medicine for costive pockets.[1]

If we look through the columns of any newspaper today we see that the writers of complaints and criticisms are always more numerous than those who express praise or gratification. It would be unwise, therefore, in studying the social structure of any age to gauge the attitude of people in general from reading the effusions of the vocal few. The revolt of the peasants caused for some days what might be called a national emergency, but it is as well to bear in mind that the peasants who did not take part in it were probably far more numerous than those who did, and that, of the total peasant population, large numbers suffered little change, or put up without complaint with what changes there were.

The same may be said about the Church. For the most part parish priests went quietly about their business. Their flocks, realising that they were no more than human, were probably tolerant towards a reasonable measure of human frailty. The abbots, abbesses and priests continued their work of mercy, visiting the sick and succouring the poor, while the friars car-

[1] Wright, *op. cit.*

ried the evangel to the common folk in homely sermon, story and parable.

In our day, when a person may adopt whatever faith he pleases or none at all, when the churchgoing population numbers no more than a mere fraction of the whole, it is hard to imagine the hold the Church had on the life of European man in the fourteenth century. Religion was then not a thing apart, which might be donned like a cloak; it was part of the flesh and bone of existence. Out of the many faiths existing within the Roman Empire there now remained one only, adopted as the state religion by the Emperor Constantine. It had emerged from the confusion of the Dark Ages with complete dominion over the mind of man, and was a powerful organisation capable of humbling kings and emperors, possessed of wealth and temporal power over vast estates. Its influence reached down from the Pope through the Papal hierarchy of cardinal and bishop, to the labourer in the field. The sacrament was his spiritual comfort, and spiritual consolation through the Church was as important to him as his daily food. However poor his village, the Church was the repository of all that was best in it, its vestments, crosses and plate paid for out of the peasant's meagre substance, its walls covered with sacred paintings which served as his Bible and his book of Saints.

To question Church doctrine was heresy and to abide in heresy meant to quit the physical world by the ordeal of fire.

During this century the Roman Church passed through one of the worst periods of its history. In 1305 the newly-elected Pope Clement V, a Frenchman, set up the Papal court at Avignon where it remained until 1377, largely under French influence. In that year Gregory XI was persuaded by Catherine of Siena to return to Rome, but in 1378 he died and the troubles broke out again. The subsequent election of Urban VI was challenged by a group of cardinals who, under the protection of the French King, elected another Pope, Clement VII. This Great Schism as it was called, with one Pope in Rome favoured by the English, the Italian States and the Holy Roman Empire, and another, known as the Anti-Pope in Avignon, supported by France, lasted until 1417.

The effect on the morale of the Christian world was totally bad. Church discipline grew lax. Sinners, who according to the doctrine of absolution should have confessed to their priests, often absented themselves. Those who were brought up in the Church courts were allowed to pay for absolution rather than do penance for it. Priests neglected their duties, many caring more about their tithes and other perquisites than about the spiritual welfare of their flocks.

In the Church hierarchy things were no better. The bishops were appointed, not by the cathedral chapters or by the Pope, but by the King, the Pope having only the power to ratify the appointments. They were therefore as much the servants of the state as of the Church, and were employed as trained administrators, treasurers and diplomats. The Church was a career which attracted the best brains in the land, and the reward was affluence and power for the bishops themselves and preferment for their families and friends.

> How many of all these princes of the Church observe such duties (after the pattern of Christ) in these days, do you think? Travel through the provinces and look at the cathedral churches, and you will find them replete with 'flesh and blood', the nephews and grand-nephews of bishops, I perceive. Well do the princes of the Church procure the services of their own flesh. The services of other men subject to them, approved by God in wisdom and holiness of life, they utterly neglect and despise. And thus, these latter languish in poverty.[1]

It was vital to the King that he should keep in his own hand the appointment of such useful servants as the bishops. For this he was willing to forgo control of the lesser ranks. Archdeacons, deans and the cathedral clergy were appointed by the

[1] *Literature and the Pulpit in Medieval England*, G R Owst, Cambridge University Press, 1933.

36

Pope. Many of them were cardinals and, at least before 1377, Frenchmen, too. This was an absurd situation since England and France were at war. These cardinals seldom visited England and when they did they rode like princes. The revenue from their English property went abroad, and much of it was probably used to pay for arms used against the country providing it. Yet, though Parliament passed such acts as the Statute of Provisors (1351) to prevent such evils, the King was willing to allow them to go on.

It was in this department of Church affairs that corruption reached its disgraceful peak, and extortion went on uninterrupted. Throughout all the protest against the injustices of the Church runs one principal theme – money; 'the Lady Pecunia' rules all. She is the fount of all hypocrisy, fawning and double dealing. To the Church, the sinner who brings with him the Lady Pecunia, be he never so vile, is more thought of than the honest poor man who is alone. She ruins the monasteries, emptying them of their monks, she corrupts the priests who have given themselves up to sloth and she rules the church courts which...

> ... for every vice and for every sin ... prescribe only a single medicine – that which is called by the popular name of 'pecuniary penalty'. This certainly appears to be well called 'a penalty' because it is very 'penal' to many; nevertheless whether it ought to be called a 'medicine' I do not know. Yet, in truth I think that if it is a medicine it deserves rather to be called 'a laxative medicine for purses', than 'a medicine for souls'.[1]

The number and variety of clerics in the regular clergy (monks, friars, canons, nuns) and the secular clergy (prelates, priests and clerks) was very great. It is estimated that at least one in thirty of the adult population of England got all or part of their livings from the Church. Of Chaucer's thirty pilgrims there were no fewer than twelve connected with the Church.

[1] *Ibid.*

It would have been strange if, in such a universal institution, there should not have been a few rogues. Chaucer's clerical pilgrims do not, on the whole, show up well for devotion and self-sacrifice. The monk prefers good food and hunting to good works and prayer. The friar is a first-class lady's man, 'the beste beggere in his hous' who could wheedle the halfpenny out of the poorest widow with no conscience at all. The summoner whose flaming face and great black beard frightened all the children, is 'lecherous as a sparwe'. The pardoner, with a wallet 'brimful of pardoun come from Rome all hot', can with clever sales-talk palm off an old pillow-case as the Virgin's veil, a piece of rag as part of St Peter's sail, and a few pigs' bones as the relics of saints:

> And thus with feigned flaterye and japes,
> He made the parson and the peple his apes.

The only principal characters in which true virtue reveals itself are the clerk who 'gladly would learn and gladly teach', and the good man of religion, the parson, who ...

> ... Cristes lore and his apostles twelve
> He taught and first he folwed it himselve.

Chaucer's, at most, is gentle satire. For true protest we must go again to the poor preachers, the men of the lowest social classes who shared the humble fare of their hearers and slept in their hovels. What did they have to say of their greedy and unscrupulous fellowclerics?

> ... those priests who should be most spotless upon the breast of God have now become most foul in the Devil's service. For with those hands with which at night they handle the prostitute's flesh, with those same hands, I say, in the daytime they handle the Flesh of Salvation. . . . But alas! it must be bewailed of many priests, that those who should be an example

of good conversation in good works have now become an example of perdition in their own evil examples and evil works of whom it may be said in the words of Jude in his epistle (v 18) – 'There shall come mockers in the last time, walking after their own ungodly lusts'. . . .[1]

Some of the higher clergy such as Bishop Thomas Brunton, Bishop FitzRalph of Armagh and William de Rymington, Cistercian Prior and Chancellor of Oxford University, are even more scathing. Rymington chastises the unworthy priest with intense fury:

> O wretched modern condition of the clergy! O marvellous perversion of the priesthood! O abominable confusion of the *curati* whom from the obscenities of lechery, the embraces of the prostitute and the public keeping of harlots Reason does not restrain, Sacred Authority does not withdraw, the Love of God does not attract, nor fear of the Almighty repel, and Shame of public scandal wholly fails to prevent. . . . Rightly, as I think, it would please God better and be more profitable to His Holy Church not to have any priest save one only for a distance of ten leagues, rather than this disreputable modern crowd of presbyters.[2]

William Langland, author of *The Vision of Piers Plowman*, a repository of medieval lore as well as a pungent commentary on the times, dismisses them with one curt line: 'Christ at His coming may curse the whole lot of them.'

In all this there was no hint of heresy, no criticism either of church doctrine or discipline; it was the observance of doctrine and the enforcement of discipline that was at fault. The Church was no less holy because its servants were vicious, it was no less loving because its minions dealt in hatred and oppression. In all the literature of complaint, there is no criticism of the confessional, no denial of the Pope's power to bind and loose, no opposition to the sacraments, least of all to the doctrine of Transubstantiation, that is, that the bread and wine were trans-

[1] *Ibid.*   [2] *Ibid.*

39

muted in substance into the body and blood of Christ. Then in about 1374 a new national figure appeared.

John Wycliff, one of the most prominent scholars in the country, was born in about 1320 in north Yorkshire. Most of his life had been spent in Oxford where, as Master of Balliol College, his learning and skill in disputation had earned him many followers, and his judgments on matters connected with theology and the Church carried great weight. In the spring of 1374 Wycliff was presented to the rectory of Lutterworth in Leicestershire, where most of his later important works were written.

Wycliff's first attack was on the material possessions of the Church. There was nothing new in this, for other writers had asserted for the best part of a century that the Church, being of the spirit, should have nothing to do with material things, and that poverty was the self-appointed lot of every priest. The open scandals in the Church during the fourteenth century and the violent protests of one section of the clergy had made this only too obvious. Wycliff went further. He held that God, having created all material things, these must be considered as being held in trust of Him by men, and that their lordship is only justified by righteousness. The clergy, because of their wickedness, and the Church in general because of its greed, had proved themselves unfitted to exercise this lordship, therefore the civil power, the state, might lawfully take away the Church's property. Indeed, the Church would be all the purer for losing it.

Wycliff was a man who carried his arguments to their logical conclusion. He recognised that to put into practice his theory of dominion would reduce the whole community to violence and confusion. He acknowledged that it was a theory and he did not go so far as to admit that a man might take away his neighbour's property simply because he believed him to be unrighteous.

These pronouncements did, however, bring Wycliff into the

political arena. During the dotage of Edward III, the most powerful man in the state was his third son, John of Gaunt, who had put himself at the head of the baronial party. He cared nothing for the theory of dominion beyond seeing in it a pretext to take over the property of the Church. On the other side were the bishops headed by Courtenay of London who, unable to harm Gaunt, attacked Wycliff.

The crisis lasted from 1376 to 1378. The first time Wycliff faced his accusers at St Paul's, John of Gaunt rescued him from a stormy scene when the Londoners burst into the Cathedral and broke up the council meeting. A second time at Lambeth, Joan, mother of the young King Richard II, forbade his accusers to harm him, and the mob demonstrated in his favour. Had this not happened, Wycliff might never have lived to found a new faith.

He began his public life as a scholastic; he ended it as a rebel. From 1378 until his death, a succession of writings on all the important religious questions of the day flowed from his pen. In this period his rebellion against Papacy and Church was not merely one of politics; it became an even more important one of doctrine.

Wycliff's denial of transubstantiation struck at the very roots of the medieval Church. This was even more than his old allies, John of Gaunt and the Baronage, would support, and from 1381 onwards Wycliff's followers were, not the nobility, not the peasantry, but mainly the country gentry, the traders, artisans and the lower classes in the towns. His gospel therefore had little to do with the uprising of the peasants.

Nevertheless it was political because it represented a protest against the wealth and power of the bishops. One by one the accepted teachings of the Church were condemned – no priest, according to Wycliff, was qualified to administer the sacrament if he was in mortal sin; no confession was valid unless it was accompanied by sincere repentance and effort to amend; the ceremony of the Mass was of the Church and had not been

ordained by Christ himself. All the charges ever levelled by
the fourteenth-century preacher against idle monks and dissolute friars, against abbots who mopped up country livings and
put them in charge of ignorant, ill-paid vicars, and the way the
Church fawned on the rich and spurned the poor, found expression in his works. He taught a purer religion in which salvation depended on a man's own self, redemption on repentance
and subsequent reform, and access to God was through Christ
and not through an elaborate church ceremony performed by
an unworthy cleric.

This immediacy of contact between God and man meant the
freeing of man from the shackles of superstition in which the
Church had locked him. Wycliff had two ways of doing this.
The first, undertaken it is believed as early as 1377, was the
sending out of his own poor preachers who should go from
place to place like Christ's disciples, in simple garb, with
neither scrip for their journey nor shoes to their feet, to preach
openly, and especially to teach the Lord's Prayer, the Ten
Commandments and the scriptures. Moreover, in order that
men should know the scriptures better, he undertook the first
translation of the whole Bible into the English tongue. Thus he
hoped to counter the activities of those friars who were interested in the suppression of knowledge of the scriptures in
their own interest. The number of poor preachers increased;
learned and able men gave their lives to the work and so great
was their impact that by the end of the century it was said, in
Leicestershire at least, that every other man was a Lollard.

Lollardy, as it was called, existed in England as a kind of
religious nonconformity until the Reformation when its remnants gradually became merged with the various Protestant
movements. Late fourteenth-century England, devastated by
war, pestilence, political upheaval and social unrest was in a
mood to receive it. Mystics such as Richard Rolle, Dame
Juliana of Norwich, Walter Hilton and the anonymous author
of *The Cloud of Unknowing* had already spoken of the dark-

ness of the soul, and the silence in which man seeks and may perceive the 'naked intent unto God'. Thus mysticism, by dwelling on the direct contact between individual and God, helped to foster heresy.

The century ended without any major upheaval. Lollards were particularly active in the Midlands and the West of England, but, since the stress laid by the preachers was rather on the points of doctrine than on the question of Church property, the bishops preferred not to stir up trouble for the time being. Nor were the first generation of Lollards the kind of stuff of which martyrs are made, for when they were taken and were brought up for trial they recanted, one and all. In 1395 King Richard II, distressed at the death of his Queen, went to Ireland. While he was away a small number of Lollard members of the Privy Council prepared a petition on Church reform for discussion in Parliament. When it was not taken up, they nailed their *Twelve Conclusions* to the doors of St Paul's Cathedral and Westminster Abbey for the public to read. The bishops, alarmed, sent messengers to the King asking him to return to England.

In May 1395 Richard reached London in haste, vowing that he would hang all Lollards. The leader of the petitioners immediately recanted, the King promising 'that if you ever break your oath I will slay you by the foulest death that may be'.

In 1399 Richard was defeated and dethroned by his cousin, Henry of Derby, who ascended the throne as Henry IV. From this time onwards, pressure on the Lollards increased and there were several martyrdoms. In 1410 a body of knights of the shire presented proposals to Parliament that the King should seize the property of the Church and use the proceeds to endow 15,000 priests, establish fifteen universities, build and endow almonries, still leaving some £20,000 a year for the King's treasury. Henry, however, had always been insecure on the throne and badly needed the support of the Church. In any circumstances he could never have accepted such a proposal,

43

and the petitioners received no answer. The only effect was to stir up the bishops towards the more vigorous repression of heresy.

Prince Henry, the King's eldest son, ascended the throne as Henry V in 1413. For many years he had stood at his father's right hand and, though reputed to be a young man of dissolute life, had served him well both in the council-chamber and on the field. He had seen enough of rebellion and controversy to convince him that national unity must be achieved at all costs. In 1410 he had stood before the stake at which the Lollard, John Badby, was to be burned, and tried in vain to persuade him to recant. Now it was time for him to set the bishops on the track of one of his own greatest friends, Sir John Oldcastle.

Oldcastle had rendered distinguished service to the country as a commissioner on the Welsh border, and by marriage to the heiress of Lord Cobham had come into the estates in Kent where he openly encouraged the people of his own faith in their worship. In vain the King pleaded with him to renounce it, and in the end he was cited to appear at the ecclesiastical court where he confessed his faith as a follower of Wycliff. While he was in prison a Lollard plot was discovered, the object of which was to capture the King, to advance on London and take over the government. Forewarned, the soldiers were waiting and as the bands from the counties converged on the capital they were taken prisoner one by one. Oldcastle escaped, and for three years lived as an outlaw in the Welsh mountains before he was captured and executed. Thus died a hero, and thus ended the hopes of the Lollards of any effective resistance to the bishops. The reformed religion had been crushed in Oxford, the place of its birth; most people of consequence had forsaken it or were practising it secretly, and it was no longer a threat to the stability of either Church or state.

4

The New Society

IN 1367 TWO princes were born. The elder, Richard, son of
the Black Prince, mounted the English throne ten years later
on the death of his grandfather. The younger, Henry, was the
son of John of Gaunt. Though for the most part Henry supported his cousin against the Duke of Gloucester's faction, he
was banished from England in 1398 and when in the following
year his father died the Lancaster estates were forfeited. Henry,
who was now heir to the throne, assembled an army and invaded England. Within a very short time Richard was deposed
and murdered, and Henry seized the throne.

Thus opened the fifteenth century, an age as troubled, as
bloody and as gloomy as any in the country's history;
troubled by the endless bitter feuds between the children of
one family; bloody because of the long and useless slaughter
inflicted on the people of a neighbouring state followed by a
war at home through whose fury and barbarity thousands of
England's finest youth were slain; gloomy because of the hol-
lowness of life in a world where men pursued their own ends
before those of society, where chivalry was but a gaudy cloak
hiding brutality and barbarism, where the Church of Christ
was universal only in name, where the things of the spirit
were lost in the search for material and sensual pleasure and
the promise of heaven could no longer destroy the terror of
death.

Europe was gripped by the general malady that goes with
the decay of a civilisation. 'The world,' said a French poet, 'is
like an old man fallen into his dotage. He began by being in-
nocent, then in his full manhood he was wise, virtuous and
strong; now in his old age and weakness he is cowardly, greedy

and confused in thought and word. All goes ill, and the end is approaching.'

In England the lowest point was reached in mid-century. In 1453 the state of war with France, which had lasted with only brief intervals of disturbed peace since 1336, finally came to an end, with the loss of all England's possessions in France, save Calais. Meanwhile at home the long struggle between York and Lancaster had begun. Because of a quarrel with Burgundy, trade with the Low Countries had come to a standstill. No wine came from Gascony and cloth exports diminished. Privateers, French and Genoese, preyed on shipping on the high seas and in the Mediterranean.

The effects of bad trade and industrial depression were made worse by the heavy taxation, and injustice. People were restive, especially in the south and east, and there were sporadic outbursts of violence, directed principally against the 'evil advisers of the King', and against the clergy 'because they do not provide examples of good life, nor do they preach to the people, but collect money and do not visit churches nor display hospitality'.

On the 29th June 1450 the Bishop of Salisbury was dragged from the chancel at Edington where he was celebrating mass, and murdered by an angry crowd because he was the King's confessor and had done nothing to remedy the evil state of affairs. On the very same day, all Kent broke out in rebellion under the mysterious leader known as Jack Cade. This was no peasants' revolt. Of the insurgents a hundred at least were gentlemen and half the whole number were husbandmen and craftsmen, goaded to rebellion by the corruption within the court, the constant miscarriage of justice, the extortions of the taxgatherers of the Treasurer Lord Saye and Sele, but above all by the deep humiliation felt at the loss of England's pride and power for, it was said, the King had traitors around him who had lost 'his land, his merchandise, his common people destroyed; the sea is lost, France is lost, and the King himself is so set that he cannot pay for his meat and drink'.

Their demands for the dismissal of William de la Pole, the hated Duke of Suffolk, whom they considered responsible for the disgrace and corruption, and for a new government of 'true barons' headed by the Duke of York gives us a glimpse of one of the earliest popular movements with a political aim. Even then, the cry for the repeal of the Statute of Labourers shows that the old grievances still existed. The rebels advanced from Kent, and for a short while Cade was master of London. Lord Saye, the second Treasurer of England to lose his life at the hands of the people, was beheaded before the rebellion came to an end.

England was still in the throes of civil war. For ten more years the baronial factions of York and Lancaster fought it out until in 1461, after the battle of Towton, Edward of York had himself crowned as Edward IV. Apart from the destruction and devastation on and around the battlefields and on the lines of march, the Wars of the Roses had little effect on the lives of the middle and lower classes who went on quietly with their trades and occupations.

Meanwhile Europe was recovering. Under Louis XI of France the power of Burgundy was broken, and with the coming of peace, trade began to flow along the old routes between the Mediterranean and the north. England, a main producer and buyer, could not long remain outside the circle. Given stability, expansion was certain. That stability was achieved in some measure with the accession of Edward IV, and the slackening of tension brought the biggest revival ever. For the cloth of gold and damask of Venice, for the fruits, oils and spices of the East, the wine of Spain, Portugal and southern France, England exchanged cloth from East Anglia and the Cotswolds, iron from Surrey and the Midlands and lead from Derbyshire and the Mendips. Bristol and Southampton flourished. The Merchant Adventurers became the largest English trading concern of its kind, exporting every kind of commodity except wool. London was soon one of the largest trading centres in Europe, her merchants as prosperous as ever those of Flanders had been in the previous century. The sons of country gentry did not consider it below them to take up apprenticeships in the companies where they rose to wealth and civic dignity. Many of them bought up manors and landed estates, especially in the home counties, and not a few found their way through marriage and service into the new nobility.

Industry and trade must have capital, and large sums can only be obtained by borrowing. Usury was a crime in the Middle Ages for which manor courts had often punished villagers. The medieval preacher, while admitting that there may be a place in God's scheme for the citizen and the trader, denounced the usurer as a servant of the Devil. Yet the lord of the manor did not scruple to lend money to his tenant, taking for the loan of it so many days of ploughing. 'Was not that interest?' asks the pamphleteer. Though usury in theory was condemned for two hundred years more, it came into common practice at this time.

In economic and social matters the protestor is almost always a conservative. He wishes to keep the old because, being poor, he fears that innovation will be made a tool to grind him down. Thus in the general pessimism that comes with the decay of old institutions, it is impossible for the prospective victim to take the long view, or to estimate at its true value the new one. 'Usury,' says the preacher, 'is of a miserable, bare and abject mind; therefore some, to cover their sin and to uphold their credit, have devised cloaks to shroud their ragged garments, and have begotten a more cunning and subtle traffic on the world.' Yet, on the very usury which the preacher denounced, the whole fabric of modern industry and commerce was later built.

How far the revolt of 1381 freed the peasantry from feudal services has long been a doubtful question, but the situation was gradually changing throughout the century. A static and even a declining population in the first half of that century meant that more land was available than could be taken up, and there was a tendency for the poorer soils to pass out of cultivation and revert to waste.

Meanwhile trade was increasing, the towns were growing and drawing the agricultural labourer away from the countryside. Land was therefore easier to buy, to sell and to lease. The increase of trade put more wealth into the hands of the merchants. Some, like the de la Poles of Hull, had already found their way into the nobility through their services to Edward III and there were many more who followed the same path in the succeeding century. The natural progress of a gentleman's son from the provinces was to come to London, engage in trade in one of the companies and, having amassed a certain amount of wealth, to acquire an estate in the home counties and found a family. The natural desire of an enterprising farmer was to add to his holdings wherever he could, and to build up his own small estate.

England, however, still lived under the old manorial system. In the olden days the lord of the manor had lived on the services of his vassals and on their tribute in kind, but all that was gradually changing. In the case of the bondsman, his labour service was now almost everywhere commuted to money payments in the shape of an annual quit-rent and extra sums at specified times, such as the fine when a tenant died or sold land and a new tenant entered into possession. The security the bondsman had for the holding of his land was the small piece of parchment on which was written the copy of the court roll referring to it. He was therefore known as a copyholder.

The standpoints of lord and vassal compared with what they had been in the previous century were now completely reversed. Then, the lord had wanted to change money payments back to services, now his main desire was to get all the land he could under his direct control so that he could let it on lease and live from his rents. On the other side were the men with capital acquired in trade, who wanted to establish themselves as landed gentlemen. The wealthier ones were on the lookout for the lordships of manors, the rest sought smaller pieces of land which they could take on long lease.

All this had a profound effect on the character of the medieval village. It was no longer the self-sufficing, solid, protected community it had once been. The lord had probably leased his demesne land to a stranger who was able to ride roughshod over age-old manor customs, taking into his land part of the waste, interfering with streams and water supplies, turning his beasts out on the common to eat up the pasture which was the peasant's right, cutting wood that was not rightfully his, letting his animals wander over growing crops and inflicting a thousand petty injuries on the villagers who were no longer able to get satisfaction from an absentee lord with no interest in their welfare.

This conflict of interest became evident even among the villagers themselves. The freeholders were secure in their tenancy, and nobody could expel them from their holdings. Many sought to increase them through leases, and to benefit from the movement to enclose. Even the copyholders came to be divided. Some who had taken extra plots on lease had thus gained a certain independence and even power, but the poorer ones who had nothing but their copyholds tended to fall victims to the greed of the enclosers. The manor rolls had once contained the evidence of men's bondage. In 1381 the peasants had cast them into the flames, but a century later they came to be the only means by which they could claim their legal rights. In 1481, the copyholder valued his scrap of parchment, the title to his land and privileges, more than anything else in the world.

The shape of the medieval manor was altering in two ways. Firstly, among the tenants themselves there was a movement to draw together their scattered strips in the common fields by exchanging with each other, also getting a share of the common meadow and pasture land which they could make into one

50

large field and enclose with hedges. This, bringing about considerable saving in labour and cartage and an increase in output, was all to the good where it was well and justly carried out. Many holdings, however, still remained scattered and on a large number of manors were not affected at all.

The second movement was towards the enclosure of the common land. Before the Black Death this had been the normal way of bringing land into cultivation to cope with population increase, but in the later fifteenth century it took a sudden and alarming form.

To the medieval villager the common was as important as the land he cultivated because it gave him summer pasture for his beasts and from it he could take such things as clay, turves, gravel, reeds and brushwood, when they could be found, for the walls and roof of his hovel and to drain his paths. To take the common land away was to deprive the peasant of a good part of his living.

The wealthy men, the newcomers to the village who arrived either as manorial lords or as leaseholders, had no regard for the old custom or for the rights of the poor inhabitants. They were interested mainly in possessing large estates, not necessarily to improve the yield of the land, but rather to build their new and spacious houses with pleasant parkland around them, and to use the rest as they pleased.

Part of the process of estate-building was, where necessary, to buy out the freeholder, to rearrange the leaseholds by admission and eviction to suit the new landlord's convenience, and to get rid of the copyholder. There were various legal, if hardly moral, ways of forcing out the leaseholders, such as raising rent or questioning the legality of the lease. A family might thus have farmed land for a hundred or more years, invested money and labour to make it produce, only to find that according to law the land was not leaseable.

The Tudor landlord who wanted to clear out his tenants had not so many ways of creating nuisances as the modern one who, to get the occupiers out of a block of tenements, has holes bored in the roof and walls, scatters filth, lets rats loose, cuts essential supplies and employs strongarm men. Copyhold quitrents were fixed by manorial custom, but fines and reliefs could be raised almost at will. Many a young man, therefore, inheriting his father's copyhold, after all the fines and reliefs had been paid, had hardly enough capital left to buy tools and seeds. Then, when his cottage fell into disrepair and his fields lay waste, he could be taken to court and ordered to put his holding to rights or pay a fine. If he failed to do either, he could be thrown out. Other tenants who were not evicted could be compelled to give up their copyhold and take land elsewhere on lease. In any case, it was the end of security for the tenant.

The merchant looked at the land in an entirely different way. For the old manorial system, a way of life based primarily on cultivation, he had little respect. In previous ages England had grown rich on the export of raw wool, and Edward III, seeing the advantages to his country in encouraging cloth manufacture, had brought Flemish craftsmen to work in London, York, East Anglia, the Cotswolds and many other districts. Now that there was a worldwide market for English wool and cloth, not only the owner of the large estate but also the small farmer became interested in sheep, in addition to the growing of corn. Enormous quantities of wool were shipped yearly from England to the Continent and everybody who had enough land sought a share in the fat profits. Sheep-rearing absorbed less labour than agriculture, and where it was introduced, especially on the large consolidated estates, labourers lost their employment and some with their families were thrown out of their homes.

Sir Thomas More in his *Utopia* (1616) bewailed the plight of these poor evicted cottagers:

> . . . forsooth my lord (quoth I) your sheep that were wont to be so meek and tame, and so small eaters, now as I hear say, be

become so great devourers and so wild that they eat up and swallow down the very men themselves. They consume, destroy and devour whole fields, houses and cities. For look in what parts of the realm doth grow the finest and therefore dearest wool, there noblemen and gentlemen, yea, and certain abbots, holy men no doubt . . . not contenting themselves with the yearly revenues and profits, that were wont to grow to their forefathers and predecessors of their lands, not being content that they live in rest and pleasure nothing profiting, yea much noying, the weal publique . . . leave no ground for tillage, they enclose all into pastures, they throw down houses, they pluck down towns and leave nothing standing, but only the church to be made a sheep-house . . . and so that one covetous and insatiable cormorant may enclose, poor people have to sell . . . by one means therefore as by other, by hook or by crook they must needs depart away, poor, silly, wretched souls, men, women, husbands, wives, fatherless children, widows, woeful mothers with their young babies. . . . Away they trudge, I say, out of their known and accustomed houses, finding no place to rest in. . . . And when they have wandered abroad till that be spent, what they then else do but steal, and then justly (pardy) be hanged or else go about a-begging.

This kind of eviction was by no means general, and large areas of England were not touched by it. It is estimated that between 1485 and 1515 about one half per cent of the total area of twenty-three counties was enclosed, the most severely affected being in the Midlands (Northamptonshire 2·21 per cent). Probably over this period some five to eight thousand people were displaced. This out of a total population (excluding London) of some three to four millions may not seem much, but the strain on the limited charitable services of the day told heavily, the plight of the poor evicted families evoked both pity and protest, and no tragedy can be played down when it strikes, as sometimes it did, at the livelihood of most of the people in one unfortunate village, where houses were allowed to fall to ruin while the sheep grazed peacefully around the crumbling walls. Protests and complaints abounded.

Envy waxith wonders strong,
The Riche doth the poore wrong:
God of his mercy sufferith long
*   the devill his workes to worke.*
The towns go down, the land decayes:
Off cornefeyldes, playne layes;
Gret men mekithe now a dayes
A shepecott in the churche.

The places that we Right holy call,
Ordeyned for christyan buriall,
Off them to make an ox stall
*   thes men be wonders wyse.*
Commons to close and kepe;
Poor folk for bred [to] *cry and wepe;*
Towns pulled downe to pastur shepe:
*   This ys the new gyse!*

A favourite simile in all ages has been to compare the community to the human body. Thomas Starkey, writing in 1538, likens the hands to the craftsmen and the warriors who furnish and defend it. But the body cannot stand without feet, and these are 'the plowmen and tyllarys of the ground, because they by theyr labour sustayne and support the rest of the body'.

The old medieval figure of speech died hard. Shakespeare's Coriolanus and Hobbes in his 'Leviathan' were to repeat it. And in a body, everything depended on the balance of the functions. To the philosopher and the statesman the encroachment of any one of these was an aberration, a departure from the ideal. Tillage was the foundation industry on which all others rested, and the tiller of the land must not be sacrificed to the unscrupulous rackrenter. There were many practical reasons for upholding the theory. To destroy the small farmer meant not only to cut down the supply of food; evictions diminished the income from taxes, and since the yeoman was

54

also the backbone of the shire it lopped Leviathan's fingers, his means of defending himself. Every statesman of note from Wolsey to Cecil was against excessive enclosure for sheep-farming, and from 1489 to 1597 a long series of acts were passed to check it, to restore 'common to common'. They all failed, for the old system was worked out. England was on the march to a new way of living and nothing law or government could do would stop it in its tracks.

Life in communities was rapidly becoming more complex. Free labourers, once a rare phenomenon on the English scene, were now too numerous for comfort. The natural attraction was to the towns which, with the expansion of trade, were growing fast. But even in villages labour was becoming specialised, and men were finding profit away from the land, in extra occupations such as tiling, thatching, saddlery, the tanning of leather, barrel-making, charcoal-burning, carrying and so on, in which occupations so many modern surnames have their origin. There was more personal freedom than there had ever been before, for the days when every man had his lord were gone. This mobility of labour was all to the good in times when trade was brisk, but in times of recession England was confronted with a new and ever-growing unemployment problem.

This agrarian and social revolution, which had started in such a small way after the Peasants' Revolt, thus gained momentum throughout the Tudor period and not only brought about a new way of life, but completely altered economic thought.

5

Church and State

THOUGH THE SOCIAL evils resulting from enclosure were already pronounced before 1540, the full volume of protest did not come until the middle of the century. The reasons are twofold.

Firstly, the weight of a protest depends to a large extent on the number of people making it, as well as on the force with which they express themselves. John Ball's peasants, for all their zeal, had hardly any means of propaganda beyond the passing of slogans and catch-phrases from mouth to mouth. Such limited means of communication were bound to slow up the progress of any popular movement. Not that it made such a movement any the less serious, for the second effect was also to check the awareness of active discontent in the minds of those in authority.

It is, however, with the spread of the printed word that we are able to gauge something of the intensity of popular discontent as well as to appreciate the arguments of the protestors and the critics. Caxton set up his press at the Red Pale, Westminster, in 1476, but it was fully fifty years before the press became an effective vehicle for the spread of opinion and propaganda.

In 1517 Martin Luther nailed his ninety-five theses to the door of the Castle Church at Wittenberg. These academic arguments against indulgences were hardly calculated to raise a storm, but such was the demand to read them that the university could hardly produce enough printed copies for the public. A century before that time the Papacy and the princes had successfully beaten down the far more serious heresies of Wycliff and Huss. Yet from this relatively minor incident arose the great religious movement known to us as the Reformation. This, like the Wycliffite movement, was a direct challenge to the doctrine of the Roman Church.

Luther believed that sacraments were of no value without faith, and that the Christian who truly repented had already received a pardon from God without the need to purchase an indulgence from a professional pardoner. In 1519 at a great disputation at Leipzig it was proved to Luther that some of his views had been held by Huss and Wycliff. He refused to recant. His revolt against the Church spread; some German princes took up his cause and as a result a large part of northern Europe broke away from the Catholic Church.

In matters of religion Henry VIII of England was a rigid conservative. Theological argument had always fascinated him, and the Lutheran heresy gave him the chance of entering into the lists in 1521 with the only complete book he ever wrote, a defence of the sacraments against the attacks of Luther. On the 12th May 1521 occurred the first public burning of books in England when Luther's works were cast into the flames before Paul's Cross, Bishop John Fisher of Rochester preaching the sermon.

At this point religious differences became political matters, and they continued to be for almost two centuries. The Tudor sovereigns believed that England could only survive as a powerful nation if the people were united, and that religious schism would be the first step to dissolution. As long as Wolsey lived there was no burning of Protestants, but from 1531 onward martyrdoms went on and continued for one reason or another for the rest of the century.

Religion was political, and became more political when Henry, to obtain his divorce, detached his country from the Catholic Church and made himself Supreme Head of the Church in England. But Henry's Church was to remain in all other respects as Catholic as that of the Pope. Here the picture of protest becomes more confusing, for we have on the one hand the Catholics, Sir Thomas More and Archbishop Fisher, who condemned Henry's assumption of ecclesiastical supremacy, and on the other the young men, strongly attached to the new German doctrines, who were faced with the alternatives of recantation or the flames.

More and Fisher voiced in public what many other persons thought in private. Both had been friends of the King and as such had earned the jealousy of Wolsey. Both knew what Henry's favour was worth. 'If my head would win him a castle in France,' More said to his son-in-law, 'it should not fail to go.' When the question of Henry's divorce came to the fore, neither man favoured it. Fisher, who was Catherine's confessor, appeared on her behalf before the legates at Blackfriars, and wrote a treatise against divorce. More, who was Lord Chancellor at the time, asked to be relieved of his post and retired into private life. When he was later invited to be present at the King's wedding with Anne Boleyn, he declined, and for this Henry never forgave him.

The breach between the King and his two servants was complete. At that time the country was startled by the revelations of a young Kentish woman named Elizabeth Barton, whom the country people believed to be God-inspired. One of her prophecies was that should Henry put away his wife he would no longer be King, but would die the death of a villain. Both Fisher and More believed her ravings for a time, and corresponded with her. Fisher was charged with misprision of treason, and an attempt was made to incriminate More on many charges but with no success.

Then in 1534 the Act of Supremacy passed through Parliament. Neither More nor Fisher would acknowledge Henry as Supreme Head of the Church. Fisher was tried on the 17th June 1535 and executed on Tower Hill five days later. More's trial was more sensational, for by his skill he had already more than once escaped sentence. This time the trial was by a special commission. Both Thomas Audley, the Lord Chancellor, and

Richard Rich, the Solicitor-General, were the King's creatures and the jury was packed. The issue was decided when Rich came down from the bar and presented himself as a witness for the Crown. He declared on oath that, while on a visit to More in the Tower of London, he had heard the prisoner declare that no Parliament had the right to make a king supreme Head of the Church.

'If this oath that you have taken be true,' replied More, 'then I pray I may never see God's face.'

He was beheaded on 7th July 1535.

Thus ended one of the earliest episodes of Catholic protest. More's head was exposed on London Bridge. Rich and Audley were both later rewarded with baronies.

In Germany the spread of the Lutheran movement had already plunged the country into chaos. The peasants, oppressed by their feudal lords and the Church, had long been ripe for revolt, and the teaching of Luther gave them promise of freedom in a new and juster society. Luther was himself the son of a peasant, and might have been expected to sympathise with their demands for the abolition of feudal dues and of tithes. But when the disorders threatened to develop into general rebellion, Luther did all he could to prevent it. His appeals to the peasants to keep the peace failed, and he then turned to the nobles, urging them to put down the revolt fiercely and mercilessly. The lot of the unhappy peasants was now worse than before, but their defeat did not bring about peace. The reforming movement was split, and new sects came into being. Civil war broke out in Switzerland between the Catholics and the reformers under Ulrich Zwingli, and from Westphalia a fanatical doctrine called Anabaptism spread into the Netherlands. In the Middle Ages Christendom had been one, for all the infinite variety that existed within it. That unity was now being shattered into fragments, each sect pursuing its own course with no universal system to hold them all together.

Toleration of another's point of view in religious matters

had always been a thing unknown, indeed impossible under the Church Universal, and in the sixteenth century could obviously not suddenly come into being. Not only Catholics, but also Protestants envisaged a world where all the activities of man would be governed by one law as they had once been governed by one Church, and that that law would be the Law of God. But each sect had its own idea of how the Law was to be expressed, and would admit of no other. Against such an attitude the protest of the individual could not but be unavailing. Even among the rebels this was an age of conformity in which no man might dare to stand alone. Protest in religious matters was therefore never successful if it was in the cause of one man's freedom of thought and expression.

The new reformed doctrines were repugnant to Henry VIII, and he wished to avoid at all costs the social stresses that were likely to arise from them. Hence the persecution of the Protestants that occurred during the latter part of his reign. The 'heretical' teachings of Luther could not possibly be kept out of England altogether, and these appealed particularly to a few intelligent young students and priests in Cambridge. These included Thomas Cranmer, Hugh Latimer, Miles Coverdale and William Tyndale.

In 1523 Tyndale had been accused of preaching heresy and in the following year had migrated to Germany where he visited Luther and completed his translation of the Bible. His fame and his teaching spread from the Continent to England, and Henry VIII asked the Emperor to send him back to be tried for spreading sedition. In 1535 he was betrayed and imprisoned in a castle near Brussels and the following year was tried, condemned and executed.

The martyrdom of Protestant preachers was in the cause of that political and doctrinal unity without which Henry believed the country could not exist as a state. Another Cambridge man, Robert Bilney, was summoned before Wolsey and in 1527 imprisoned in the Tower on a charge of heresy. On his release two years later he again began to preach in the open and was arrested at Norwich. He was burned at the stake in London in August 1531.

Many English and Scottish reformers visited Luther at Marburg in Germany, among them Patrick Hamilton, Tyndale and John Frith. Hamilton was burned in Scotland in 1528, Frith in London in 1533 and six or seven others later.

Thomas Cranmer followed a different course. In 1529 he had left Cambridge for Great Waltham in Essex, where he met Henry VIII. Here, in the course of discussion on the question of divorce, and the Pope's refusal to grant it, he made the suggestion that the King might get around the difficulty by consulting the most learned doctors in the universities of Europe. 'This man I trow,' exclaimed Henry, 'has got the right sow by the ear.' It was the beginning of Cranmer's advancement. Within four years he was the Archbishop of Canterbury. In private he shared the views of his Cambridge friends, but he served the King before all other considerations, and during his long period of service he influenced him greatly. Had Henry lived longer, he too might well have become a moderate reformer.

The last great personage among these Cambridge men was Hugh Latimer. A priest of great humanity, and the finest preacher of them all, he had forsaken Romanism in 1523. Though his preachings and writings went very near to heresy, he approved of the royal divorce, and his friendship with Cranmer brought him to the notice of the King, whose favour kept him out of prison. Neither Henry, nor his Chancellor Thomas Cromwell, was averse to tolerating a little heresy in a useful servant. Providing Lutherans did not make nuisances of themselves by preaching and controversy, they were reasonably safe. With the few Anabaptists who appeared in England it was different; for them there was no mercy.

Wycliff in his day had condemned the holding of large estates by the Church as being the source of evil and corruption. In 1536 Henry began the great takeover of these estates for a very different reason, but in replenishing the royal treasury out of the spoils he did much to destroy the unity which the country so much needed. Socially as well as in religion the people of England were torn farther apart, and their differences were not merely differences in belief, but in ways of living. On the one hand, there were the greedy nobles, keen to seize on the pickings of the great confiscation, lords who had long coveted the ecclesiastical manors lying near their estates, lawyers who had furnished the King with advice on the conduct of his complicated religious negotiations, and diplomats who had furthered his interest in the struggle for prestige among the European princes. On the other hand there were people, especially in the north and east of England, who had long cherished grievances of many kinds against lords of whatever nature. The event which brought all these grievances to a head came in 1536 when the property of the smaller monasteries was taken over by the King.

In itself it was a calamity. True, there were many religious houses whose incumbents had long ceased to serve society, whose abbots and priors were as extortionate as any lay landlord, but there were many others, especially in parts more remote from London, which were the only source of comfort and charity to the poor, and whose imminent disappearance raised the threat of eviction when their properties changed hands. The protest which the Dissolution provoked was thus partly religious, partly agrarian.

On the banner of the Lincolnshire rebels was embroidered a ploughshare, the symbol of cultivation, and their cry was, 'What will ye do? Shall we go home and keep sheep?' Those in Cumberland marched behind the Four Captains of Penrith – Faith, Poverty, Pity and Charity – and, having heard Mass, set out to destroy the power of the gentlemen. Yet Robert Aske, the acknowledged leader of the revolt, who marched under the banner of St Cuthbert with the Badge of the Five Wounds, was himself a gentleman and the son-in-law of John, Lord Clifford.

Everywhere the rebels went they reinstated monks and nuns in their old quarters and, gathering forces, they made themselves masters of the whole of the north of England from Newcastle to Hull. A clash between the rebels and the King's army under the Duke of Norfolk at Doncaster was only avoided by the promise of pardon from the King, which Aske persuaded his followers to accept. Like many rebels before him, Aske did not consider himself as being disloyal to the King, but went forward in the full conviction that if only Henry could be made to realise the distress that was being caused by the Dissolution, he would change his mind and come to the help of his people. He was encouraged in this belief by receiving a safe-conduct to London so that he could explain the position of the northerners to the King himself. At this period he wrote down a full account of the rebellion and its causes which puts very clearly the dislocation in social life brought about by the Dissolution:

> The temple of God is now razed and pulled down, the ornaments and relics of the Church of God [are] irreverently used; the tombs and sepulchres of honourable and noble men pulled down and sold. No hospitality [is] now, in those places, kept, but the farmers for the most part let and tavern [underlet] out the farms of the same houses to other farmers for lucre and advantage to themselves.
>
> ... Also divers and many of the said abbeys were in the mountains and desert places where the people are rude of condition and not well taught of the law of God. And when the said abbeys stood, the said people not only had worldly refreshing in their beds, but also spiritual refuge both by the ghostly living of them, and also by spiritual information and preaching.

The wording of this last statement shows why the Pilgrimage of Grace started in the north of England and why, even after the country had become Protestant, Catholicism lingered in these remote parts. The abbeys had been, as Aske put it, the spiritual comfort to man's soul, the earthly support of the people, with charity, meat and wages, the educators of the young in school and nunnery, the maintainers of sea-walls and dykes, highways and bridges. Their destruction caused more harm and distress here than anywhere else in the whole country.

The last lot of the peasant was infinitely worse than the first. Between 1536 and 1540 millions of pounds in property were passed from the Church to the Crown, and this was handed over sometimes as a grant in payment of a debt, sometimes as a sale. The sudden release of large estates for sale caused an abnormal drop in land values. Old monastic buildings were converted into country mansions by young lawyers and financiers who had served Henry in the Court of Augmentation, the body that had managed the extensive land transfers. Many of them even bought estates and paid for them in instalments. Others, particularly the smaller men, often bought at second-hand and, on a rising market, sold later at a profit. Never before had there been such a fury of land speculation, and though Henry obtained about £1½ million from the sales and an average of £130,000 a year from leases, he received nothing like the real market value of the land confiscated.

In every case it was the tenant who suffered. If the land he held was wanted for sheep, he was turned off; if not his rents were raised to breaking point, and with the rise in prices, he suffered privation.

> More for a penye wee have before seene
> than now for fowre pense, whoe list to compare.
> So goethe hee to hys bedde hungrelye,
> and risethe agayne with bellies emptye;
> whiche turnethe to tawnye their white englisch skyn,
> like to the swarthie coelored Fflawndrekyn.
>
> Wheare they weare valiaunt, stronge, sturdy and stowte,
> to shoote, to wrastle, to dooe anye mannys feate
> to matche all natyons dwelling heare abowte,

64

as hitherto manlye they holde the chief seate;
if they bee pinched and weyned from meate,
I wisse, O kynge, they in penurye thus pende
shall not bee able thye Royalme ro defende.

By the time Henry died (1547) the reformed religion had taken strong root in England. Under the influence of Cranmer, even the King had made some concessions to it. The English Bible, translated by Miles Coverdale, was authorised for circulation (1536) though only the nobility and gentry were permitted to read it. Religion was, however, more and more freely discussed. England, already turning towards Protestantism, was thrust into it by the Protector Somerset, ruler of England for the young King Edward VI. All Henry VIII's laws against heresy were repealed, restrictions on the printing of the Bible were lifted, images and relics were removed from the churches, a new form of public prayer was introduced with the First Prayer Book, and the old books used in the Catholic Church, the antiphonaries, missals, graduals, processionals and others, were abolished. Over all England precious church furniture and relics disappeared in an orgy of burning and destruction. All chantries and religious gilds were suppressed and their endowments confiscated, and the lands belonging to the bishoprics were taken over. Though Cranmer would have liked to see the proceeds of all this go to help the poorer clergy, they were greedily lapped up by courtiers and the speculative buyers.

The fall of Somerset and the rise to power of the Earl of Warwick accelerated the rush to a more extreme form of Protestantism. From his stronghold in Geneva Calvin exhorted the King and Cranmer to root out the last remnants of Catholicism. Altars in churches were replaced by plain communion tables, and in the second Prayer Book introduced in 1552 the communion service was made no more than a service or remembrance of the Last Supper. By the Second Act of

Uniformity this form of worship was imposed on all, and a minimum of churchgoing was made compulsory.

During this period, religious and economic unrest were again intermingled. In 1549 the introduction of the First Prayer Book aroused the villagers in the West of England who rose in protest, and in many places parsons were forced to put on their vestments and celebrate Mass according to the old rites. Devon and Cornwall, which, like the North, were the counties farthest from London and the new religious thought, clung to the Catholicism of Henry VIII. The leaders were principally peasants and priests, and their aim was to restore the Mass in Latin and to keep the ancient vestments, pictures and images. They had no sympathy from the more progressive towns, especially Exeter, which resisted them, and when the revolt was over they received no mercy from the soldiery who subdued it.

The movement of the peasants in Norfolk was hardly as much a rebellion as a mass protest against the gentry who had enriched themselves by enclosure at the expense of the Church and the poor. Robert Ket, who became the leader, though not the instigator, of the movement, was lord of one of the manors of Wymondham, and one of the few members of the gentry who took part in it. He obviously thought that the Government would listen to his plea and reason with him, for though sixteen thousand men are said to have assembled on Mousehold Heath, they conducted themselves at first more like a Chartist open-air convention than an army. Twice Ket was offered a pardon and refused it because he maintained he had done no wrong.

He sought not to hinder the Government but to co-operate with it in achieving the things he asked for; the stopping of further enclosures, the control of land prices, a reduction of fines on the transfer of copyhold estates, the restoration of commons, an end of personal bondage, the checking of rabbits and other pests on private estates and many other things. His most important proposition was for a commission to see that such measures were taken. The request that he and the men he nominated should serve on that commission indicates that he considered his movement far from being a rebellion.

The real fighting did not begin until a peasant boy insulted the herald reading the offer of pardon 'with words as unseemly as his gesture was filthy' and was shot by a member of the herald's retinue. The rest of the story is quickly told. The rebels, as they then became, moved on Norwich and took it. Up to this moment Somerset had had a certain amount of sympathy with them but it was obvious that they had to be crushed, and the man most able and eager to do this was Somerset's rival for power, the Earl of Warwick. With an army he entered Norwich and routed the insurgents at Dussingdale.

This happened in 1549. Within thirty years the complexion of public affairs had changed completely. New factors, among them Protestantism, the great trade revival, the free market in land, the increased mobility of labour and the circulation of printed literature, had brought about a great awakening. The commons were no longer mute. Not even in the twentieth century, reputed to be one of speed, have conditions changed more quickly. The old man in 1549 who remembered the early days of the Tudor despotism must have wondered what the world was coming to. Men who had once accepted the word of priest and lord were asking questions, discussing in tavern and at street corner. Luther, Columbus and Caxton between them had created a new world, new doubts, new discontents, new directions and new hopes. In the thirty years the unitary state of Henry VII had been shattered to fragments, bereft of the binding force once exerted by land obligations and a universal form of religion. Now every man, in pursuance of his own interests had forgotten that he had his duty to a greater society.

But had this power for unity really been lost? The new forms of prayer asserted it, the Act of Uniformity was there to enforce it. What was essential in the mind of the thinking person was that religion, man's duty to God, should of his own volition be carried into daily life and expressed in loving-kindness and charity to his fellowmen. Only in this way could the common weal be realised.

If anybody by exhortation could have rooted out the evils of the day the men who preached this doctrine of common weal would have done it. They were not a political party; they were not even a group or a society as much as a number of separate individuals inspired by an ideal which could only be realised by willed obedience to God's laws. They were all reformers. Some of them had been imprisoned for their faith and might well have been put to death had they not discreetly recanted and subsequently kept a bridle on their tongues. Among the best known of them were Hugh Latimer, Bishop of Worcester, John Ponet, Bishop of Rochester, Thomas Becon, Chaplain to the Duke of Somerset, the priests Robert Crowley and Thomas Lever, and John Hales, Member of Parliament for Preston. Latimer, Ponet, Becon and Lever were famous preachers, Crowley was an Oxford scholar turned propagandist and printer who issued his own works from his press in Holborn.

For all their reforming zeal, the commonwealth men, as they were called, were bound by the traditional ways of thought. Their condemnation of the vices of the age, their word-pictures of the greedy usurer, the rapacious landlord and leaseholder, the brawlers, dicers, bawds and cozeners in the London streets are in the true spirit of the medieval preacher. In their opinion the first requirement for the salvation of England was that all men should look into their own souls and, having seen the evil there, should strive to mend their ways.

This applied in particular to the rich men and the land-owners, for the fate of the country lay in their hands. Again the likeness of the state to the body appears. The upper members, the head, neck, arms, chest and heart, which are the directing force, should clothe the lower members, for it is on them that the body is carried. This is true common weal.

How strong feudal ideas still remained in the minds of men is borne out by its preachers. Land and riches were not the sole property of the individual to do as he pleased with; they were held of God and to God the evil leasemonger, the encloser of commons and the usurer would one day have to render account.

> Thou shalt not think that thou maist take
> Thy rente to spend it at thy wyll,
> As one that should no reknyng make
> For ought that he doth well or yl.
>   But thou shald fynd that thou art bound
> And shalt answer much more strayghtly
> Than the pore men who tyll the ground
> If thou regard not thy duty.
>   Thou shalt not fynd that thou mayst reise
> Thy rent, or levy a great fyne
> More the hath bene used alwayes
> For that only is called thine.

Thus wrote Crowley in his book, *The Voyce of the Last Trumpet* (1550). On the leasemongers and rent-raisers he is especially scathing in his *Of Pleasure and Payne, Heaven and Hell* (1551).

> The pore, the pore and indigent
> Come unto you ofte tymes ye knowe
> And you sawe them wepe and lament,
>   Yet would ye not on them bestowe
>   The least frute that to you dyd growe,
> That other gave them for my sake.
>   Your hertes were harder than the flynt —
> In them no pitie could be founde.
> Youre greedie gutte coulde never stynt
>   Tyle all the good and fruitfulle grounde
>   Were hedged in within your mownde.
> Yow wycked sorte, how used ye
> The londes and goodes ye had of me?

69

The two rebellions in the west and in Norfolk had both been put down in 1550. In that year Crowley published his *The Waye to Wealth*, in which he analysed from the point of view both of rich and poor the causes of sedition:

> The causes of Sedition muste be roted oute. If ye shuld demaunde of the pore man of the countrey what things he thinketh to be the cause of Sedition, I know his answere. He would tell me that the great fermares, the grasiers, the rich buchares, the men of lawe, the marchauntes, the gentlemen, the knightes, the lords and I cannot tel who . . . men without conscience. Men utterly voide of Goddes feare. Yea, men that live as thoughe there were no God at all! . . . Cormerauntes, gredye gulles; yea, men that would eate up menne, women & chyldren are the causes of Sedition. They take our houses over our headdes, they bye our growndes out of our handes, they reepe our rentes, they levy great (yea unreasonable) fines, they enclose our commons. No custome, no lawe or statute can kepe them from oppressying us in such sorte, that we knowe not whyche waye to turne us to lyve. . . . In the countrey we can not tarye, but we must be thyr slaves and laboure tyl our hertes brast, and then they must have al.

Thus speaks the poor man. The rich man has another explanation:

> Nowe if I should demaund of the gredie cormerauntes what they thinke should be the cause of Sedition, they would sai: 'The paisant knaves be to welthy, provender pricketh them! They knowe not them selves, they knowe no obedience, they regard no lawes, they would have no gentlemen, they wold have al men like themselves, they would have al thinges commune! They would not have us maisters of that which is our owne! They wil appoint us what rent we shal take for our groundes! We must not make the beste of oure owne! These are ioly felowes! They wil caste doune oure parckes & laie oure pastures open! They wil have the law in their own handes! They wil play the kinges! They wil compel the kinge to graunt theyr requestes! But as they like their fare at breakfaste they had this laste somer, so let them do againe! They

have ben metely wel coled, and shal be yet beter coled if they quiet not themselves. We wyll tech them to know theyr betters. And if they once stirre agayne or do once cluster togither, we wil hang them at their own dores.

'Give me leave to answer for the pore idiotes over whom ye triumphe in this sorte,' writes Crowley. He points out that the first crime was that of the landlords for enclosing the commons and in disobeying the continual proclamations to return common to common. 'Own your offences,' he cries, 'lest God serve you as he did the Egyptians . . . and doubte ye not, you leasemongers, that take groundes by lease to the entente to lette them oute agayne for double and tryple the rent, your parte is in this plage. The Lord shall take his Spirite from you.'

Though the commonwealth men were scathing in the condemnation of unjust landlords, they were as severe in their disapproval of any act of force on the part of the peasants. They were not without pity for their poor countrymen whose blood had been 'metely well coled' by the swords of Warwick and Russell, and whose lifeless bodies lined the highways of the east and west country. It is hard to imagine that the survivors could have had much comfort from the exhortations of Thomas Lever:

Meate was provided for the Commens of Englande and ready to have ben delivered. But when they were bydden to syt downe in quietness they rose up by rebellion, and have lost the chere of that feast. Yet that notwithstandyng, I trust that those whiche sat quietly indede shall soone be fed with plentye, if they sytte styll, untyll it may conveniently be disposed. I pray God they may; I trust they shall. . . . Wherefore, ye people, if ye fele your burden is heavye, and your yocke grevouse, pacyently suffer, and call unto the Lorde, for then he wyll heare thee, and he wyll relieve thee, and he wyll delyver thee.

Lever's picture of the commonalty waiting for the preparation of a feast was far too rosy. Though Somerset was on their

71

side and legislation to deal with some of their grievances was already in being, landlords were not likely to give way so easily.

Crowley's reprimand is far harsher. He urges everybody, peasants, servants, tenants, yeomen, even beggars, to be content with their lot. If not, God will visit both rebels and tyrants with the same punishment:

> *The wycked sorte that dyd rebell*
> *Agaynst you, when you dyd them wronge,*
> *Shall have theyr parte wyth you in hell,*
> *Where you shall synge a˙dolefull songe.*

Truly medieval this! Indeed, the whole tenour of the gospel of common weal was medieval, the return to a unitary state where every man was his brother's keeper, whose rackrenting was impossible and usury abhorrent. The idea of commonwealth brought forth the accusation that its apologists wanted all men to possess everything in common, but this was stoutly denied. Their doctrine was one of stewardship.

> Take me not that I should go about these wordes to perswade men to make all thynges commune; for if you do, you mistake me. . . . But I woulde wysh that the possessioners woulde conseder whoe gave them theyr possessions. – Crowley, *An information and Petition agaynst the Oppression of the Poore Commons.*

How, said Lever, could anybody preach the common holding of property when there were so many lazy parasites in society?

> . . . How be it ther can be nothyng more contrarye or further disagreying from that phantastical commennesse, or rather from that develyshe disorder and unrighteous robberie where as Idle Lubbers mighte lyve of honest mennes labours, then to have all thynges common as the Apostles hadde. – *A fruitful sermon made at Paules Church,* 1550.

What, then did the commonwealth men do?

Their contribution was threefold. First, they kept alive the land question. Their works were an inspiration for other commoners for generations to come. Somerset fell in 1549, and with his fall ended the fruitful period of their writing and preaching, but there were problems arising from enclosure and sheeprearing for a hundred and more years.

Their second contribution, slight though it may have been, was in the realm of education. Crowley in one of his epigrams muses on the fate of the abbeys and their schools: while walking alone, he thought of all the abbeys he had seen which were gone, suppressed by a law.

> O Lorde, (thought I then),
> What occasion was here
> To provide for learnynge
> And make povertye chere?
> The landes and the jewels
> That hereby were hadde
> Would have found godly preachers.
> Which might well have ladde
> The people aright
> That now go astraye,
> And have fedde the pore
> That famyshe everydaye.

The schools were sacrificed with the monasteries and the chantries. It was a sad blow to education, and especially to the yeoman families who had been used to sending their sons to these schools. Latimer, himself the son of a yeoman, preaching before Edward VI at Paul's Cross in 1549, spoke plainly about the effects of enclosure on education:

> Well, well, this is one thing I will say unto you; from whence it cometh I know, even from the devil. I know his intent in it. For if ye bring it to pass that the yeomanry be not able to put

their sons to school (as indeed universities do wondrously decay already); I say ye pluck salvation from the people and utterly destroy the realm. For by yeomen's sons the faith of Christ is and hath been maintained chiefly.

Lever delivered the same condemnation of the rapacity of the landlords and the callousness of the government in failing to stop this great gap. The re-establishment of a few schools which had previously been disendowed, now known as the Edward VI Grammar Schools, was the direct result of the agitation of a few commonwealth men.

Of all the stars of this movement none shone more brightly than Hugh Latimer, whose sermons before Edward VI at Paul's Cross were heard by fascinated crowds. His discretion had saved him from the Henrican persecution of Protestants to help in the building of the new Church, and though the work he did with his superior, Cranmer, in this direction was temporarily undone, it was not utterly lost.

In 1548 his tongue was loosed, and his sermons are classics of their kind. He had the gift of clothing his ideas in simple homely language, his points illustrated by a wealth of narrative culled largely from his memories of youth in a country household. Fearlessly he lashed out at the landlords and the oppressors, and his language still stirs the heart and paints a picture of social England more vivid than that painted by many a textbook. Like his fellowmen of the common weal he wanted to see a united happy country, not only politically but socially, bound by a united Church. His lively denunciation of German Protestantism, the very antithesis of Church unity, is only one of a thousand homely, humorous allusions.

> Germany was visited twentie years with goddes word but they dyd not earnestlye embrace it, and in lyfe follow it, but made a myngle-mangle and a hotchpotch of it. . . . They say in my contrye, when they cal theyr hogges to the swyne troughe, Come to thy myngle-mangle, come pyr, come pyr; even so they made a myngle-mangle of it.

74

Nobody had more influence than Latimer on the minds of man in his day.

The third effect of the agitation of the commonwealth men was in the achievement of their man of affairs and legislator, John Hales.

Hales, born in Kent and living in Coventry where he founded a free school, was a Member of Parliament and in 1549 held the office of Clerk of the Hanaper. He was almost certainly the author of *A Discourse of the Common Weal of this Realm of England,* written in 1549 and one of the most informative books of the period. In its way it is a text-book of commonwealth beliefs. The work is a dialogue between the Knight, probably representing Hales himself, the Doctor, whose original may have been Hugh Latimer, and three others, a capper, a merchant and a husbandman. These five figures pass in review all the major questions of the day – enclosure, the decay of towns, agriculture and sheeprearing, credit, coinage, defence and alliances, and they suggest remedies for the evils which exist. The theme of the whole book is that man does not live of himself alone.

> We be not borne to ourselves but partly to the use of oure countrie, of our parentes, of our kinsfolkes and partly of oure friendes and neighbours, and therfore all goode vertues are grafted in on us naturally, whose affectes be to doe goode to others, whan it shewethe forthe the Image of God in man, whose propertie is ever to doe goode to others, to distribute his goodness to others abroade, like no nygarde nor envious thinge.

This natural goodness of man is hindered by more powerful faults, which combine to create social chaos and make for the decay of the realm. The chief of these faults is avarice:

> To tell you plainely [says the doctor], it is Averice that I take for the principall cause therof; but can we devise that all covetousnes mai be taken from men? No, no more than we can make men to be withoute Ire, withoute gladness, withoute

feare, and withoute all affections. What then? We must take awai from men the occasion of covetousnes in this parte?

The remedy is legislation. By such measures as price-fixing, coinage reform and regulation of imports and exports, sheep-rearing can be made to bring less profit and husbandry more, thus restoring the balance on the land, and by regulation of foreign trade the wellbeing of different sections of the community may be ensured.

Hales tried to put into practice what he preached. Through his friendship with the eminent lawyer, Sir Thomas Smith, he had the goodwill of Somerset, who was himself interested in the protection of the husbandman. The first Act which Hales brought into Parliament was the Subsidy Act of 1548, which was intended to remove one great evil, that of the purchase of provisions by the Crown. When the King was on a journey his dreaded purveyors went on in front of the retinue to buy goods either at a grossly reduced price or by giving 'wooden money' in the form of tally-sticks which were often never honoured. A royal journey often laid waste a whole region.

'for they march,' said the fourteenth-century preacher, 'not at the King's expense or their own, but at the expense of the churches and the poor, whom they spoil in their path. And if they do happen to buy anything, they give nothing but tallies in payment. Christ fed five thousand on five loaves. These men do a greater miracle; for they feed ten thousand on little tallies . . . not once or twice, like Christ, but frequently.'

Hales proposed to abolish purveyance and to substitute a tax on sheep and cloth. Parliament accepted his bill, for it meant relief for the landowner, and in any case it would probably be easy to evade the taxes.

Hales' second measure was the appointment of an Enclosure Commission. This was the body which, said Lever, might have put before the peasants that feast which was being prepared for them. Accounts were to be given of all land enclosed since 1489, of all flocks of sheep over 2,000 strong, and to whom they belonged. Hales himself was a member of the committee dealing with six midland counties, and some enclosers were actually presented by grand juries, their fences levelled and the plough driven over the enclosed land. The landowning classes were infuriated by this, and also by the bills which were subsequently presented to rebuild decayed houses, to forbid speculation in foodstuffs and to encourage cattle grazing at the expense of sheep. In view of their attitude, there was little prospect that the peasants would have taken part in any feast even if they had not risen in revolt.

They suffered the vengeance of their lords, but the most notable victim of the unrest of 1548 was Somerset himself. His brief tenure of power had been a succession of mistakes and misfortunes. By a fruitless invasion of Scotland, a further debasing of the coinage to help pay for it, the plunder of the chantries, the destruction of church plate, furniture and vestments, the reclaiming of commons and leniency towards the peasants, he had alienated almost every influential section of society – Catholics, reformers, nobility, merchants and landlords. The Council turned against him, the army failed to come to his support, and he was imprisoned in the Tower. Though he was later released, his popularity in the country districts was a menace to the power of Warwick, who was now the leading man in the Council. Two years later, after a travesty of a trial, Somerset was beheaded.

This was the end of common weal. Under Warwick, who was now Duke of Northumberland, the Enclosures Commission ceased to function, no more measures were taken to protect tenants, and an Act was passed making it a felony for peasants to meet together to break down fences. Hales left the country; Crowley, Bacon and Latimer wrote and preached in vain. But the work they had done was not lost; its record remained as an inspiration to future generations of protestors.

77

Three years later the commonwealth men suffered the same fate as many other prominent reformers, for under the Catholic government of Mary, England became too hot for them. In the German and Swiss citadels of reform they waited for the tide to turn. 'What is exile?' asked Ponet. 'A thing painful only in imagination provided you have the wherewith to exist.' He died in Strasbourg in 1556.

With the death of Queen Mary in 1558, the exiles returned, but things were never the same again. Crowley, now a priest, was deprived for a time in 1566 for refusing to preach in the surplice. In 1576 he was given a living in London and became a freeman of the Stationers' Company. He died in 1588.

The story of Latimer is too well known to be repeated. He was led to the stake at Oxford on the 16th October 1555 in company with Nicholas Ridley, Bishop of London, he who had first cast down the church altars in the orgy of Protestant destruction. Latimer's last words were in keeping with the character and preaching of a great Englishman.

'Be of good comfort, Master Ridley, and play the man; we shall this day light such a candle by God's grace in England as, I trust, shall never be put out.'

6

The Elizabethans

IN THE UNITARY state such as existed under the Tudors there were two kinds of protest; the first that of a section of the people, active even to the point of taking up arms, the second that of individuals, holding on to some faith or belief repugnant to the rulers and persisting in their refusal to obey authority whatever the consequences. The first we have seen in the Pilgrimage of Grace, and the rebellions of 1549, the second in the case of the Protestants martyred in the reign of King Henry VIII. There were to be still more of both kinds in the days to come.

Jane Grey and her husband were the unfortunate tools of an unscrupulous, ambitious and unpopular statesman, and all three paid for one man's folly at the executioner's block. The acclamation of the excited crowds who flocked to Mary's standard in Suffolk, and the warmth of her subsequent reception in London proved that the old Tudor magnetism had not lost its strength. England was still Catholic enough to acquiesce in the restoration of the Mass, and the sacred vessels, vestments, images and books, which had been thrown out three years before, were brought back. The country was still mainly Catholic at heart, and the convinced Protestant gentlemen, who felt they could not live under the new regime, were allowed to move abroad with the expelled foreign clergy. There remained a minority of malcontents, especially in London and the south-east, and a few Protestant bishops of whom the most important were Cranmer and Latimer.

The first protest of the reign was provoked by the Queen's decision against the will of her counsellors, her parliament and the bulk of her people, Catholics and Protestants alike, to marry Philip of Spain. Her motives, to bear a son who would one day be king of a country restored to Catholicism, were both political and religious; the movement against her marriage was purely the former, for there were even many Catholics to whom the idea of a Spanish king on the throne of England was repugnant.

Sir Thomas Wyatt was the son of the famous poet and courtier of the same name, of Maidstone, Kent. Early in life he is said to have accompanied his father on his missions abroad, and there to have been shocked by the brutality of the Spanish Inquisition. The rebellion that takes his name was the most dangerous of all in Tudor times, for the men who took part in it were both better armed and better disciplined than the peasants. Like the rising of Jack Cade, this took place in and near London, the nerve-centre of the kingdom. If the Queen had taken the advice of some of her counsellors and left the capital, both it and the crown might have fallen. Wyatt, with four thousand Kentishmen at his back, was prevented from crossing the Thames at London Bridge and the move to Kingston was his undoing. When he arrived at Ludgate the city was closed to him and a force under the Earl of Pembroke blocked his retreat at Temple Bar. His surrender and execution were the end of the only armed protest against Catholicism.

The number of Protestants who died in the Marian persecution was small compared with that in many other countries. The reason for the burning of at least some of them appears trifling today, and the manner of their deaths was appalling. Cranmer, Latimer, Ridley and Hooper had taken part in the stormy politics of England and vengeance against them is to some extent understandable. Other bishops and clergymen, whose business it was to preach the gospel, were burned because they persisted in their open opposition and would not desist from preaching. Some gathered congregations in the woods and on the heaths, only to be betrayed to men like the infamous Richard, Lord Rich, who handed them over for examination.

The south and east of England, always open to trade and communication with the Protestant Netherlands and the Rhineland, had more than two hundred martyrs, and Essex alone had seventy-three. These were not gentlefolk, for the bulk of the Protestant gentry had already gone into exile. They were in the main ordinary men and women who, when their preachers had been taken from them, persisted in their worship, meeting secretly in each other's houses where, said one accuser 'they keep their privy conventicles and schools of heresy'. Most of them were artisans and housewives, or young men and girls hardly out of adolescence, with little learning but great zeal. Some person, jealous, bigoted or evil-minded, would denounce them as being of unsound doctrine, when they would be hunted down, examined by the bishop, found wanting and yet refusing to recant. Theirs was an early example of passive resistance and non-cooperation.

During the reigns of Mary and Elizabeth I, religious differences threatened the unity of the state to such an extent that one is apt to forget the seriousness of the enclosure problem, and the evils that sprang from it. Sporadic risings took place all over the country accompanied by the tearing down of enclosures and the driving away and selling of the sheep. The most important disturbances took place in Kent in 1550, in Buckinghamshire in 1552 and in Derbyshire in 1569. Here the villagers of Chinley tore down the hedges put up by a lease-holder who, on producing warrants against them, was threatened with murder. One of the demands of Wyatt's followers was that pasture lands seized by those in power should be restored. In 1595 high prices caused unrest in Oxfordshire and there were more threats against those who had enclosed land and forced them up. The government, ostensibly on the side of the peasants, passed laws against depopulation, including the well-known one of 1589 forbidding the leasing of labourers' cottages unless they had four acres of ground attached. There was neither the will nor the power to implement these at the time, and the disturbances went on. In 1598 the Rev Thomas Bastard's epigrams on enclosures appeared:

> *I knowe where is a thiefe and long hath beene,*
> *Which spoyleth every place where he resortes:*
> *He steales away both subjects from the Queene,*
> *And men from his owne country of all sortes.*
> *Howses by three, and seaven, and ten he raseth,*
> *To make the common gleabe, his private land:*
> *Our country Cities cruell he defaceth,*
> *The grasse grows greene where little Troy did stand,*
> *The forlorne father hanging downe his head,*
> *His outcast company drawne up and downe,*
> *The pining labourer doth beg his bread,*
> *The plowswayne seeks his dinner from the towne.*
>   *O Prince, the wrong is thine, for understand,*
>   *Many such robberies will undoe thy land . . .*
> *Sheepe have eat up our medows and our downes,*
> *Our corne, our wood, whole villages and townes.*
> *Yea, they have eate up many wealthy men,*
> *Besides widowes and Orphane children:*
> *Besides our statutes and iron laws*
> *Which they have swallowed down into their maws.*
>   *Till now I thought the proverbe did but jest,*
>   *Which said a blacke sheepe was a biting beast.*

All through the first half of the following century the disturbances continued, and the complaints of the unprivileged classes found expression in the programmes of the Levellers and Diggers.

The economic revolution, the conversion of arable to grass, the dissolution of the Monasteries, the flood of evictions, the increase in trade, the rise in prices, all these had created a class whose presence was a visible protest against the injustices of society. These were the numbers of unemployed who tramped the country, often in gangs, the demoralised remnants of what once had been an industrious agricultural society. Their complaints are seldom recorded, but their ruses to get money, clothing and food are set out in such accounts as Harrison's *Description of England*, Audeley's *Fraternitie of Vacabondes*, Harman's *Warning for Common Cursitors*, and Dekker's *Gull's Handbook*.

In Elizabeth's day England was still paying the price for the devastation wrought by her father, in the spectacle of a country scarred by the unsightly remains of what had once been stately churches and monastic buildings, and by the slums put up, especially in London, on their former precincts. The country was still more scarred by the ruins of humanity who infested town and countryside, the sturdy beggars or rufflers, the courtesy men who dealt in confidence tricks, soldiers and sailors discharged to get a living as best they could, with their doxies, dells and morts. Their method was to deceive, to arouse fear or pity, their justification, the right for all to live, for, said one, 'Is not this a great labour, to run from one town to another to get our meat? I think we work as hard as other men do.'

No doubt they did. The days had gone when a poor man was accounted blessed and used as a sounding-board for the virtues of the rich. Then, he could squat outside the abbey gates or by the side of the highway, and to serve him was to open the way to heaven. But in the sixteenth century with the founts of charity running dry and the number of applicants increasing, there was no living to be got out of squatting with a clap-dish. The poor and indigent had to learn new tricks.

The hearts of men had hardened. Puritan and mercantile morality taught that if men did not work neither should they eat, and labour, once deemed the Curse of Adam, had become the *summa virtutis*. 'Go to the ant, thou sluggard, and be wise.' Thus the beggar, once a necessary part of social and religious life, was to be abhorred and spurned. 'They are as rotten legges or armes that droppe from the body,' wrote the preacher Thomas Preston. '. . . to wander up and downe from yeare to yeare to this ende, to seek and procure bodily maintenance, is no calling, but the life of a beast.' The tramp was the dread of every respectable man and woman.

Unemployment and vagabondage would have resulted in any case from the loosening of feudal bonds, and the changes in the use of land, but they had been vastly increased by the events following on the Dissolution. Thus, this problem, created in the reign of Henry VIII, was inherited by the state under Elizabeth. It was a problem the country had never had to deal with before, and it took time before those in authority realised that unemployment cannot be cured by trying to suppress its symptoms, that no amount of setting vagrants in the stocks, whipping them at the cart's tail, branding and earlopping could make a man find work if it did not exist.

The beginnings of a remedy, the provision of relief for those who were too ill or too old to work, of houses of correction for the sturdy and able-bodied who would not, of homes and hospitals for the sick and the children, were first undertaken by towns such as London and Norwich out of voluntary gifts made by citizens. The giving of charity that had once been the work of monasteries was now thrown by the government on to the parishes and the Justices of the Peace. At first parsons were urged to collect voluntary alms, then in 1549–50 they were given the power of calling in the bishop's aid should their gentle exhortations prove inefficacious. In 1563 power was given to the civil magistracy, if neither the bishop nor the parson could do anything, and this led in 1573 to the appointment in all parishes of overseers of the poor who were empowered to secure the approval of justices to compulsory poor rates. All this culminated in a series of acts between 1597 and 1601 which codified everything that had been done and for two hundred years and more formed the basis of the English Poor Law.

England, in its newly-developed local government, in its

poor law, its flourishing trade, growing towns, expanding industries, its adventurous seamen, its poets, dramatists and scholars, and above all the high spirits and national pride of its people under a queen respected and loved, had the beginnings of all that was best in its national life. In the squalor and corruption in its towns, the laxity of morals, the festering vagrancy problem and above all the religious intolerance that made men ready to maim and slay their neighbours over points of doctrine that were beyond any man's knowledge or understanding, it possessed the elements of everything that was worst, and this was to lead to a further century of loss and destruction, with the sacrifice of some of its finest and most talented sons.

The country had seen first a sort of state Catholicism under Henry VIII, then a lapse into rabid Protestantism followed by just as violent and intolerant a reversal of religious policy under Mary. In the sixteenth century when the whole fabric of medieval Catholicism came crashing down, even within the Church of Rome itself, and northern Europe was thrown into a series of convulsive reactions under Luther, Zwingli, Mün zer, Calvin and a dozen other self-announced prophets, fanaticism would have flourished and been transported into England in any case, but the rapid change from one official doctrine to another as the state religion, the persecution of those who opposed it, and the bitterness and hatred engendered by it, must have contributed to the increase of the number of fanatics. This was an age when a man would fight to the death to see his own particular faith tolerated, but would be just as ready to deliver the deathblow to anybody who did not share it.

This was, however, more than a mere question of doctrine; it was a difference between ways of life which cleft the English people as cruelly as any problem of colour; even more so, because a sudden act of conversion could split irreconcilably members of one family. The Mass and the Puritan conventicle were poles apart; their adherents did not even speak the same language or inhabit the same world though they may have been living next door to each other. These two were the extremities, the Right and Left of English religious and social life. Between them was the bulk of the people, the Anglicans who assented to the forms of the Elizabethan Church. They were the great majority but as always happens, the voices that were loudest were those of protest from the two extremes, Papist and Puritan.

Elizabeth faced the position not without hope. She desired, as much as ever her father and sister had done, to see England united. Her object was, by taking reasonable measures of compromise, to draw these extremes nearer together, to brace the country to face all the other serious problems, internal and external, that confronted it. This was the reason for what is called the Elizabethan Settlement, embodied in the measures of 1559 which made Elizabeth Supreme Governor of the country 'as well in spiritual or ecclesiastical things as temporal'. Edward VI's Second Prayer Book was restored and religious uniformity throughout the kingdom was demanded. Attendance at church was made compulsory on pain of a fine of a shilling for every absence, and though other vestments were abandoned the parson had to use the cope for sacraments and the surplice for all other ministrations.

All the bishops but one and the majority of the clergy were deprived of their livings, though many more left off wearing the surplice and were only ejected when they were found out. The wholesale return of exiles from the Continent strengthened the Puritan element, especially in the south and east, and here in particular protests against wearing the 'rags of Antichrist' were very strong. Harrison, who was himself a parson, describes the surplice as 'comely, and in truth more decent than ever it was in the Popish Church when the priests went either in divers colours like players or in a garment of light hue . . . so that to meet a parson those days was to behold a peacock that spreadeth his tail when he danceth before the hen'.

86

The refusal of parsons to wear the surplice went on for years and provoked both amusing and moving incidents. One vicar, having been presented to the Archdeacon's Court for this lapse, armed himself with his bow and arrow and went in search of the offending churchwarden who, however, lived to tell the tale. In many parishes the congregations urged their vicars and rectors to give way on such a small issue:

> Wee . . . fully persuaded that God hath sent you . . . it is our great grief that your mouth is shut up and that we are deprived of our spiritual comfort. We do also understand that your liberty may be redeemed also by wearing the surplice. . . . It is a thing we wish with all our hearts . . . for we look to have such an one thrust upon us that we shall be constrained to beare greater things than the surplice, and want our godly instruction. We wish rather to beare with that, and so have your preaching, than to beare not only that but much more and to be without teaching. We do therefore intreat you as you render our soules and as you regard that account that you must make unto God for them, not to forsake us for such a trifle. . . .

The letter is signed by twenty-eight parishioners – 'Your hungrie sheep'.

Francis Quarles, the Jacobean minor poet, put the matter very clearly in one of his poems in which he imagines God calling his shepherds to account at the Last Judgment. Their answer runs:

> *We have been silent, canons struck us dumb.*
> *Thy Great Ones would not let us feed thy flock*
> *Unless we played the fool and wore a frock.*
> *We were forbid unless we'd yield to sign*
> *And cross their brows, they say, a mark of thine.*
>   *To say the truth, great Judge, they were not fed.*
>   *Lord, here they be, but Lord, they are all dead!*

Now the parsons have to suffer God's bitter reproof:

Ah, cruel shepherds, could your conscience serve
Not to be fools, and yet to let them starve?
What if your fiery spirits had been bound
To antick habits, or your heads been crowned
With peacock's plumes; had ye been forced to feed
Your Saviour's dear-bought flock on a fool's weed?
He that was scorned, reviled, endured the curse
Of a base death on your behalf, nay worse
Swallowed the cup of wrath, charged up to th' brim.
Durst ye not stoop to play the fools – for HIM?

One of the worst features of the period was the second fury of destruction which accompanied the settlement. What had been restored under Mary again perished under the hammer and in the flames. Roods, altars, pictured windows, water stoups, vestments, plate, statues, most of them vanished. Nobody knows what treasures of art, sculpture and music the country lost and how much richer not only England but the world would have been today had they been preserved.

While externally the unifying forces were welding the English into a virile and powerful nation, internally the forces of dissension were tearing the country apart. Yet even here the causes were to be found in large measure outside the country. Religious at the outset, the Catholic offensive was sparked off by the political problem arising out of the claim of Mary Stuart to the English throne.

Mary was without doubt the next heir. She was a descendant of Henry VII through his daughter Margaret who had married James IV of Scotland. Since the days of Edward I, with a few very short breaks, Scotland had been in league with France, and James V, son of James IV and Mary, had married the daughter of Claude, Duke of Guise whose family were the champions of Catholicism in the great religious struggle that was on the point of breaking out there.

In the year after Elizabeth's accession to the throne Mary

Stuart, then a girl of seventeen and married to Francis II, King of France, assumed the arms of England and the name of Queen, claiming that Elizabeth, being the daughter of an irregular marriage of her father Henry VIII, was illegitimate. In 1560 Francis II died and Mary returned to Scotland. Here Catholicism had already given way before the vigorous offensive of the extreme Protestants under the reformer, John Knox, with the support of most of the Scottish nobility.

Elizabeth favoured Protestants both in Scotland and in France. At the same time, if Mary became strong enough to defy Knox and the Protestant lords in Scotland, Elizabeth would be in danger of losing her throne and England would probably be plunged into the great armed conflict that had now broken out all over western Europe between the two faiths.

Politics and religion had been intermingled in the reigns of Henry, Edward and Mary; they were more so than ever now, and as the years passed by Elizabeth's position became more and more hazardous.

All this was complicated by a stiffening of attitudes on both sides. In 1540 a new order of priests called the Company of Jesus was founded within the Catholic Church, its aim being to combat the spread of the Protestant heresy. The Jesuits, as its members were called, became the spearhead of the counter-Reformation. They were organised on military lines under a supreme officer called a general, and every man took vows of unquestioning obedience to his officers. Because they so often worked in secret and wore no distinctive religious habits, they were able to enter every country and all walks of life.

Between 1545 and 1563 the Council of Trent met. Its work was mainly to reform and purify the doctrine and discipline of the Catholic Church, to fit it for the great revival. Its decrees, published in the latter year, removed abuses among the clergy and strengthened the Catholic Church for the struggle that was ahead. The year 1566 marked the accession of a new Pope, Pius V, a man in full sympathy with the Decrees of the Council. There followed a drastic reform of his court and a concerted drive against heresy. The Inquisition was revived, persecution was intensified and no mercy was shown to anybody, high or low, who was suspect wherever the Pope's power extended. Pius was the advocate of militancy. He urged the Catholic nobles in France to wage war on the Protestants, even to the point of extermination.

One of his aims was to have Elizabeth deposed and to get the Catholic princes to invade England. In 1570 he issued a Bull excommunicating her, declaring her illegitimate and commanding her subjects to resist. After this time nobody in England could obey the Pope without being a traitor to the Queen. For most Catholics who were still intensely loyal, such a course was unthinkable, but the way was open for agitators to stir up discontent and foment conspiracies.

Other impulses from abroad were not long in coming. In 1568 Mary Stuart, after her scandalous life in Scotland and her defeat by the Lords of the Congregation, fled to England and threw herself on Elizabeth's mercy. It was the signal for the plots to begin. In 1571 and 1572 two were discovered, in one of which the Duke of Norfolk was implicated.

Meanwhile the Catholic revival in England was also continuing on a lower level. This was largely the work of William Allen, an Oxford scholar and priest who had been deprived of his living in 1559. He left England in 1565 and founded a college in Douai where he was joined by other exiled students from home. Soon they began to return, coming into the country largely by stealth, first in a trickle, then, as they were joined by English Jesuits, in a flood. They were taken in by the gentry in whose houses small groups of neighbours gathered together to celebrate mass.

Liberty to practise their religion would have satisfied most Catholics and most priests, but after the excommunication of Pius V, Catholicism had officially become tied up with support for a rival claimant to the English throne. With the open fomenting of conspiracy and the danger of invasion, the religious problem remained political. In the hunt for agitator and plotter, all had to suffer. Penalties for hearing Mass were increased to a fine of 100 marks (£66 13s 4d) and a year's imprisonment, and for absence from church the fine was increased from the original shilling a service to £20 a month (1581). Jesuits and priests were expelled; any who remained were deemed guilty of high treason and those who sheltered them were tried as felons.

Catholic recusancy was the protest of the individual against repressive laws, and took the form of a battle of wits. Promises were made to conform and to attend church, but these were as lightly broken. Priests were harboured and kept for months, then, when the searchers came, were hidden for hours and sometimes days in deep, narrow and dark priest-holes such as may be seen to this day at places like Sawston Hall, Cambridgeshire, the ancestral home of the Huddleston family. East and north Lancashire, still under the sway of the local gentry, was the home of recusancy and supplied a larger number of missionary priests than any other part of England. Catholicism survived there because the local gentry, whom the Tudors had made into the arbiters of country affairs, were almost solidly on the side of Rome. Payment of fines was avoided, lands which the government wanted to seize were made over to others, but in spite of all they could do many families were gradually bled of their possessions.

Young men from the best families in England went abroad to Douai to study and came back to risk their lives. Father John Gerard, Long John with the Little Beard, swarthy, hawk-nosed, high-templed and black-haired, toured East Anglia from his headquarters with the Yelvertons at Grimston. Most unlike a monk, dressed in satin doublet garnished with gold and silver lace, with velvet hose and a coat of buff leather, he was a constant and welcome guest at the houses of his friends. Nicholas Owen with his bag of tools went from house to house sounding walls, quietly removing floors and constructing deep holes in the most unlikely places. 'Uncle James' in the north tramped the roads with his chalice and paten of tin, his boxes of bread and his old mass book. John Payne, a recusant priest from Warwickshire, went from house to house saying mass until he was betrayed by George Eliot, known as 'Judas', an apostate Catholic, a profligate and a thief. Eliot swore that Payne had been the chosen instrument of the Pope and the Jesuits, and had tried to persuade him to join in a conspiracy to kill the Queen and Walsingham. Eight months later, after being tortured in the Tower, Payne, his hands hardly able to form letters, set down his protest of loyalty.

> First touching her Majestie, I pray God long to preserve Her Highness to His Honour and her hartes desire; unto whom I alwaies have, and during life will wishe, no worse than to my own soule. If her pleasure be not that I shall live and serve her as my sovereigne Prince, then will I willingly die her faithful subject, and, I trust, God's true servant.
>
> Touching the State, I protest that I am, and ever have been, free from the knowledge of any practise whatsoever, either within or without the realme, intended against the same; for the verity wherof, as I have often before you and the rest of Her Grace's Commissioners called God to witness, so doe I now again; and one day before His Majestie the truth not now credited will then be revealed.

His confession did not save him. He was hanged at Chelmsford on 2nd April 1582.

> After all, very meekly, when the ladder was about to be turned, he said 'Jesus, Jesus, Jesus!'; and so did hang, not moving hand or foot. They very courteously caused men to hang on his feet, and set the knot to his ear, and suffered him to hang to death, commanding Bull, the hangman of Newgate, to despatch in 'the quartering of him' lest, as they said, he should survive, and rebuked him that he did not despatch speedily. All the town loved him exceedingly, so did the keepers and

92

most of the magistrates of the shire. No men seemed in countenance to dislike him, but much sorrowed and lamented his death; who most constantly, catholicly, patiently, and meekly ended this mortal life to rise triumphantly, his innocency known to all the world.

Edmund Campion, the first and foremost of all the Jesuits, had suffered with two companions at Tyburn on the 1st December 1581. Some three hundred suffered in all, approximately the same number as that of the Marian martyrs. Large numbers were imprisoned, some for long periods. In 1594 Jane Wiseman, a widow of Broadoaks, Wimbush, was condemned for the withholding of evidence, to *peine forte et dure*, and would have been crushed to death by heavy weights laid on her had not Queen Elizabeth, for mercy's sake, interfered and forbidden it.

'Is there to be no end of the shedding of blood?' the Queen is reported to have cried during the last sad years of executions. She had never been in favour of them. She would have banished the priests and spared the life of Mary Stuart had she had her own way. But it was too late. England had been saved from the Spanish menace, and the Anglican form of worship had been preserved, but the cost had been great. The Catholics now constituted a permanent minority, mostly loyal, but for two hundred more years distrusted and under-privileged. While Elizabeth mourned the divisions that had set her people one against another, the Catholics lamented the decay in faith and manners:

> *Weepe, weepe, and still I weepe,*
> *For who can chuse but weepe,*
> *To thyncke how England styll*
> *In synne and heresye doth sleepe.*

> *The Christian faythe and Catholick*
> *Is everywhere detested,*

The holy service and suchlike
  Of all degrees neglected....

Our churches gaye defaced be;
  Our altars are thrown downe,
The walls left bare, a griefe to see,
  That once cost many a crowne.

The monuments and life of Sayntes
  Are brent and torn by vyolence;
Some shead the holye sacramentes,
  O Christe, thy wondrous pacyence! ...

Now favour hyndreth equytie,
  And ryches rule the roste;
In vaine the poore crye Cheritie
  God healpe you, saye the moste.

7

The Puritan and Parliamentary Protest

THE CATHOLIC OFFENSIVE, backed as it was by powerful influences abroad, would alone have been enough to damage the prospects of an Elizabethan compromise. The Puritan offensive delayed all promise of agreement on religious affairs for more than a century.

Puritanism had been born on the Continent, in the rigorous atmosphere of Geneva under Calvin and in the Protestant meetings which the English exiles attended in Basle, Strasbourg and Frankfurt. Their faith was rooted in the word of God as revealed in the Scriptures; their belief was in a personal relationship with Christ without the interposition of a hierarchy of priests imposed on them from above. Their worship was simple and direct, with no need for elaborate ceremony, images, altars or vestments. They believed in predestination in that, while some were destined for salvation even from birth, the rest of mankind were eternally damned. But the ardent Puritan was convinced that though the lot of others might be eternal torment his own salvation was certain. Their code of morality was strict; the belief in the virtues of industry and thrift appealed to the rising mercantile classes, and attracted industrious artisans and craftsmen. Their simplicity in all things earned them the name of Puritans, at first a term of disparagement.

From the highest to the lowest, Puritans were always good rebels. The records of the Archdeacons' courts are full of instances of petty nonconformity, and sometimes of the most extraordinary behaviour. One member of a congregation 'refuseth to bow at the name of Jesus', another 'sweareth and curseth in church', and a third 'calleth the Churchwarden a knave and the pulpit a calf's coop'. The Occasional Conformity Act of 1593 compelled all to go to church at least once a month, and forbade attendance at any conventicles or assemblies on pain of a prison sentence; and if the culprit persisted in his disobedience – exile. This affected Puritans and Catholics alike.

Without doubt the fact that a number of zealous Puritan parsons had been deprived of their livings lowered the quality of the clergy in general. The Puritans at least had a very poor opinion of most of the men who were brought in to take their places. A list drawn up by them about the year 1586 gives not only names but in some cases not too favourable character sketches. 'Some time a serving man, a grocer, a pedlar, a mender of saddles and pannels, a sow gelder, a pettifogger, a higgler, a wheelwright, a popish priest, a friar.' Such remarks could conceal a perfectly good character, but there is also a fair sprinkling of alehouse-haunters, common barraters, gamesters and men of scandalous life.

Case histories abound; there are men who have put away their wives, who have got maids with child, and neglected their families through playing bowls and cards. The parson of Leaden Roding was 'a notorious swearer, a dicer, a carder, a hawker and a hunter, a very careless person. He is a quarreler and a fighter, for he fought with the parson of Stoke in a common inn in Chelmsford'.

The parson of Ugley was 'a common swearer, a proude and careless man, a riotous man; he hath been absent from his benefice and preacheth not'.

While the petty skirmishes were going on in a thousand parishes and in the Archdeacons' courts, battle was joined on a grander scale in Parliament itself. The Puritans were still part of the Church of England, for there could be no question of secession. Their aim therefore had to be to reform the Church from within, to change both its spirit and organisation. They abominated a church run from above and would have made an end of bishops. They wanted parsons who had not been imposed

96

on congregations, but appointed by them, men who were leaders, examples of good living, and 'good preaching ministers'. The Prayer Book, the sacraments and all the 'trappings of Popery', as they were called, they wished to abolish. Such reforms as these, however, could only come through measures taken in Parliament and with the consent of the Queen.

Puritanism had by now taken fully as firm a hold on one section of the population as Catholicism had on the other. It was preached and discussed in the universities, while in Parliament, besides a core of Puritan members, there were a large number who were favourable to limited Church reforms. But the ardent reformers came into direct conflict with the Queen herself. She had, by the Act of 1559, established the Church of England in the form it took and had no intention of making changes in the fabric that had been set up with such difficulty. In any case, she regarded parliamentary interference in a matter such as this as a direct attack on the royal prerogative.

Though the Commons had first been called into counsel in the thirteenth century, they were still brought together only when the monarch needed them, and that was principally to make grants of money. What power they possessed was gained through their ability to withhold these grants until their grievances had been redressed. Edward III had constantly had to call on them for funds to carry on the war with France, and in the reigns of Henry IV and Henry V they were sending petitions to the King which, if they obtained his assent, became statutes. Their decisions were reached by debate among themselves, and in these discussions they claimed freedom of speech. In 1523 Sir Thomas More begged leave of Henry VIII to allow every man 'to discharge his conscience, and boldly in everything . . . declare his advice, and whatsoever happeneth any man to say, it may like your noble Majesty . . . to take all in good part, interpreting every man's words, how uncunningly soever they may be couched, to proceed yet of a good zeal towards the profit of your Realm and honour of your Royal person. . . .'

A fortnight later when Wolsey descended on the Commons to demand a large grant of money not one of the members answered, but all remained silent for the Speaker to make reply. In 1565 freedom of speech in Parliament was so generally accepted that Sir Thomas Smith, one of Elizabeth's most trusted Protestant counsellors, included it in his account of parliamentary procedure.

This question of royal prerogative brought about the most striking act of parliamentary protest that had so far been made. It happened in 1571, when a member of the House of Commons made proposals for changes in the Book of Common Prayer.

The dispute about the Prayer Book marks the beginning of that long struggle between Anglican and Puritan that rose to a climax during the Commonwealth and ended in the Restoration settlement. It also marks the beginning of the duel between King and Parliament which brought forth Laud, Strafford, Pym and Hampden, and ended in the episode of the Five Members and the Civil War.

These two causes, Puritanism and parliamentary privilege, were so intimately connected that they can hardly be seen apart, and what began in 1571 as protest continued in the seventeenth century as civil strife.

The principal figure in this contest for parliamentary liberties was Peter Wentworth. His father, a member of an old Yorkshire family, held lands at Lillingstone Lovell in Oxfordshire and was chief porter at Calais in the service of Henry VIII. In the 1571 Parliament Wentworth was member for Barnstaple.

We first hear of him as a member of the Committee of the House of Commons which visited Matthew Parker, Archbishop of Canterbury. The deputation arose out of a motion by Walter Strickland, 'a grave and ancient man of great zeal', but like many other zealous Puritans, hot-tempered and forthright. Strickland wanted to see the Church reformed on Puritan lines, and many 'errors and abuses such as pluralities, the promotion of mere boys to high spiritual posts, and the wide difference between the incomes of rich and poor livings, rooted out,' so that all things should be brought back to the purity of the primitive church 'without too much chopping and changing of religion'.

The Commons, though very much in sympathy with the motion, wisely refused to consider a bill until the bishops had been consulted, and Wentworth was a member of the committee which was appointed to meet them. When Archbishop Parker asked why the Commons had included nothing in their proposals about homilies or the consecration of bishops, Wentworth replied that they had not had time as yet to consider how these matters agreed with God's word.

Parker replied by pointing out that such things were the concern of the bishops, and surely the Commons would be willing to leave such questions to them.

'No,' said Wentworth, 'by the faith I bear to God, we will pass nothing before we understand what it is, for that were but to make you popes. Make you popes who list, for we will make you none.'

Five days after Strickland's motion (7th April), the question arose of a grant of supply to the Queen, and one member proposed that this should be linked with redress of grievances; in other words, no redress, no money. Here was a situation in which both subsidy and prerogative were under attack. The Queen wanted neither of these controversial questions to be debated. On the 10th she sent a curt message to the Speaker to read to the House, commanding its members to spend little time in motions, and to avoid long speeches.

It was clear that these two questions were closely linked. On the 14th, when Strickland's bill for Church reform was read for the first time, the Lord Treasurer reminded the House that there were certain matters which were not within the power of Parliament to decide. On the other proposal Sir Humphrey Gilbert, another member of the Court Party, warned them against encroaching on royal prerogative: 'What difference is to say the Queen is not to use the privilege of the Crown and to say she is not Queen? . . . It is not good to sport or venture too much with princes.'

The Bill, however, passed the Commons and had been read once in the Lords when the Queen stopped it on the grounds that Church reform had nothing to do with Parliament. During the Easter recess Strickland was called before the Privy Council to be examined and was then forbidden to leave his home – an early instance of house arrest.

It was no uncommon thing for Tudor monarchs to dictate to Parliament, but the Puritan members considered the action of the Queen as a serious affront. Wentworth must have thought deeply over it during the recess, for on the day Parliament opened he denounced the conduct of the Court Party. The speech of Sir Humphrey Gilbert, he said, had been an injury to the House. His fawning and flatteries of the Queen he compared to the chameleon 'which can change into all colours (saving white), even so, this reporter can change himself into all fashions but honesty'. This, he said, tended to no other end than to inculcate fear into those which should be free, and he requested care for the credit of the House and for the maintenance of free speech.

This, the boldest utterance so far in the history of Parliament, was followed by a heated argument, the Lord Treasurer and others vainly trying to restrain the Puritan members, to urge them to be wary and 'neither venture further than our assured warrant might stretch, nor to hazard our good opinion with Her Majesty on any doubtful cause'. Sir Christopher Yelverton, while admitting that it was reasonable for princes to have their prerogatives, held that they should at the same time be 'straitened within reasonable limits', for the Prince 'could not of herself make laws, neither might she of herself break laws'. Whatever the reason, Strickland was released and appeared the following morning, to the great rejoicing of the House, who accounted it a triumph.

In the Parliament of 1572 Wentworth was just as forthright.

The Queen commanded that no bills having to do with religion should be brought before the House unless the bishops had previously considered them. As it happened the country was passing through a crisis. Parliament had been called because of the discovery of the Ridolfi Plot. The Duke of Norfolk had been sentenced to death for his part in it and Mary Stuart was disgraced. Parliament reacted to this peril loyally, and Elizabeth replied with a gracious message. A motion was put that the thanks of the House should be conveyed to her by the Speaker and a small deputation 'for the good opinions conceaved of us', the which, said Wentworth, 'I did not think Her Majestie deserved'. He declared to the House his opinion that the message of thanks should not be sent.

Elizabeth, in continuing to forbid the introduction of bills dealing with religion, blocked all the reforms the Puritans had in mind. On this and other subjects, Wentworth had seen the coercion of members through fear of the Queen's displeasure, one member having been confined to his house because he had spoken his mind, and others voting against motions which he knew they favoured in private, so that they might be on good terms with 'the best sort'. In February 1576, when a second session of the 1572 Parliament was called, his anger and resentment had mounted to such a pitch that he could no longer contain them. The question was far vaster than the mere subject of Church reforms; the Queen's actions opened up the whole issue as to whether a member of Parliament had the right to express himself freely in the House. Early in the session he astounded the Commons by a speech, the subject-matter of which he had pondered for years. It was the speech of the century:

> I find in a little volume these words, in effect: 'Sweet is the Name of Liberty, but the thing itself has a value beyond all inestimable treasure.' So much the more it behoveth us to take care lest we, contenting ourselves with the sweetness of the name, lose and forego the thing. . . .

> I was never of Parliament but the last, and the last session, at both which times I saw the liberty of free speech, the which is the only salve to heal the sores of this Commonwealth, so much and so many ways infringed, and so many abuses offered to this honourable Council as hath much grieved me, even of very conscience and love to my Prince and State.

Without free speech, he went on, it was a mockery to call the House a parliament, for it could be no more than 'a very school of flattery and dissimulation and so a fit place to serve the Devil and his angels, and not to glorify God and benefit the Commonwealth', for in whatever was undertaken, one of two things was said, either 'take heed what you do; the Queen's Majesty liketh not such a matter', or 'the Queen's Majesty liketh such a matter; whoever speaketh against it she will be much offended by them'. Thus, all was rumour and messages.

He pointed out that even a prince could be wrong and favour a perilous cause. It followed that if a subject, knowing this, dissembled and agreed for private gain, he should be counted as a hated enemy 'for that he giveth to Her Majesty a detestable Judas kiss'. Open and severe criticism of the Queen herself followed:

> It is a dangerous thing in a Prince to oppose or bend herself against her nobility and people. And how could any prince more unkindly intreat, abuse and oppose herself against her nobility and people than Her Majesty did the last Parliament? . . .
>
> . . . I beseech God that Her Majesty may do all things that may grieve the hearts of her enemies, and may joy the hearts that unfeignedly love Her Majesty; and I beseech the same God to endue Her Majesty with his wisdom, whereby she may discern faithful advice from traitorous sugared speeches and to send Her Majesty a melting, yielding heart unto sound counsel.
>
> Nay, I will discharge my conscience and duties unto God, my Prince and Country. So certain it is, Mr Speaker, that none is without fault, no, not our noble Queen, sith then Her

Majesty hath committed great fault, yea, dangerous faults to herself.

Thus he developed his theme of liberty, attacking all traitors, two faced gentlemen, such as 'sit or rise with the best sort', and the bishops. 'We are incorporated in this place to serve God and all England and not to be time-servers, as humour-feeders, as cancers that would pierce the bone, or as flatterers that would fain beguile all the world . . .'

He never concluded his speech, for upon this 'the House, out of a reverent regard for Her Majesty's honour, stopped his further proceeding'. He was committed by the Commons to the Serjeants' Ward and his examination took place the same afternoon in the Star Chamber. He would not revoke a word that he had said, and was imprisoned in the Tower. He remained there for just over a month and then two days before the end of the session the Queen, probably thinking he could do no more harm, intervened and he was released.

His stormy career was by no means over. The 1586 Parliament was called after the discovery of the Babington Plot to assassinate Elizabeth and make Mary Stuart Queen. On 8th February 1587 Mary was beheaded at Fotheringhay and the Puritan element considered this a favourable juncture to bring in a bill for Church reforms. It was introduced by Anthony Cope, Member for Banbury, on 27th February, and the Speaker sent it to the Queen, who refused to tolerate any attempt to reform the Church.

The question was again one of freedom of speech, and Wentworth immediately went into attack by preparing a list of questions to define what the rights of the House were. Could the State be maintained by the Queen without Parliament? Could any council but Parliament make or abrogate laws? Was not free speech vouchsafed to all Members by law? Was it not an injury for the Prince or the Privy Council to send for a Member in parliamentary time, as had so often been done? Was Parliament there to receive complaints or merely to act as humble suitor to the Queen? Should not those who carried tales to her be punished as enemies, and finally, was not a prince or a state which infringed the liberties of Parliament an enemy to God? A definite answer to these questions would have settled the question of parliamentary privilege for ever, but such a thing was impossible. He was asked to hold up his motion to await the Queen's pleasure, but he refused.

The end was sudden. The Queen sent for the Speaker before the parliamentary business ended and ordered him to send the members home. Wentworth was again imprisoned in the Tower and was joined there next day by his collaborators.

Like most loyal subjects, Wentworth was deeply concerned about the succession to the throne if the Queen should die. She had chosen to remain single much against the will of her counsellors, and though her life had been in peril she had constantly refused to name a successor.

About the year 1586 Wentworth wrote a booklet on the subject, *A Pithie Exhortation to Her Majesty for establishing her Successor to the Crown*. His words to her were as forthright as they had ever been, even though his political vision was this time more clouded.

> . . . whensoever it shall please God to touch you with the pangs of death (as die most certainly you shall) . . . your Grace shall find such a troubled soul and conscience, yea ten thousand helles in your soule, even such bitter vexation of soule and hart for the perilling of the Church of God and of your naturall countrie as to be released thereof you would give the whole worlde. . . .

He painted a doleful picture of a whole country, nobility, counsellors, and people up in arms as soon as the breath left the Queen's body, the Queen herself lying on the ground unburied, leaving behind a name of infamy, the realm rent to shivers, with slaughter and murder, and nothing remaining sacred. He implored the Queen to follow the example of Moses, Hezekiah, David and her own father, and to speak.

He did not publish the booklet, but handed a copy to a Buckinghamshire minister who sent it out to be copied. Before long, and without Wentworth's permission, it was in the hands of the public.

In August 1591, brought before the Privy Council, he refused to change or recant a single word, confident that when the Queen read it she would understand and appreciate the loyal feeling that prompted its composition.

Until February 1592 he was under house arrest. On the 21st he went to the House with his speech and a copy of his petition all ready. It was never given, for the Queen, after all, did not understand. Indeed, she was very angry.

From that day until his death this loyal, well-meaning, tactless and unrepentant old man remained a prisoner in the Tower. The Queen put off the decision about a successor until almost at the point of death when she acknowledged James Stuart. 'Who should that be, but our cousin of Scotland.'

By that time her constant and faithful critic had also passed on, his last words, like those of many a servant spurned:

> The case is very hard with us poore Parliament men, when we deserve to hang in hell if we neglect His [God's] service or the service of our own Prince or State, and may neither serve God or Prince or State truely but are sure of displeasure and punishment therefore.

8

Resisters and Pamphleteers

As LONG AS Queen Elizabeth lived, Parliament was the petitioner and the predominant power was the monarch. Under James I the relationship between these two altered, for though the powers of the King were nominally the same as they had been under his predecessor, protest and petition soon resolved itself into conflict.

All through her reign Elizabeth had managed in one way or another to stifle parliamentary protest. Only on one major issue, that of monopolies, had it been even partially successful.

The desire for foreign trade had led to the foundation of a number of companies, each engaged in its own part of the world and enjoying, under the charter, the protection of the Crown. In Elizabeth's day this grant of monopoly had also been extended to the production of articles of everyday use such as salt, starch, iron, leather, books and soap. Monopoly had its uses if a trade was to be protected in its early stages, but it could easily be continued too long, or it could be granted on some article already under manufacture when there was no economic need for it. In either case it became a nuisance. This grant of a monopoly was a convenient way for the Queen to reward those who had served her in the past, by giving them the sole right to manufacture, to trade in or to organise the trade in certain classes of goods. Thus there came to be a rush for monopolies among the speculators and fortune-hunters who had some influence with this or that minister or court favourite. Then, when they had once cornered the market, they could raise the price to as high a level as the consumer could pay.

The Reverend Thomas Bastard put the case of the complaining public in one of his epigrams (1598):

Ye Courtiers, so may you in courtly sorte
With manners old, old courtiers long remaine,
So that some upstart courtiers ye refraine,
Unworthy of a peerelesse princes port.
As courtier leather, courtier pinne, and sope,
And courtier vinegeer, and starch and carde;
And courtier cups, such as were never heard,
And such as shall not court it long, we hope.
  The true gentilitie by their owne Armes
  Advance themselves, the false by others harmes.

In 1601 the long drawn-out war against Spain was still going on. A Spanish force which had invaded Ireland had failed to join up with Irish rebels and was forced to surrender; English troops were still fighting in the Netherlands. The Queen wanted money, and Parliament, which was called in November, immediately launched an attack on monopolies. It was in vain that members like Raleigh, who held the patent on tin, tried to justify them as being for the public good. When Sir Robert Wroth read the long list of patents granted since 1597 one member interrupted saying that if steps were not quickly taken the country would soon see a monopoly on bread.

This was a direct challenge to the Crown, much more dangerous than that of Wentworth's had been, and no amount of expostulation or excuses on the part of the court could silence it. Threats of retribution were unavailing against general opposition, and Elizabeth knew how to give way graciously. A declaration followed in which the Queen promised to remedy matters and to allow no monopoly that was irregular.

This was the first real triumph the Commons had against royal prerogative. On the last day of November 1601, the Speaker and 160 members met in the Council Chamber to accord their thanks on their knees. The Queen had been their mistress more than forty years. She had seen the country through its days of peril, and she was sure of their respect and affection, therefore she could afford to yield in a queenly manner. In her speech she dwelt on her affection for her people and her life of service to them. Then she touched on the question of monopolies:

> Of myself I must say this, I never was any greedy scraping grasper, nor a strict fast-holding prince, not yet a waster, my heart was never set upon any worldly goods, but only for my subjects' good. What you do bestow on me I will not hoard up, but receive it to bestow on you again; yea, mine own properties I account yours, to be expended for your good, and your eyes shall see the bestowing of it for your welfare. . . .
>
> Since I was Queen, yet did I never put my pen to any grant but upon pretext and semblance made me that it was for the good and avail of my subjects generally, though a private profit to some of my ancient servants, who have deserved well; but that my grants shall be made grievances to my people, and oppressions shall be privileged under colour of our patents, our princely dignity shall not suffer it. . . .
>
> And if my princely bounty have been abused, and my grants turned to the hurt of my people contrary to my will and meaning, or if any in authority under me have neglected or converted what I have committed unto them, I hope God will not lay their culps [faults] to my charge. . . .
>
> . . . for my own part, were it not for conscience sake to discharge the duty that God hath laid upon me and to maintain His glory and keep you in safety, in mine own disposition I should be willing to resign the place I hold to any other, and glad to be freed of the glory with the labours, for it is not my desire to live nor to reign longer than my life and reign shall be for your good. And though you have had and may have many mightier and wiser princes sitting in this seat, yet you never had nor shall have any that will love you better. . . .

After 1603 a subtle change from this master-servant relationship between King and Parliament took place. Political philosophers had already put forward the theory that the prince occupied his position by the goodwill of and by virtue of his services to the people. John Ponet had expressed it as early as 1556 in his *Short Treatise of Politique Power*. Christopher Goodman, once Lady

Margaret Professor, and friend of John Knox, preached the resistance of the people to an ungodly ruler: 'When the Kings become blasphemers of God and oppressive of their subjects,' he wrote, 'they are no more to be regarded as kings, but as private men, and are to be condemned and punished by the Law of God.' Mary Tudor decreed that any person found in possession of the works of Goodman or Knox should be executed. Elizabeth, though not in Goodman's sense a blasphemer or an oppressor, was so angry at the very mention of his name that he dared not return to England until 1565. Such ideas as these were common currency in the late sixteenth century among the reformers. Elizabeth knew well enough about them, and knew she was fighting a losing battle.

The new king had none of her advantages. Elizabeth's age and sex had commanded respect; because of them the Commons had kept their demands in check. Her long experience as a queen had taught her what the monarch's difficulties were, and her natural ability in dealing with people had been of unfailing service to her in meeting the demands of her ministers and her parliaments. Only on one question, that of monopolies, had she lost the initiative.

Apart from age and sex, James Stuart differed from his cousin in almost every respect. His background was that of feudalism in a land of tribal chieftans which was off the main stream of European culture. He was intelligent and well-read, but the deference always paid to him, plus his natural weakness of character and judgment, had produced a kind of pedantry and self-conceit which was bound to sort ill with the urge towards independence in the Commons and among the religious sects. Even before he had come to England he had claimed that its kings were absolute rulers of all the landed property in the country. In the *True Law of Free Monarchies* he stated that.

.... The Bastard of Normandy set down the strangers his followers in many of the old possessors' rooms, as at this day well appeareth, a great part of the gentlemen of England being come of the Norman blood, and their old laws, which to this day they are ruled by, are written in his language, and not in theirs; and yet his successors have with great happiness enjoyed the crown to this day.

Belief in the Divine Right of Kings was not unnatural in days when it was common for those who had privileges or power to claim that they were theirs by the express will of God, but James miscalculated the forces which inspired the parliaments with which he had to deal, and he committed the grossest blunders. In particular, his constant reiteration of his pet theory and the innuendoes that often appeared in his speeches to Parliament did nothing to smooth over the strained relations that existed between them.

In the latter part of Elizabeth's reign the Commons had begun to feel their strength. Now that she had died nearly half a million in debt and they held the purse-strings, they were no longer beggars or remonstrators, but challengers. From 1603 every move was part of a great game in which they held the initiative. The goal was not only control of religious and foreign policy but also the undermining of the royal prerogative.

In 1603 the war of precedents began. The Commons could point to a time recorded in chronicle and statute when Parliament had acted as a check on the Crown, which the Court Party could show that many so-called parliamentary rights had never been fully acknowledged by the ruler. James quickly made an attempt to put Parliament in its place, declaring that kings were not only God's lieutenants upon earth, sitting on God's throne, but even by God himself they were called Gods. Parliament reacted immediately with an assertion of their rights 'to debate freely all matters which properly concern the subject and his right or state, which freedom of debate being once foreclosed, the essence of the liberty of Parliament is withal dissolved'.

Wentworth's actions were bearing fruit. This was no protest of a single person or a small group as in his case, but a declaration by the majority. There were still casualties after this time, such as when Pym and Coke, opposing the projected marriage of Prince Charles, were imprisoned in 1621, but they were casualties not of a protest movement, but of a great constitutional struggle.

We should not therefore be misled by the familiar names, petition, protestation, apology and remonstrance. After Sir Thomas Shirley, a member of Parliament, was imprisoned for debt and Sir Francis Goodwin had been prevented by the King from entering the House of Commons, the members published an Apology, not apologising, but in the old sense of the word *apologia*, defending their privileges. In 1621 they urged James to break off the hated Spanish alliance and to support the Protestants in Germany. On his reply commanding them not to meddle in foreign affairs they entered a *Protestation* in their journal. James sent for the offending book and tore out the page. *The Petition of Right* of 1628 was an expression of their grievances to Charles I and an invitation to the King to remedy them. *The Grand Remonstrance* of 1641 was another statement of all that had gone wrong since the King's accession with a demand for redress.

These are part of history, moves in the great war of principle in which new and heroic figures step on the stage: John Pym, acknowledged leader of the dissidents in Parliament; John Hampden and John Eliot, both of whom refused to pay the forced loan of 1627 and were imprisoned, and Sir Edward Coke, the great jurist, who in his support of parliamentary privilege repeatedly braved the anger of the King.

The Petition of Right gave rise to the last grand gesture of protest on the part of the Commons before the King embarked on the eleven years of personal rule. In spite of the Petition Charles had collected tonnage and poundage, and had distrained on the goods of merchants who had refused to pay it. The session of 1629 was brief and ominous. Eliot prepared a threefold proposition condemning religious changes and the arbitrary imposition of taxes. The Speaker refused to read the paper, but as he rose to quit the chair he was seized by two members and held down while it was read, put to the vote and carried by acclamation. When Parliament again met in 1640, protest was fast ripening into revolution.

We go back to religion. In 1603 both Puritans and Catholics had looked forward to the coming of James with high hopes. Was he not the product of the Scottish Reformation, brought up on the counsel of Presbyterian lords? On the other hand, was not his mother a Catholic, daughter of Mary of Guise? A number of Puritan clergy signed the Millenary Petition requesting toleration of their beliefs. In 1604 James met their principals at Hampton Court, only to disappoint them grievously when he told them in the last stormy session either to conform or to be harried out of the land. As a result three hundred Puritan clergy were ejected from their livings, to preach and worship in secret conventicles and further to embitter the parliamentary opposition that aimed to blast away the royal power. The most famous act of protest on their part was the departure of a small minority of devout Puritans in 1608 to Leyden and a still smaller minority in 1620 to New England.

The Catholics fared little better, though James at first abolished the £20 fine for recusancy, hoping that with freedom of private worship they would be loyal to him. Suddenly recusants who had been forced to attend the Anglican services disappeared from the congregations, and priests toured the country openly. James, shocked at the sudden apparent spread of militant Catholicism, issued a proclamation ordering all priests to leave the country. Some who did not were hanged, and the fines for recusancy were reimposed.

The fiasco of 5th November 1605 embittered relations between Catholics and Protestants for two hundred years.

For those who would take the Oath of Supremacy, the fines were lifted, the rest, silent protestors, were subjected to every form of persecution and ignominy. Popery fell more out of favour with the mob whom it was easy to scare with the spectre of a Jesuit round every corner.

Then in 1619 James embarked on his ridiculous quest to make an alliance with Spain and to seal it by the marriage of his son Charles with the Infanta. Raleigh, the old enemy of Spain, who had come back empty-handed from Orinoco, was executed to satisfy James' hoped-for ally. That Gondomar, the Spanish ambassador, should have so complete an ascendancy over an English king enraged the London mob who attacked the embassy, assaulted the ambassador's servants in the streets, and in 1623 brought a building, in which a congregation of a hundred people were listening to a Jesuit priest, crashing to the ground. When Charles came back, the whole absurd business having fallen through, the bells of London rang, bonfires were lit in the streets, prisoners were let out of gaols and the crowds went mad with joy. It was the most popular moment of the young man's life.

Charles became King in 1625 and it was made clear in the first four years of his reign that whereas he was not pleased to have parliament as a master, parliament was not satisfied to be no more than a royal servant. The uneasy relationship was broken off on that day in March 1629 when the angry and excited members streamed out of the council chamber having acclaimed Eliot's resolutions in the face of the Speaker's prohibition. This was the end of parliament for eleven years, and Charles broke the financial deadlock by stretching royal prerogative to its utmost limits. The gentlemen of England were subjected to impositions on matters of which they had never heard. Those with lands worth more than £40 a year which they held by military tenure were fined for having neglected to be knighted; owners of land which had once been royal forest but which at some time or other had been 'assarted' or brought into private ownership, were compelled to acknowledge the assart and to pay, in some cases thousands of pounds. A brisk trade in monopolies brought in more money and though many of the London merchants temporarily closed their businesses as a protest against Tonnage and Poundage, they could not resist for long.

The climax was reached in 1637 when John Hampden refused to pay 20s Shipmoney Tax due on his estate for that year. The case was tried by twelve judges of the Exchequer, of whom five only gave judgment for Hampden. The result of the trial amounted to a denial of the right of Parliament to control supply, and the legalising of the royal claim to an indefinite extension of prerogative. The clock had been turned back to the Middle Ages with a vengeance. Yet Hampden's protest was not in vain. Though the tax was levied after 1637, it was one of the most unpopular of all impositions and the example of the Buckinghamshire squire was a spur to resistance.

Arbitrary taxation was distasteful enough, but the one subject that was still capable of raising tempers to boiling point was religion. Though persecution had failed to extinguish Catholicism and though many sects of Puritans were firmly established in England, it was still the firm hope of William Laud that he would be able to restore in England a 'comprehensive' Church, with one belief and one form of worship for all.

Laud, born in 1573, had even as a student shown his predilection for Church organisation on the ancient lines and for old-established ritual in a thesis that there could be no Church without bishops. From this standpoint he never departed, believing that as opposed to congregationalists, bishops existed *iure divino* – by divine law – which was even more than by royal enthronement. James I had never gone so far, but after Charles became King, Laud, who in 1628 had been made Bishop of London, was allowed to go his own way.

After the dissolution of Parliament in 1629 Laud became the King's chief adviser in matters of Church and state and, armed with the power his position gave him, he set about the reintroduction of the old usages and forms so abhorred by Puritans. Communion tables were taken from the body of the Church and placed at the extreme east end, vestments and images were reintroduced. The Puritan lecturer who had been specially engaged by congregations to provide sermons in parishes where the priests were 'non-preaching' were dismissed, and the Puritan Sunday, a day of rest and solemnity, was done away with by the introduction of Sunday games according to the re-published Book of Sports written by James I. Justices of the Peace were given instructions to deal severely with all those who attended conventicles and parishes were overlooked by frequent visitations. In 1633 Laud was made Archbishop of Canterbury.

When repression is vigorous, those who indulge in open criticism are few, and their careers are generally short. The preachers of Puritanism had been driven underground. By a proclamation of 1624 all who wished to publish a book had to have the consent of an archbishop, the Bishop of London, or the Vice-Chancellor of Oxford or Cambridge. This amounted to nothing less than the censorship of the press. During the years in which Laud ruled England, Puritanism was gagged.

In spite of this, protest had a way of bursting out in one form or another. Conventicles, for all the watchfulness of the authorities, were held in private houses and in out-of-the-way places. Secret presses turned out an abundance of libellous and scurrilous pamphlets and broadsheets, and more were imported from Holland. Prophecies of evil abounded, especially when some minor disaster or other occurred. The Court of High Commission gave short shrift to dissenting authors, publishers and printers, especially if they refused to take the oath, while the Star Chamber, a royal court set up by Henry VII, was used by the bishops to fine, imprison and mutilate offenders. Its judges condemned Alexander Leighton, a Scottish minister who had written the book, *Zion's plea against Prelacy*, to be whipped, put in the pillory, to lose one of his ears, to have one side of his nose slit and to be branded on one cheek. A week afterwards the barbarous process was repeated on the other side of his face and he spent the next ten years languishing in the Tower. Gestures of defiance were legion, but outside the courts the voice of protest was an undertone, whispered from house to house and from street to street.

One man was not content to whisper. William Prynne was the son of a farmer of Swainswick, near Bath, a graduate of Oriel College, Oxford and a bencher of Lincoln's Inn. Though a Puritan, he was no extremist, nor was his quarrel with the Church of England as such. What he attacked violently in his pamphlets was the direction in which the Church was going under Laud. Laud had elevated the bishops beyond their true estate, claiming divine right for them, and in so doing he was even placing them above the King, to whom Prynne was intensely loyal. Just as the peasants in the fourteenth century had hoped to free their young king, Richard II, from the evil counsellors surrounding him, so Prynne in another way hoped to open the King's own eyes to the evils that were threatening him from the rising pretensions of Laud and the bishops. His ideal Church was that of the Elizabethan settlement, the Church defended by Jewel and Foxe, whose ceremonies were modest and without ostentation. He deplored the Laudian innovations, the moving of the communion table and the placing of the railings round it, the bowing at the name of Jesus, and the other so-called 'trappings of Papacy' that were being forced into the Church. His early pamphlets also denounced the Church's approval of such customs as theatre-going, Sunday games, the drinking of healths, dancing and the new extravagant fashions, such as the wearing of colourful clothing and long hair.

This, and his attack on the Laudian reforms of the Church, marked him out, for all his professed loyalty to the Crown, as an enemy to be dealt with. In 1633 his famous pamphlet *Histriomastix* was published. This was not merely an attack on stage plays, but also on all the other evils he had already condemned. However, since at that time the Queen herself was rehearsing a part in the play, *The Shepherd's Pastoral,* this was an opportunity to bring charges against Prynne. His criticism of the court was construed as disloyalty and his intemperate language as incitement to sedition. He was imprisoned for life, fined £5,000, deprived of his Oxford degree, expelled from his profession and condemned to lose his ears in the pillory.

The only part of the punishment that was remitted was the fine. The loss of his ears and his imprisonment in the Tower aroused sympathy among all who opposed Laud, and in spite of confinement, more pamphlets from his pen were smuggled out of the Tower.

Meanwhile other kindred spirits had appeared. One was John Bastwick, a physician of Colchester who had travelled on the Continent, served in the Dutch army and graduated at the University of Padua. In Holland he had already written two anti-Catholic treatises which had given offence to the bishops and caused him to be fined £1,000, prohibited from practising and imprisoned. The second, Henry Burton, was a clergyman who had been in the King's household before his accession but had lost his post and had joined the opposition against Laud. Both were busy writing tracts.

Bastwick in one of his later works told how he had been urged by a much-persecuted Puritan named Thomas Wharton to write, not in Latin, but in English. He did so, and produced a book called the *Letany*, one of the bitterest attacks on the bishops ever written. With this one book he fully made up for the shortcomings of his previous ones. He castigated the prelates unmercifully, sometimes unreasonably. They were, he said, 'the tail of the Devil', and his fight against them took on the aspect of a crusade.

With all his virulence, Bastwick advanced the anti-episcopal gospel no further. It was left to Burton, who did not hesitate to involve the monarchy in the dispute. In his pamphlet, *An Apology of an Appeal*, while exonerating the King from any part of the bishops' guilt, he emphasised that the King's power was God-given, but was also confirmed by the law of the land. To alter the form of religion or to suppress those who preached it would therefore be an offence against God and the state.

Among the many pamphlets published at the time was one entitled *Newes from Ipswich*, a virulent attack on Bishop Matthew Wren and conditions in East Anglia. Who wrote the pamphlet is even now in doubt, but its appearance was an excuse for the Star Chamber condemnation of all three, Prynne, Burton and Bastwick, to lose their ears and to be imprisoned for life.

Thus in July, the London crowd in Palace Yard saw these representatives of three great callings, the law, medicine and the Church pilloried and mutilated. To Prynne it was a second mutilation, for beside losing what was left of his ears he was also to have the letters SL – Seditious Libeller – branded on his cheeks. Such punishment, common enough and applauded when carried out on thieves, rogues and vagabonds, was inflicted this time before a sympathetic crowd, moaning and weeping that honourable men should thus be tortured, and when the hangman clumsily cut off part of the cheek with the remnants of an ear, a howl of indignation arose.

Now Puritanism had a martyr, and strangely enough the martyr was the most loyal of all the pamphleteers. His biographer relates how the foremost of the crowd bent down and soaked their kerchieves in the blood to keep as relics, and how the King and Queen when they appeared in public failed to draw a fraction of the crowd that would come to see Master Prynne. He was banished to the Channel Islands, and on the way to the coast the villagers turned out everywhere to see him and give him an ovation.

The sad meeting in the Palace Yard which the soldiery, for all their efforts could not disperse, was something of a novelty. In former days people and government had been so far apart that the only way in which the one could impress its ideas on the other had been to attach itself to some self-appointed leader and march in rebellion. This was no rebellion, but a demonstration, a sign that the man in the street was becoming politically conscious and was learning how to express himself; it was a warning, too, to Laud and the ruling party. Few demonstrations had taken place before but many were to be organised after that time, and thus demonstration became the most favoured way of airing popular protest and discontent. Less than six months later another scene occurred which shocked all London. This was the public whipping of John Lilburne.

Lilburne was a young man of good family, born in the Royal Palace at Greenwich where his mother had been a lady-in-waiting. His boyhood was spent mainly on the family estates in the north of England where the family had gone to escape the plague. When he was old enough he returned to London to become an apprentice to a cloth merchant. Intelligent, eager, amiable and idealistic, he devoured the works of the Protestant and Puritan fathers, and in 1636 was introduced by a friend to John Bastwick who at that time was in the Gatehouse prison. Several meetings took place, and soon the young enthusiast was busily engaged in the reading and distribution of forbidden literature.

At the time of the triple mutilation of Bastwick, Burton and Prynne, Lilburne realised that the authorities were on his track and he left the country for Holland with a few pounds in his pocket. Here he was soon engaged arranging shipments of Puritan books and smuggling them into England. The clandestine trade was quickly discovered when his associate in London, to save his own skin, betrayed Lilburne to the authorities. In December 1637 Lilburne, at great peril to himself, came to London where he was again betrayed by the same associate and taken.

In a preliminary interview with Sir John Banks, the King's Attorney and his clerk, he was so vigorously cross-examined that after a few minutes of rapid-fire question and answer he refused to say another word, and was committed for trial to the Star Chamber. There, before the most eminent judges in the country, he refused pointblank either to pay the customary fee to the clerk or to take the usual oath. Both Lilburne and his old friend Wharton, who had been committed on the same charge, were fined £500. Lilburne was sentenced to be whipped at the cart's tail from Fleet Bridge to Westminster, a distance of more than one and a half miles, and there to stand in the pillory.

Lilburne welcomed this barbarous punishment in the spirit of a Christian martyr, and with such steadfastness that even the officials of the Fleet prison who stripped him to the waist were moved, and marvelled. He was tied by both hands to the tail of the cart which was drawn out of the gate. 'Well, my friend, do thy office,' he said to the executioner, who replied, 'I have whipped many a rogue, but now I shall whip an honest man.'

'Blessed be Thy name, O Lord my God,' cried Lilburne as the first stroke fell, 'that hast counted me worthy to suffer for Thy glorious Name's sake.'

Now the gruesome procession set off over the Fleet Bridge and up Fleet Street, the knotted cords falling on his back at every two or three steps and the dust from the wheels choking him. The crowds lining the streets marvelled that such a frail body could bear the cruel punishment. As they went towards Charing Cross, people surged forward almost within reach of the lash to encourage him and at Westminster a vast multitude awaited. He was then loosed and taken into a tavern where a surgeon dressed his back, now lacerated with weals 'thicker than tobacco pipes' and his shoulders 'swollen to the size of penny loaves'. He was offered to be excused the pillory if he would retract, but refused and stood there for two hours, haranguing the crowd and denouncing the bishops.

With his hands, which were free, he drew out of his pockets three copies of Bastwick's *Letany*, and throwing them out into the crowd denied that there was anything in them against the King or the state. At last, on his refusal to be silent, the Warden of the Fleet commanded that a gag should be put into his mouth, and thus he stood for another hour. When at last the gag was removed and he was taken down he cried, 'I am more than conqueror through him that loved me. *Vivat Rex* – Long live the King.'

While Prynne, Bastwick, Burton and Lilburne were suffering, other dissentients were expressing their protests in a less voluble way. In 1620 the hundred or so emigrants had sailed out on the *Mayflower* to found new homes, and though in the first hard winter half of these had perished, thirty-two more arrived in 1622 and another ninety-six in 1623. In March 1629 the Massachusetts Bay Company was founded. During the following ten years some twenty thousand English men and women followed their compatriots, fleeing from Laud's persecution. Massachusetts was populated and flourished, but those who went out to seek 'freedom to worship God' sought it only for themselves. In the new colony, religious tests were as rigorous as ever they had been in England. In 1637 a church synod catalogued eighty-two 'opinions' as being blasphemous, erroneous or unsafe. The Massachusetts government was a more rigid theocracy than Laud's had been, for no man who was not a member of a Congregational Church and agreed with every one of its tenets was allowed the franchise. The seventeenth century was no time for religious toleration, either in the old world or the new.

The state might well have lived through the discontents caused by irregular taxation, but it could not weather the religious storm. The attempt of Laud to force episcopacy in Scotland resulted in strange scenes. It was such as these, the stool of Jenny Geddes flung at the dean's head with the cry, 'Out, thou false thief! Dost thou say the Mass at my lug?' that brought down Charles' personal government in Scotland and England. There followed the Bishops' War, a royal demand for a parliamentary grant, the Short Parliament and the Long Parliament.

Burton and Prynne entered London in 1640 amid scenes of wild enthusiasm. 'Never here such a like show: about a thousand horse, and, as some of good note say, above four thousand: above a hundred coaches and, as many say, above two hundred: with a world of foot, every one with their rosemary branch.' Alexander Leighton, mutilated, deaf and blind, was carried out into the light from the cell in which he had expected to die. A petition to free Lilburne was presented to Parliament by a member named Oliver Cromwell. Bastwick arrived from the Scillies to the sound of trumpets, torches burning and a thousand horse for convoy. All received compensation for their wrongs.

One demonstration followed another, especially in London, the heart of the kingdom. Strafford lost his head at the block, Laud was imprisoned in the Tower while the cries of London's populace against thirteen bishops impeached by the Commons gathered strength.

> *The oyster-women lock'd their fish up,*
> *And trudg'd away to cry, No Bishop.*
> *The mouse-trap men laid save-alls by,*
> *And 'gainst evil counsellors did cry.*
> *Botchers left old clothes in the lurch,*
> *And fell to turn and patch the Church.*
> *Some cry'd the Covenant, instead*
> *Of pudding-pies, and ginger-bread.*
> *And some for brooms, old boots and shoes,*
> *Bawled out to purge the Common-House:*
> *Instead of kitchen-stuff, some cry,*
> *A Gospel-preaching ministry;*
> *And some for old suits, coats, or cloak,*
> *No surplices nor Service-book.*
>
> Butler, *Hudibras, part i, canto ii*

The revolution, political, religious and social, had begun. A new world was in the making, and with it, new matter for protest.

9

'England's New Chains'

'IF THE PRESSES were open to us,' exclaimed Bastwick speaking of Laud, 'we would scatter his kingdom about his ears.' In 1640 Laud's system broke and collapsed, and in December of that year he was impeached by the Long Parliament. All restrictions gone, the country was flooded with pamphlets, and two-thirds of these were about religion. 'Let religion be our premium *quaerite*,' said one of the authors, 'for all things are but etceteras to it.' Laud had set the nation on fire.

Yet though the Puritans had been united in condemning the Church of England, there was no one Puritan body or organisation, for the name itself embraced a multitude of sects whose attitudes to life were similar, but which differed greatly on points of doctrine and organisation, to the modern mind of little apparent importance but to the members of each one of these sects, vital.

For this reason, once the presses were freed and once the incubus of the Laudian tyranny had been cast off their shoulders, and every man able to speak his mind, the conflicting elements of Puritanism split apart. Pym would have imposed on England a state Puritan Church in which Parliamentary lay commissioners exercised control in place of the bishops and in which neither Anglicanism nor Catholicism would have been tolerated.

But this was not to be. In 1643 Parliament, to obtain the support of the Scots, had to accept the Solemn League and Covenant agreeing to set up a Presbyterian Church on the Scottish model and to enforce the Presbyterian form of worship over the whole country. Religious toleration had no place here, as the first clause of this famous document indicates:

That we shall sincerely, really and constantly, through the grace of God, endeavour in our several places and callings the preservation of the reformed religion in the Church of Scotland, in doctrine, worship, discipline and government, against our common enemies; the reformation of religion in the kingdoms of England and Ireland in doctrine, worship, discipline and government, according to the Word of God, and the example of the best reformed Churches; and we shall endeavour to bring the Churches of God in the three kingdoms to the nearest conjunction and uniformity.

Pym had completed his great task of building up a parliamentary party and backing it with military force and an alliance with the Scots. The Solemn League and Covenant had been concluded and was to be imposed on every county in England and to be affirmed by all county officers, including Members of County Committees, magistrates and churchwardens. Copies of it, signed with the names of the chief parishioners, appear in many parish registers. But in spite of their affirmation, Presbyterianism was a faith of foreign extraction and did not take deep root in England. A large number of Puritans refrained from attaching themselves to any sect, for Puritanism to them was rather a way of life than a set of rules. All these could have been brought under the general term of 'presbyterians' just as the hospital patient or the recruit who is unattached to any religious body today allows himself to be classed as C of E. The Presbyterian organisation, with its Church Elders and its counties divided into *classes* or groups of churches, was probably universal throughout the country. The experience of ministers under this system proved that Presbyterian intolerance was as rigid as ever that of Laud had been. Many were sequestered from their livings or censured for such offences as bowing to the east, churching women, preaching that Papists as well as Puritans could be saved, ('but a Papist must go a little further about it'), for conversing with malignants, drunkenness, incontinency, and suffering youth to play lewd games on Sunday afternoons. Lawrence Washington, reputed ancestor of George, who was vicar of Purleigh, is described in the report of the Commission for the Sequestration of Scandalous Ministers as being –

> a common frequenter of alehouses, not only himself sitting tippling there, but also encouraging others in that beastly vice, and hath been often drunk, and hath said that Parliament have more Papists belonging to them in their armies than the King hath about him in his army, and that the Parliament army did more harm than the Cavaliers, and that they did none at all, and hath published them as traitors that did lend to or assist the Parliament.

Washington was obviously a royalist and the condemnation not entirely true, for some more sympathetic Justices refer to him as 'a worthy pious man, a very sober person, and had one of the best benefices in those parts, and this was the only cause of his sequestration . . .'.

Under such circumstances as these it is understandable why the foreign persuasion of Presbyterianism did not take firm hold, or that other sects continued to flourish.

Of these others, the chief were the Independents. At first they were in a minority, for at the beginning of the Civil War few Members of Parliament would have had the temerity to rise and set forth the belief of the Independents that other sects besides Presbyterians should be tolerated. But, as the war passed into its second year and pressure on the parliamentary army increased, it was of the utmost importance to its leaders to maintain the allegiance and morale of every man in it. Presbyterian discipline was too demanding to ensure universal support. What was needed was a more tolerant outlook, and the Independents supplied this. The founder of the sect, Robert Browne (1550–1633), laid down its three main principles, religious liberty, the election of ministers by the congregations, and the exclusion of magistrates from all ecclesiastical authority. The Brownists, Independents, or Congregationalists as they were later to be called, would thus have split the Church completely off from the state. The army officers, realising that strength depended on toleration, encouraged the admission into the ranks of all kinds of sectaries, every one of whom was fighting as much for his own creed and sect as for the victory of all. Puritans were always good rebels, and the sectaries contributed largely to the final victory of Parliament in the First Civil War.

An even more important contribution was made by this 'harvest of armed men from the soil'. The most earnest of them were profound thinkers, nonconformists of the nonconformists, and once their tongues were loosed and their pens given full play they produced a harvest of political ideas such as had never before sprung to life in England in so short a time. The activities of these Sectarian Fathers had therefore two notable characteristics. They involved protest, but to the protest of most of them was added constructive thought and programmes which, however preposterous and dangerous they might have seemed to the independent majority, had within them the seeds of doctrines such as Republicanism, Pacifism, Chartism and Communism. While studying the protests and the events that followed, it is impossible entirely to neglect their more valuable results in fashioning the political theories of future generations.

The Independents had two notable advantages, first, the army of forty to fifty thousand well-trained, well-disciplined men, and secondly a leader of undisputed genius and authority. Thus, whereas Parliament up to 1646 was supreme, its members were too blinded by a mistaken idea of their own power to realise that its foundation was in the army, and they committed the most stupid blunders in attempting to conciliate the moderate Royalists, persecuting the sectaries even to the infliction of the death penalty for Unitarians and life imprisonment for others, and finally in ordering the disbandment of the New Model.

Such actions completed the work the Self-denying Ordinance had begun in splitting off one from the other, and in inspiring Cromwell to take possession of the most important asset of all

– the person of the King, who had by this time been surrendered to Parliament by the Scots. The progress of events from this point to the conversion of the army by Independent preachers, the occupation of London, the rapprochement between part of the Presbyterian sect and the Cavaliers, the Second Civil War, Pride's Purge, the trial and execution of the King, proceeded as if decreed by some inexorable fate. Long before this last bitter climax England had one paramount power – the army with Cromwell at its head.

When the army purged Parliament and the Rump, 'the hind-quarters of the Beast', appointed a commission to try Charles, a tremor ran through the country. To some, who had signed the Solemn League and Covenant, it was a feeling of regret that the revolution had gone to such extreme lengths. Others held that whatever the King might have done, his person should still be regarded as inviolable. How many protests were sent to Parliament at the time of the King's trial and execution is not known. One, from the ministers of the gospel within the province of London, was delivered to Cromwell on 18th January. Two days later another, a truly Presbyterian document was received, signed by sixty-three persons, including eleven ministers, from the hundred of Rochford in Essex. It is bold in the extreme:

> We neither do nor can approve of the violence and force done by some of the Army upon the House of Commons in surprising, imprisoning and excluding so many members thereof going to the House to perform their duties. . . . Neither can we approve of the present actings of the Army with the remaining members of the Commons in proceeding against the King as a traitor.

The document goes on to list the Army's many offences. Another, called the Essex Watchmen's Watchword, penned after the King's death, shows in its bitter reproaches something of the shock felt at the sudden tragic turn of events:

. . . persuaded of the loyalty of their [Parliament's] intentions towards His Majesty's Person Posterity and Crown, and being fully assured of our own, having this witness in Heaven and in our own hearts that that calamity which hath now befallen the king and threatens his posterity was exceedingly far from our designs and desires. . . .

But O, how amazed are we to behold the sad issue the war is now driven into! To see the war, begun for the Defence of the King ending in the death of the King: a war begun for the defence of the Parliament ending in the violation of the present and mutilation of future parliaments both in point of election and constitution!

'*This is a lamentation and shall be for a lamentation.*' (*Ezekiel XIX, 14*).

The Civil War had been undertaken by Parliament to safeguard its liberties against the King, but it was barely three years after its outbreak that at least one citizen spoke openly for the liberty of all citizens against the tyranny of Parliament. The spate of pamphlets issuing from innumerable presses had been watched with great concern by the Stationers' Company who had repeatedly complained to Parliament about them. In June 1643 an order was therefore issued forbidding the printing of any unlicensed publications whatever. Thus, press censorship, so violently attacked in the days of Charles I, returned in full force under the rule of the Presbyterian House of Commons. From this point the protest on behalf of the freedom of the individual grew in intensity and spread throughout the Independent ranks and among the London populace. Its apostle was John Lilburne.

Lilburne had suffered in 1637 for his religious convictions, but he was now to oppose another government on the much wider question of the liberty of the subject in all matters. Since 1637 he had grown to full manhood and experience. He had at the beginning of the Civil War espoused the cause of Parliament, which he believed at the time to be the true defender of political liberty. On 23rd October 1643 Captain John Lilburne had faced the King's Guards in a bloody struggle at the battle of Edgehill. Three weeks later he had been taken prisoner at Brentford, condemned to death for high treason, and only saved by Parliament's threat, if any of their men were executed by the Royalists, to inflict the same punishment on their own captives. Later he fought at Marston Moor and was prevented from taking by storm a royalist castle at Tickhill through the over-caution of the Earl of Manchester. Then, when in 1645 the Solemn League and Covenant was imposed on all members of Cromwell's New Model Army, Lilburne, vowing that he would dig for turnips rather than fight to set up a power to make himself a slave, resigned his commission.

Once in London, Lilburne was the centre of the clique of Independents and sectaries who opposed the pretensions of Parliament to regulate all matters of Church and state without regard to the claims of the individual conscience. Assuming for themselves the freedom they claimed for others, these pioneers of religious and political thought sat together and probed into the eternal questions of the relations between God and Man, and all the social implications that arose from them. In William Walwyn, an elderly merchant, Lilburne found an ideal teacher who appealed to reason and intellectual honesty, and in Richard Overton, a pamphleteer who had the gift of putting forward the group's theories with force, and in language the ordinary man could understand, while Lilburne himself, the fearless propagandist, was the idol of the London populace. Together these men captured both the people and the army for the Independents and thus indirectly contributed to their victory over the Parliament.

Many things were to happen, however, before that day came. The Presbyterians were only too anxious to get Lilburne out of the way, and in July 1645 he was arrested on the evidence of John Bastwick for having made, in private, an accusation against the Speaker of the House of Commons. When called before the Committee of Examination he refused to answer until he had been given the reason for his commitment. He told the Committee:

> I am a free man, yea, a free-born denizen of England, and I have been in the field with my sword in my hand, to adventure my life and my blood against tyrants for the preservation of my freedom, and I do not know that ever I did an act in all my life that disfranchises me of my freedom, and by virtue of my being a free man, I conceive, I have as true a right to all the privileges that do belong to a free man as the greatest man in England, whatsoever he be, whether Lord or Commoner, and the ground and foundation of my freedom I build upon the Grand Charter of England . . .

. . . that no free man should be arrested, deprived of his free-hold nor in any way harmed unless by the judgement of his peers or by the law of the land. He was sent back to gaol where he remained until the sessions. No charges were brought against him and he was released on 14th October.

Even in gaol he had not been silent. Four days before his release appeared the pamphlet *England's Birthright Justified*, the confession of faith of the men who were later to become the leaders of the sect commonly known as the Levellers. The first half of the pamphlet, with its clear reasoning and pungent, compact writing, shows evidence of Overton's work; its unequivocal statement of the fundamental rights of Englishmen is undoubtedly that of Lilburne.

These rights, according to Coke, were grounded in the common law of the country 'beyond the memory or register of any beginning, and the same which the Norman conqueror found within the Realm of England'. The native English, the Saxons, had been free men, equal in rights, in power and dignity. William the Conqueror had deprived them of their rights and their property and, to perpetuate his robberies, had imposed on the English tyrannical laws in a foreign language. This was a double-edged theory, for while the oppressed based on it their claim to freedom, the propertied classes could use it as a justification of their own privileges by ancient conquest. Lilburne justified Magna Carta and the Petition of Right as indicating a return to the conception of freedom. The rest of Lilburne's pamphlet attacked monopolies, especially that of printing, which interfered with both people and Parliament, and was only good for spreading lies and prejudice.

This was one of the first pamphlets in the great outpouring of Leveller literature between the years 1645 to 1653. To the men who had fought in the Parliamentary forces for this freedom and who now had little to do but think and argue, such ideas spread like wildfire.

In June 1646, Lilburne was again in prison for an offence against Parliamentary privilege. Visitors were forbidden and he was deprived of writing materials. There, for more than a year he lay, as Walwyn put it, 'a Pearl in a Dunghill', while the activities of his friends went on without him. Overton published in July the *Remonstrance of many Thousand Citizens and other Free Urban People of England to their Owne House of Commons.* Again he persisted that the Commons were the trustees of the people, and that they were elected to work for the people's deliverance.

> Wee are your Principalls, and you our Agents; it is a Truth which you cannot but acknowledge: For if you or any other shall assume, or exercise any Power, that is not derived from our Trust and choice thereunto, that Power is no lesse than usurpation and an Oppression, from which wee expect to be freed, in whomsoever we finde it, it being altogether inconsistent with the nature of *just Freedome,* which yee also very well understand.

Then he proceeded to remind the Commons that they had lately become as tyrannical as any king with all his prerogatives and privileges:

> To accuse or prosecute any of you, is become dangerous to the Prosecutors. Yee have imprisonments as frequent for either Witnesses or Prosecutors, as ever the Starre-Chamber had, and

131

yee are furnished with new devised Arguments, to prove, that yee onely may justly doe these grosse injustices, which the Starre-Chamber, High-Commission and Counsell-board might not doe.

Accusations follow one on another – a gagged press, a form of religion enforced on all, exorbitant taxes and customs, the unjust pressing of men for the war, monopolies, the selling of justice and imprisonment for debt. On this point the manifesto rises to a climax of scorn:

> . . . yee are Rich and abound in goods, and have need of nothing; but the afflictions of the poore; your hunger-starved brethren, ye have no compassion of; Your zeal makes a noise as far as Argiere, to deliver those captived Christians at the charge of others, but those whom your owne unjust Laws hold captive in your own Prisons: these are too neere you to thinke of; Nay, yee suffer poor Christians, for whom Christ died to kneel before you in the streets, aged, sick and crippled, begging your halfe-penny Charities, and yee rustle by them in your Coaches and silkes daily, without regard, or taking any Course for their constant reliefe, their sight would melt the heart of any Christian, and yet it moves not you nor your Clergy.

What then was the remedy? Nothing but perfect confidence between people and a parliament elected freely by all men, without fear and favour.

> And if any Person without exception, shall write Letters, or use any endeavours to incline the choosers to choose any man, or use any means to disturbe or pervert them from a free Choice, then that all such sinister dealing be made punishable, or a most haynous crime.

In this alone the Levellers were far ahead of their time; in the totality of their programme they anticipated the Chartists. Overton was arrested in the following month for another pamphlet in defence of Lilburne. He refused to walk to prison and was dragged through the streets to Newgate where he was beaten and put in irons. His house was pillaged, his wife and brother arrested and his three children thrown out into the streets.

The London populace were solidly behind 'Freeborn John' and his friends, and petition after petition followed, demanding their release. The last of these was not answered by the Commons and when the petitioners pressed for a reply, they ordered it to be burned by the common hangman. After this it was realised that nothing could be done in face of the high-handed actions of a parliament that hugged its privileges and incarcerated all who challenged them. The only possible appeal left was to the rank and file in the army. By this time Parliament had produced its scheme for disbandment, and this had met with spirited protests both from officers and men. Another petition caused Ireton, Pride and two more officers to be called to the bar of the House of Commons, and in the stormy meeting which followed, Holles for Parliament and Ireton for the army almost came to the point of duelling.

At Newmarket in June the officers and men bound themselves together by a Solemn Engagement and established an Army Council. Parliament by its high-handed attitude had created the force which ultimately destroyed it. Within three months Cromwell had taken the King, occupied London and entered the House. From that time (August 1647) the Independents were masters of the country. In these six months of confusion and dissension the Leveller creed was born. It had helped to infuse spirit into the army and to draw the teeth of Parliament; now it was to split the army itself into two opposing elements – officers and men.

Thus in thirty years, in situation after situation – Parliament against King, Independents against Presbyterians, Levellers against Independents – we pass from one series of protests to another.

In a last vain effort to obtain some basis of agreement with the King, Ireton had placed before Charles a treaty called the

133

Heads of the Proposals. This went a long way towards meeting the Levellers' demands in that it would have provided for parliaments every two years, free elections, freedom of worship, abolition of monopolies, the release of debtors and many other items on their programme. But like most plans to meet everybody's wishes, it ended by satisfying nobody. Rumours were spread about that the King was playing fast and loose with the army leaders, that his flatteries had poisoned the blood of Cromwell and Ireton, that they had been promised earldoms, that they had knelt before the King and kissed his hands. From his prison in the Tower Lilburne sent forth violent recriminations against Cromwell.

> . . . if these army news be true, I must bid you farewell, and must here declare myself an avowed enemy to your self pecuniary interest, and all your co-partners and shall with more zeal bend all my abilities against you all, and unmask you to my friends, than my adversaries the tyrannical and arbitrary Lords.
>
> It hath been my unhappiness to be . . . destroyed by men of guilded outsides, and . . . I must plainly and truely now tell you, I judge you to be the chiefe.

In September Cromwell met Lilburne in the Tower and in November 'Freeborn John' was allowed to leave his prison during the day on condition that he returned at night. By that time Cromwell and Ireton had failed to reach an agreement with the King, the Heads of the Proposals were out of date and a new Leveller manifesto had been published. This, *The Agreement of the People,* was a most complete statement of the political philosophy of the Levellers. All the manifold arguments so often put forward were here repeated, with all the fervour of idealism. Cromwell, the wary opponent, judged things not by the yardstick of right and wrong, but of the possible and the impossible, and he saw 'very great mountaines' in its path. The subject-matter of *The Agreement* was debated in the nave of Putney Church by the army leaders and seven representatives of the Levellers.

In this important series of debates they were at least allowed a voice, but at once the wide cleft between officers and men showed itself. The officers' viewpoint was put by Ireton, who was for preserving the old social distinctions and order, including the limited franchise for the 40s freeholder only. This would have left without votes most of the rank and file of the army. If every man was given a vote, declared Ireton, how could one be sure that the poor would not attack the wealthy? Moreover, said another officer, how could they be prevented from selling their votes or even voting for a law enacting equality of wealth for all?

The Levellers' representatives stood firm. Though they found it difficult to rebut the charge that property rights might vanish, they stressed that they were not Communists, and that many of their leaders including Walwyn the merchant, Overton the printer and Lilburne, once a brewer, were men of the propertied classes. And was not *The Agreement* the only means to preserve property? The basic principles of the Levellers' belief were laid down in the well-known words of Colonel Thomas Rainsborough, one of the officer members of the sect.

> I think that the poorest He that is in England hath a life to live, as the greatest He; and therefore truly, sir, I think it's clear, that every man that is to live under a government ought first by his own consent to put himself under that government; and I do think that the poorest man in England is not all bound in a strict sense to that government that he hath not had a voice to put himself under; and I am confident that, when I have heard the reasons against it, something will be said to answer those reasons, insomuch that I should doubt whether he was an Englishmen or no, that should doubt of these things.

This was the great doctrinal cleavage that added to the initial mistrust of the ranks for Cromwell and Ireton. In this early expression of the Social Contract Rainsborough foreshadowed the major political dispute of two centuries to follow. Cromwell, after many days of debate, saw with dismay the possible subversion of army discipline. Determined to preserve order at all costs, he declared that the suffrage clause of *The Agreement* tended towards anarchy, and got a motion passed that all should return to their regiments.

The officer clique had proved in the end as uncompromising as King or Parliament had ever been. On the 15th November, four days only after the King's escape, came the test of strength between the two factions. When the regiments were mustered at Corkbush Field near Ware, most of the men and many of their officers arrived carrying copies of *The Agreement*, and wearing in their hats slogans such as 'Soldiers' Rights', and 'England's Freedom'. As Cromwell and the other generals rode on to the field, they were greeted by angry cries, especially from the more extreme regiments. An appeal for solidarity had a response from some parts of the field, but the cavalry regiment of Robert Lilburne, John's elder brother, refused when commanded to remove the papers from their hats. With that, Cromwell, followed by other officers, rode among them, drawn sword in hand. A sudden hesitation on the men's part and all was lost. The awesome personality of Cromwell won the day as, in a rage, he rode up to some of the astounded troopers and, with his own hand, snatched the papers and flung them away. A court-martial followed, three officers were sentenced to death, and one of them, Richard Arnold, was shot.

Lilburne, having ridden from London, heard the lamentable news in Ware. The army had been cowed into submission but the memory of the martyred Leveller prevented it ever again being united in spirit. Government lapsed into little short of tyranny. All free expression in public meetings was forbidden, books and newspapers were strictly controlled, private presses were raided and broken up. Even religious freedom, the boast of the Independents, was limited through considerations of the safety of the state. With Lilburne in the Tower and the country again in peril from the Scots-Royalist alliance, the spate of pamphlets died down somewhat and for a time officers and men, facing common enemies, reached a semblance of unity.

The trial of the King in January 1649 was the signal for more petitions and pamphlets. England was bound in new chains, the chains of a spurious republic. The Commons had exceeded the tyrannies of the Stuarts. They had redressed no grievances; they had even increased the perils to individual liberty through the institution of special courts whereby ordinary legal proceedings were circumvented. Dissatisfaction again flared up in the army when eight troopers laid a manifesto before Fairfax, attacking the officers for taking away their right to draw up petitions. Five of these were sentenced by court-martial to ride with their faces towards their horse-tails in front of their regiments with their crimes written on papers fastened to their breasts. Their swords were broken over their heads and they were dismissed from the army. This disgraceful procedure brought from them a few days later a scathing pamphlet, probably penned for them by Overton. *The Hunting of the Foxes* accused Cromwell, Ireton and their faction of 'self-interested officers . . .'

> who thought they had got the souldiery fast by the brain, then decline the Agitators, decline the Engagement, slight their Declaration and Promises to the people and the Army . . . corrupting some with Places, over-awing others . . . so by Degrees they cast out the interest of the Souldiery among them . . . and broke the Faith of the Army.
>
> Was there ever a generation of man so Apostate so false and so perjur'd as these? Did ever men pretend an higher degree of Holinesse, Religion, and Zeal to God and their Country than these? These preach, these fast, these pray, these have nothing more frequent than the sentences of sacred Scripture, the Name of God and Christ in their mouths: You shall scarce speak to Cromwell about any thing, but he will lay his hand on his breast, elevate his eyes, and call God to record, he will weep, howl and repent, even while he doth smite you under the first rib.

Disaffection gave way to mutiny by thirty men of Whalley's regiment in London, but this was quickly put down. Five of the mutineers were cashiered and the sixth, Robert Lockyer, was shot, protesting that his death in peace time by court-martial was murder. London came out in a great demonstration in sympathy with the rank and file, as thousands, dressed in black and wearing Leveller ribbons, walked in front of the hearse at Lockyer's funeral. The mutiny spread to Oxfordshire where Cromwell, promising safety, lured the insurgents from their stronghold at Burford. Four were immediately shot. Their captain, William Thompson, escaped with a troop to Wellingborough where he died, fighting to the last, while scattered risings in the army took place at points in the south and west. The civilian Levellers, aided by pamphlets from Lilburne's pen, carried on the struggle. His brilliant work, *The Impeachment of High Treason against Oliver Cromwell and his son-in-law Henry Ireton,* appeared in August 1649 and exceeded in violent language anything that had so far appeared from Leveller presses. Other pamphlets asserted the right of the people to rise in their own defence against tyranny, to make all who had illegally acquired property since 1640 give it up, and to refuse to pay taxes. But the full force of Lilburne's venom was directed against 'Saint Oliver' himself.

> The present contest of the present dissembling interest of Independents for the people's liberties in general is no more but Self in the highest, and to set up the false Saint and most desperate apostate murderer and traitor Oliver Cromwell by a pretended election of his mercenary soldiers, under the false name of a godly interest, to be King of England etc (that being now too apparently all the intended liberties of the people that ever he fought for in his life) that so he might rule and govern them by his will and pleasure, and so destroy and envassalage their lives and properties to his lusts, which is the highest treason that ever was committed or acted in this nation, in any sense or kind; either first, in the eye of the law, or secondly, in the eye of the ancient (but yet too much arbitrary) proceedings of

Parliament, or thirdly, in the eye of their own late declared principles of reason. . . .

One last effort was made at compromise when Lilburne was taken before the Attorney-General but refused to recognise either his authority or that of Parliament. Later, when others were sent to his lodging to try to persuade him into compliance, he threatened to kick them out. Cromwell had listened long enough to peacemakers. Lilburne's power over the malcontents could, if allowed to grow, threaten public security. In October 1649, he was put on trial for his life on a charge of high treason.

London had not experienced such a sensation since the previous January when the King had been beheaded. The spectacle of Lilburne, the puny David, standing up to the Goliath of the military state, questioning the acts under which he was judged treasonable, damning the judges as Norman intruders, refusing to answer questions on the authorship of the pamphlets, challenging the closure of the doors of the courtroom, picking flaws in the evidence against him, refusing to plead one way or the other, demanding counsel, cross-questioning witnesses and invoking ancient laws, brought forth the admiration of the populace, so that everybody ran after the latest news. In this he proved himself as astute and learned as his accusers.

The Attorney-General concluded the prosecution. 'Brother,' said John to his brother, Robert, who had been with him throughout the trial, 'I will warrant you by the strength of God I will knock the nail upon the head.' Then at the bar he proceeded, in an eloquent speech, step by step to demolish the evidence that had been brought against him, and ended by declaring his loyalty to the free men of England, his defiance of the 'Norman Conqueror's intruders', and enjoining the jury to leave no part of his indictment to the cruel bloody men, his prosecutors.

In an hour they returned a verdict of Not Guilty. He received the verdict solemnly as one who had been within a hairsbreadth of death, but London went mad with joy. Bonfires were lit in the streets and a medal was struck in memory of the occasion.

This was the end of the Levellers as a driving force in English politics. At the age of thirty-five John Lilburne had done his work. For a time he retired to his house in the Old Bailey where he went into business as a soap-boiler. In 1650 the Rump allowed him a sum of money to make good some of his losses, and he even re-established friendship with Cromwell. In 1651, however, he became involved in a family litigation, and on his case being lost, presented a petition to Parliament and put forward his family's case in a pamphlet accusing his opponents and the court of malpractice. This was taken by Parliament as a chance to get rid of him. He was fined £7,000 and banished from England for ever. In spite of the ban he returned in 1653, was caught, tried and in the following year was transferred from the Tower of London to Jersey. Eighteen months later he returned to England broken in health and was imprisoned in Dover Castle with, however, a good deal of personal freedom. Here he spent his last days. He died in August 1657 at the early age of forty-four having fought and suffered but apparently accomplished nothing. No man ever grasped more clearly than he did the meaning of democracy, and no man held more firmly to his convictions. His actions, often hasty and ill-considered, were nevertheless from pure motives, and though his name was forgotten except by the few, many of the principles for which he gave life and liberty were rediscovered by other pioneers and later became part of the British form of government and way of life.

The Levellers had repeatedly stressed both in manifesto and debate that, while they stood for universal franchise, they were not in favour of the equal distribution of property, or of holding land and goods in common. It was otherwise with the sect known as the Diggers. Though they had neither the reputation nor the influence of Lilburne and his followers, their original line of thought and their personal bravery in putting it into action were prophetic.

It was inevitable in an age when men's thoughts ranged so widely on religious and political problems that some doctrine of common ownership should appear. In days of trouble or tyranny they had always pictured a golden age in the remote past either before all the evils in Pandora's box had been let loose to fly about the world, when all were naturally upright and noble; or, in the case of the English, they imagined that the Saxon forefathers had been equal and free from the tyranny of the usurping lords, under the just government of kings such as Alfred and the Sainted Edward the Confessor. On this free country the Norman yoke descended; the people were enslaved and their lands enclosed. The Levellers knew the doctrine and some of them believed it, but to none had it a greater appeal than to the Diggers.

Gerrard Winstanley, the leader of the sect, was born in Wigan in 1609. His parents were probably fairly well-to-do, for he had some knowledge of Latin and about the year 1629 came to London, served an apprenticeship and became a freeman of the Merchant Taylors' Company. He must have been too much of an idealist to succeed in the rough-and-tumble of business, for he says in the address to one of his tracts to the City:

> I was once a freeman of thine but, beaten out of estate and trade by thy cheating sons in the thieving art of buying and selling, and by the burdens of and for the soldiery in the beginning of the war. I was beaten out both of estate and trade, and forced to accept the goodwill of friends crediting of me, to live a country life, and there likewise, by the burden of taxes and much free-quarter, my weak back found the burden heavier than I could bear....

In this period of scarcity and sorrow his great enlightenment came.

Not a full year since, being quiet at my work, my heart was filled with sweet thoughts, and many things were revealed to me which I never read in books, nor heard from the mouth of any flesh.

This was no conversion, for Winstanley's thoughts had always been occupied with religion. The sudden advent of sweet thoughts may have been inspired by his friendship with William Everson, a soldier in the New Model Army, and one of the most extreme of the Levellers.

The leaven worked quickly in Winstanley's mind and, as he says, among the revelations came one, namely that the earth should be made a common treasury of all mankind without respect of persons. In January 1649 he produced the pamphlet, *The New Law of Righteousness*. The law in brief was, that 'none shall lay claim to any creature and say, This is myne, and that is yours, This is my work and that is yours, but every one shall put to their hands to till the earth and bring up cattle, and the blessing of the earth shall be common to all; when a man hath need of any corn or cattle, take from the next storehouse he meets with' (*Acts, IV, 32*).

This was the rule among the early Christian fathers, that all should be held in common, and it was the ultimate state of grace in which man would one day exist. In a long introduction Winstanley showed how the world was ruled by the Old Adam, 'the wisdom and the power of the flesh in every man, who indeed is the Beast . . . who spreads himself . . . into divers branches . . . hypocrisy, subtlety, lying, imagination, self-love from whence proceeds all un-righteous outward acting'. Against this Adam rises up the second man who, by the power of Christ, casts the other out of the temple of the heart and dwells in it himself.

Thus, mankind would one day live in the freedom of the spirit, not the few but all inheriting the earth, with no buying nor selling, no fairs or markets, all having enough and none too much, every man opening his barns, none claiming lordship over his neighbour and none throwing up hedges or enclosures.

> For as the enclosures are called such a man's land, and such a man's land, so the commons and heath are called the common people's. . . . For let the rich work alone by themselves and let the poor work together by themselves, the rich in their enclosures saying, This is mine, the poor upon their commons saying, This is ours, the earth and fruits are common.

Here is the germ of Winstanley's teaching. The rich need not be touched, but the poor who were made to inherit the earth should take that part of it which by name is conceded to them, and cultivate it. This was not mere preaching. To Winstanley it was a call to action. Not more than one-third of the whole of England was manured and tilled. The poor had the right to take of the rest what they needed to maintain themselves and their children.

> I have now obeyed the command of the spirit that bid me declare all this abroad. I have declared it by my pen. And when the Lord doth show unto me the place and manner, how He will have us that are called common people to manure and work upon the common lands, I will then go forth and declare it in my action, to eat my bread with the sweat of my brows, without either giving or taking hire, looking upon the land as freely mine as anothers.

Three days after the publication of this pamphlet King Charles was beheaded. The victory was won and the time seemed ripe for social changes. So far the poor had taken no part in the great upheaval, but now everybody expected to see its fruits in the establishment of a purer and juster social order. The working classes had already paid dearly. Taxation and the cost of living had risen, bad harvests, evictions and the quartering of soldiers had added to their burdens.

On 16th April 1649 a message was received by the Council of State:

On Sunday sennight last, there was one Everard, once of the army but cashiered, who termeth himself a prophet, and four more came to St George's Hill in Surrey and began to dig, and sowed the ground with parsnips, carrots and beans. On Monday following they were there again, being increased in their number. On Friday they came again, twenty or thirty, and wrought all day at digging. They do threaten to pull down and level all park pales and lay open and intend to plant them. They give out that they will be four or five thousand within ten days, and threaten the neighbouring people they will make them all come up to the hills and work.

Two soldiers were sent to Cobham to find out what was happening, and returned with the news that the affair was hardly worth notice. The leaders, Everson and Winstanley, had promised to appear before Fairfax but, it was thought, he would probably be glad to get rid of them.

The next day, 20th April, they were interviewed. They explained that the time of deliverance of the people was at hand when their liberties, lost at the time of the Norman conquest, were to be restored. The Council of State, thinking that nothing of importance could result from the actions of a few harmless fanatics, dismissed them.

On the same day as the interview there appeared the manifesto *The True Leveller's Standard Advanced. A Declaration to the Powers of England, and to all the powers of the world, showing the cause why the common people of England have begun, and gives consent to dig up, manure and sow corn upon George Hill in Surrey.* Lilburne's sect had resented the application of the name Leveller; Winstanley was proud to adopt it, for it was far more aptly applied to the Diggers who would have levelled everything including property rights. Other Digger writings claim that the franchise, privilege, the law in Latin, manorial customs, monopolies, taxation, even the jury system were thought to be of Norman origin, created to oppress and enslave the true English, and how happiness, it was believed, could not return to the blighted land until the Norman yoke was removed:

> . . . when any trustee or state officer is to be chosen, the free-holders or the landlords must be the choosers, who are the Norman common soldiers spread abroad in the land. And who must be chosen, but some very rich man, who is the successor of the Norman Colonels or high officers? And to what end have they been thus chosen but to establish that Norman power the more forcibly over the enslaved English, and to beat them down again, when as they gather heart to seek for liberty?
>
> For what are all those binding and restraining laws that have been made from one age to another since that Conquest, and are still upheld by fury over the people? I say, what are they, but the cords, bands, manacles and yokes that the enslaved English, like Newgate prisoners, wear upon their hands and legs as they walk the streets.
>
> O, what mighty delusion do you, who are the powers of England live in! That while you pretend to throw down that Norman yoke, and Babylonish power, and have promised to make the groaning [people] of England a free people, yet you still lift up that Norman yoke and slavish tyranny, and hold the people as much in bondage as the bastard Conqueror himself and his Council of War.

This doctrine was subversive of the whole basis of seventeenth-century society. If carried out to the letter, it meant everything Lilburne was fighting for, plus the abolition of copyhold and all feudal services, the throwing open of commons and the end of every landlord's privilege. Winstanley's last words were both a prophecy and a threat:

> O you Adams of the earth, you have rich clothing, full bellies, have your honours and ease, and you puff at this. But know thou, stout-hearted Pharaoh, that the day of judgment is begun, and it will reach thee ere long. Jacob hath been very low, but he is rising, and will rise, do the worst thou canst. And the poor people, whom thou oppresses shall be the saviours of the land; for the blessing is rising up in them, and thou shalt be ashamed.

If the Council could not see the danger, the local community, on whose doorstep it had arisen, feared and acted. In his *Humble Request* of 1650, Winstanley tells the sad story of how the parson and impropriator of the tithes arrived at the little settlement with hired thugs, tore down the houses, made a bonfire of them, throwing in the poor people's belongings, and turned them all away, not pitying the women and frightened children left homeless. Many were assaulted and abused. Yet Winstanley counted even this a triumph according to the teaching of Christ whom he called the Head Leveller.

> The voice of the Dragon is Kill him, pull down his house, beat him, arrest him, take him, jailor, imprison him, he is a rogue.
>
> But the voice of the Lamb is Love your enemies, let him live, the earth is his Creation right as well as mine; there-fore let us do as we would be done unto. . . .
>
> And now they cry out the Diggers are routed, and they rang bells for joy; but stay, gentlemen, yourselves are routed, and you have lost the crown, and the poor Diggers have won the crown of glory.

For a short time Winstanley was the leader of a movement. Diggers' settlements were started at various places, but were quickly and easily dispersed. In 1652 he published his *Law of Freedom*, a symposium of Digger beliefs. His act of protest was small in scale but significant, his writings are examples of the finest prose of his day, and his theories influenced profoundly the thought of all socialist leaders who followed him. He continued to live at Cobham as a small trader for some ten years, but the date and place of his death are not known.

10

Cross-Currents of Agitation

'NEVER DID THE human mind attain such a magnificent height of self-assertiveness as in England about the year 1650,' wrote Lytton Strachey. Nor were there any other periods when man probed so deeply into his inner being and laid bare his thoughts and feelings to his fellows. The study of the Puritan sects and the motives, conscious and unconscious, which produced these ideas and impulses of bewildering variety, is a fruitful field of enquiry for the historian-psychologist. The emergence of the Behmenist, Bedelian, Coppinist, Salmonist, Dipper, Traskite, Tyronist, Philadelphian, Christadelphian, Seventh Day Baptist, Seeker, Considerer, Mennonite and Muggletonian sects, to mention only a few of more than a hundred, was the result of this phenomenal religious revolution, this shaking up of the mind of man, and was born of the principle of toleration practised by the Independents.

Under any other regime these sects could never have existed at that time and the world would probably have been all the poorer for it. It is true that many were on the lunatic fringe, visionary, eccentric, idealistic, impractical and therefore ephemeral, but the ideals of some, though impossible to realise in Stuart England, sprang into vigorous life in later ages like seeds newly planted. In so far as they sought to alter the order of things established under the Commonwealth and Protectorate, they were, like the Levellers, in protest, and since Cromwell, though a revolutionary, was at heart a conservative with a profound consciousness of practical values, they were checked as soon as they became threatening. Apart from the Levellers and Diggers, the two sects whose protest became part of history were the Fifth Monarchy Men and the Quakers.

The Fifth Monarchy Men were an offshoot of the Independents, religious in origin, but with a strongly political side to their teaching. Their name originated in their belief that after the Assyrian, the Persian, the Greek and the Roman monarchies would appear the fifth, the monarchy of Christ who would reign on earth with his chosen saints for a thousand years. The priest and the lawyer, both national plagues, would be removed, and all laws would originate in the people. In this respect they had much in common with the Levellers. Their apologist was John Rogers, an Independent preacher, and its most important figure was Thomas Harrison, one of the most extreme leaders in the army, and an enemy of the monarchy. He was present at Charles' trial and was one of those who signed his death-warrant.

The Fifth Monarchy Men welcomed the advent of the republic as a step towards their expected millennium, but the Rump Parliament showed little sign of ushering it in, and when Cromwell on 20th April 1652 contemptuously sent its members home, Harrison was one of those who laid hands on the Speaker, forcing him to leave the chair. The Fifth Monarchy Men had many adherents in the next Parliament, called by Cromwell and named the Barebones Parliament after one of its members, Praise-God Barbon. It did not entirely disappoint them, for during its brief existence it attacked the clergy, demanded the abolition of the Court of Chancery, declared nobility to be contrary to the Law of Nature and proposed to abolish tithes. It was Cromwell, their erstwhile friend, who took alarm. 'Nothing was in the hearts of these men but overturn, overturn,' he said. Early one morning therefore, stealing a march on their extreme wing, the more moderate members assembled in the House and carried a vote surrendering Parliament's powers to him.

The Instrument of Government and the establishment of the Protectorate turned the more extreme Fifth Monarchy Men into violent enemies of the state. Harrison was prosecuted for plotting, deprived of his commission and put under house arrest. Rogers denounced Cromwell as anti-Christ, the Man of Sin, the Great Dragon. 'Lord,' prayed Feake, another leader, 'Thou hast suffered the tail to set itself up and rule over us in the head's place.' Fifth Monarchy became a rallying cry of fanaticism. The saints were soon to take control of the state, the ungodly were to be slain, there was to be no parliament nor any magistrates. In 1657 occurred their first rising which was put down without difficulty, though the sect continued to exist.

With the restoration of Charles II, the prospect of Fifth Monarchy receded. Harrison, the regicide, was taken, tried and executed, dying in the full conviction that he would shortly return at the right hand of Christ to judge his judges. But the fierce courage of the rest was not quelled by misfortune. In January 1661 a small number of them entered St Paul's and asked the first person they met for whom he stood. When he replied that he stood for Charles, they shot him crying 'We stand for King Jesus'.

This outburst was followed by an attempt to take London. Street fighting followed, and the last remnants, many of whom had fought for liberty in the Civil Wars, were wiped out by the soldiery in an alehouse in Cripplegate Ward. On the 19th January, Pepys went by coach to Whitehall, 'on way meeting Venner and Pritchard on a sledge who with two more Fifth Monarchy Men were hanged today, the first two being drawn and quartered'. The crushing of Venner's rebellion was the end of the Fifth Monarchy as an element of protest against the state.

With the Quakers it was different. They, like many other sects, refused to obey laws of which they did not approve, but unlike them, they had no positive political or religious doctrine, no prophecy that was likely to threaten a government, no creed with which to challenge the established Church. Their guide in religion and in conduct was the light within rather than the pronouncement of a priest. While they refused to do military service or to pay substitutes to do it for them, they did not hazard the security of the state by preaching universal franchise or common ownership of property. The object of their attacks was not any single abuse as much as the general order of things. Their crimes were therefore in the main those of non-compliance and their method quiet and deliberate resistance.

Under any other government than that of the Independents, George Fox, the founder of the sect, might have been silenced at once, especially since in the fervour of personal revelation his followers were wont to step into the steeple-houses at the time of divine service and denounce the parsons, as they stood in their pulpits, as dead dogs, hirelings, robbers and takers of tithes, or to appear in public in sackcloth, barefoot, half-naked or in garb imitating that of the old Hebrew prophets.

In one respect they differed from the majority of Puritan sects in that they believed in the inner light of personal revelation without the need for priest or ritual; in another they differed from all other sects in that they believed that it was possible to achieve complete victory over sin, not only in the life to come, but in this. The magnetic personality of Fox, and the appeal of his simple teaching to a generation already confounded by the haggling of the sectaries on this or that doctrinal point, drew to the movement recruits from among the common people, while Baptists, Levellers, Diggers and members of other sects came over to the Quakers. It was said that in 1660 they numbered more than sixty thousand.

Throughout the whole period, but especially after 1660, the Quakers were the most intractable of all the subjects of the English crown. Their protest was the claim they put forward, as much by their conduct as by their words, for the liberty to go peacefully about their business and to live according to their revelation without subscribing to anything in which they did not believe. Their preachers were flogged as vagrants and welcomed the punishment; they were sentenced by magistrates whom they treated with indifference, they refused to take oaths of supremacy of allegiance, they defied the Quaker Act of 1662 which aimed at compelling them to attend the Anglican Church for divine service, they met in conventicles, even though informers were paid to betray them, they refused to pay tithe or Church rates, and they condemned military force as wicked. The personal example of Fox and the rapid growth of the sect, especially among the manufacturing and trading classes, did much to curb the early extravagances in conduct. The faith of the more stubborn Quakers weathered the rigorous persecution of the later Stuarts and they have maintained their protests, especially against military service, until the present day.

The Revolution ended with the restoration of the Stuarts in 1660, and English history entered a new phase. The reaction was characterised by the usual vengeance, the execution and disgrace of regicides, and the barbaric treatment of the remains of Cromwell and Ireton. But these were only tokens of a more profound change in society itself. Too long, restrictions had been imposed on human conduct, too long they had been deprived of customary English pleasures, the memory of which still lingered nostalgically in the mind. Before the end of the Protectorate the rigid control of dress and manners was already breaking down. Some scenes in Hyde Park and St James's, for instance, would not have been recognised as characteristic of Puritan England, while in London itself the private theatre had come into being.

The accession of Charles II shows on the one hand a sudden release of tension, on the other a movement against those responsible for the aberrations of the former period. The offenders were eliminated, the unrepentant revolutionaries were silenced, while others who accepted the new order were amnestied. Some able men, such as George Monk (later Duke of Albemarle), Anthony Ashley Cooper (later Earl of Shaftesbury), Sir George Downing and Sir William Petty, all of whom had served Cromwell, found little difficulty in gaining acceptance into the King's service.

The new reign showed other common post-revolutionary characteristics. The first was the emergence and maintenance of a reverse process of repression through persecution. This time it was not only the extremist sects that were persecuted, but also the former ruling sects, Presbyterian and Independent alike, a persecution established by the successive measures of the Clarendon Code – the Corporation Act (1661), the Act of Uniformity (1662), the Conventicle Act (1664) and the Five Mile Act (1665). By the second of these, two thousand Puritan clergy were expelled from their livings; under the third, John Bunyan spent twelve years in Bedford Gaol, while under the Quaker Act already mentioned, some five thousand Quakers were imprisoned, many dying as a result of their treatment.

The permanent effect of the Clarendon Code was to damp down the fires of protest. Many of the smaller sects withered because the flush of idealism and enthusiasm had gone out of them. Others lost members whose faith was not deeply enough rooted to stand up to persecution much more rigorous than that of Laud had been. Many Puritans fled to America but the bulk of them, mostly artisans and small traders, worshipped in secret, succoured by the writings of the Puritan fathers and the outpourings of Bunyan.

The second characteristic was the frank return to the pleasures of life; unrestrained ribaldry and vulgarity of speech, drinking, dancing, the outspokenness of Restoration comedy, affectedness of manners and elaborate dress, both of men and women. This last drew forth protest from the more strait-laced and old fashioned. Hannah Woolley, in her book of etiquette for young ladies written in 1675, ridicules the current extravagant fashions:

> I cannot imagine whence our Ladies borrowe that monstrous and prodigious custom of patching their Faces. If they did borrow it from the French they did ill to imitate such, who, it

may be, made use of the Fashion out of pure Necessity and not involuntary: having French pimples, they needed a French Plaister.

I have read that Indians had accustomed themselves to paint the volume of their Bodies over with Apes, Monkeys and other Beasts. I know not whether our Ladies have endeavoured to epitomise their Works into the narrow Title Page of their own Faces.

For all these reasons, there was little either heroic or spectacular in the protests of the later seventeenth and early eighteenth centuries. The fires of enthusiasm had been checked. The visions of an approaching millennium, a people's parliament, manhood suffrage and the abolition of privilege were things of the past. The remnants of movements, once widespread, lingered in odd corners, their prophets fearing to make their voices heard or rotting in prison. The first revolution had ended in tyranny and had fallen to ruin, the second had given place to an administration harsher than that which had preceded the first. The result was an acute sense of disillusionment which showed itself, not in forward-looking movements inspired by hopes of better things to come, but in sporadic riots of desperate people against conditions as they were, or in tumults inspired by mischief-makers.

In the new era the organised violence of insurrectionary and repressive forces gave way to the unpredictable, sporadic and unorganised violence of the people of the streets, aptly called the *mobile* or mob. From 1660 to the mid-eighteenth century the bulk of popular protest was expressed through mob action.

The uprisings were sudden and for the most part unforeseen, though their causes were deep-rooted and enduring. In a general sense it might be said that the class struggle was beginning to show itself in a widening gap between the haves and the have-nots, and a deeping antagonism between them which showed itself both in agriculture and industry. The rapid increase in the country's wealth had its disadvantages. Industries,

153

flourishing in the middle ages, had to work in new conditions. Some decayed through the rise of the same industries in other parts of the country. The cutlery and hardware industries of the south suffered through the rising of new manufacturing districts in the Midlands and around Sheffield. The impact of war was felt especially in the coal trade where the only way to carry coal to London was by sea from the only large producing area around Newcastle. In the 1660s and 1670s there were some winters when Londoners shivered by their empty hearths while colliers in the north went short of bread.

Meanwhile the treatment of the poor increased in barbarity. The Poor Law of Elizabeth I had established the principle that every parish should care for its own paupers, appointing overseers with the power to levy rates and to spend the money raised on suitable forms of relief and accommodation. There remained one important question. What decided as to which parish a person belonged? Was it the parish of his birth, the parish where he lived, served his apprenticeship or held some parish office or other? This difficult question gave rise to endless disputation when people fell on evil days, as to who should maintain them. The Poor Relief Act of 1662 settled this point. Unless a person had rented a tenement worth £10 a year in the parish of his adoption, he could be removed by order of the justice as being chargeable to his own parish. This provision, an insult to human dignity, was elaborated in subsequent acts in 1685 and 1691, and the acts were rigorously applied to any person, employed or not, who was not able to keep himself or his family. Each parish was thus put at odds with every other, the attorneys who managed the thousands of lawsuits between them reaped rich rewards, and the poor who through no fault of their own sought relief, were deprived of every shred of self-respect.

The problem of enclosure, so long a principal factor in popular discontent, began to assume less importance, partly because the movement had gradually slowed down, but also for two other reasons. In the first place, the labourers who had been evicted had largely been absorbed into other industries, and in the second, it came to be recognised that large-scale farming was much more productive than the subsistence agriculture of the middle ages.

This is best illustrated by a pamphlet controversy of the commonwealth period. The opponent of enclosure, named John Moore, was a Leicestershire parson who had himself seen the tragic sufferings of displaced labourers. In his pamphlet, *The crying sin of England in not caring for the Poor* (1653) he condemned, not enclosure as such, but the depopulation it caused:

> Question many of our Beggars that go from dore to dore with Wife and Children after them, where they dwell and why they go a-begging. Alas, Master [they say], we were forced out of such a Town when it was enclosed, and since we have continued a generation of Beggars.

To Moore the issue was a moral one. Winstanley had put forward a solution, however impractical it turned out to be. Moore had none, save an impassioned appeal to the conscience of man:

> If the Lord Protector should impannel a Jury of all the honest hearts in Leicestershire and Northamptonshire and Counties adjacent, they must bring therein a Verdict against such Inclosure, guilty of Depopulation and decay of Tillage generally, very few if any at all excepted. Our Proof is De Facto, it is so.

There were many honest hearts who saw the problem from quite another viewpoint. Moore was answered by a writer signing himself *Pseudonismus* who, while not contradicting his facts, put forward all the economic disadvantages of openfields – damage by straying cattle, the spread of pestilence, the uneconomic use of land, the lack of proper manuring and many others. Both had to admit the facts. It was simply the first statement of a controversy which agitated those concerned with

155

production ever after – what should a man consider first, the amount and quality of a product or the health and comfort of the labourer?

Enclosure riots continued throughout the century, but controversy on the general question of enclosures diminished. One district which suffered from continual rioting was the Fens, where draining work was continually in progress. The conversion of fenland to arable was even more serious to the fenmen than the enclosure of commons to the villager, for many of them obtained a far greater proportion of their livelihood from the wild life.

Mobs gathered and destroyed the drainage works. In 1699 a body of about eleven hundred converged on Deeping Fen 'under pretext of football playing'; and a riot in the Bedford Level was narrowly averted by a declaration of the justices against unlawful assemblies. This did not prevent the purposeful flooding of much land by the fenmen to restore it to its previous wild and unproductive condition.

Thus, beneath the apparent placidity of the late Stuart period, there was the ever-present resentment on the part of a large section of the working classes, and on the part of the rest, an uneasiness lest another revolution should occur. This in itself embittered feelings between master and man, rich and poor, landlord and tenant, anglican and dissenter, and was further complicated by the abiding animosity against Catholics and the suspicion in which aliens were held. The causes of fear can hardly be said to have been real. Most foreigners were harmless, most Catholics loyal, and as for the poor, they were too disillusioned, oppressed and exhausted to throw up a champion from their ranks. The ruling class was firmly in the saddle, while protest on all except one or two occasions did not get much further than mob action.

On first thoughts, the fear of Popery may seem unreasonable, since Catholics were such a small minority, half per cent of the freeholders of England, as against four and a half per cent dissenters and 95.5 per cent Anglicans. Nor were they a vocal minority or prone to agitation. Once, however, that fear had been instilled into the minds of a semi-ignorant populace, it was not easily dispelled. Guy Fawkes and his confederates did their co-religionists a disservice, the effects of which lasted, and a hardly-justified fear of Jesuit activities kept alive the resentment.

When a disaster such as the Fire of London occurred the Papists were on hand as scapegoats. After the Fire, Parliament petitioned Charles II to banish all Catholic priests and rigidly enforce laws against Papists, while on the Monument, erected in 1677, there remained for 150 years an inscription recording their crime in setting London ablaze.

Contrast this with the last pathetic protest of William, Lord Petre, thrown into prison for complicity in the supposed Jesuit Plot revealed by Titus Oates:

I, having been five years in prison, and, what is more grievous to me, have lain so long under a false, injurious calumny of a horrid plot and design against Your Majestie's Person and Government, and am now by the disposition of God's Providence call'd into another world before I could by a public trial make my innocence appear.

I conceived it necessary for me and an incumbent duty I owe to truth and my own innocency, to make this ensuing protestation to Your Majesty and the whole world. That whereas one Titus Oates hath maliciously and falsely sworn that he saw me receive a Commission directed to me by Johannes de Oliva constituting me Lieutenant-General of an army which he pretended was to come into England: I declare in the presence of the All-seeing God before whose just tribunal I am shortly to appear, that I never saw any such Commission directed to me or to any other person whatsoever, and do firmly believe there never was any such: but of the folly as well as the falsehood of the information, the nobler part of mankind as I conceive [are] sufficiently ere this convinced.

And as for those aspersions which the ignorant and malicious have thrown upon the Roman Catholic Church . . . as if mur-

157

dering of Kings and taking up arms against our Sovereigns
were an authorised principle of that religion; I do knowingly
affirm there is nothing with more horror detested by the
Catholick Church as being expressly contrary to the command
of our Saviour and Christian doctrine; and as such I renounce
and detest it as I do all plots and conspiracies against Your
Sacred Person.

Religion had something to do with the assaults on aliens,
though political and economic motives were also present.
Dutch and Flemish weavers and clothiers were attacked in Colchester and the eastern counties. During the Fire of London,
William Taswell, a young scholar of Westminster School, saw
the crowd on two occasions beating up Frenchmen. In September 1683, the Huguenot colony at Norwich was attacked
because it was thought that the inhabitants were Catholics. In
the later Stuart period England was hardly the classic land of
political sobriety it has been sometimes thought to be. Tension was high and could easily have exploded into rioting.
Swords were drawn on the slightest provocation; robbery and
other crimes were encouraged, especially around London, by
the absence of an efficient police force. But the same violence
and ferocity was apparent in the provinces against landlords,
dissenters, Jacobites, watchmen, constables, gaolers or whoever gave offence, and sometimes at fairs and feasts when no
apparent offence had been given at all. Violence was resorted
to for violence's sake. Election disturbances, which became frequent and lasted up to the time of the Ballot Act in 1872, began to take place. Hired agitators were engaged to stir up the
rival mobs. In 1698 two of the candidates at the Westminster
election appeared on Tothill Fields with two thousand horsemen to face their rivals backed by two hundred and a great
number of rabble on foot. In 1706 at Coventry the rioters took
the Town Hall and held it for three days. When the ringleaders
– a hundred and fifty of them – came to be tried, the rival
candidates appeared, each with his mob, to make more trouble.

Such scenes were repeated all over the country.

They show the amorphous character of protest that came as a result of the Restoration and the measures of the Parliaments. There was no one cause, no ideal for which to sacrifice and work; there were simply conditions against which certain elements of society, with or without just cause, protested, sometimes in words but more frequently by thoughtless and fruitless violence.

Examination of popular discontents during this period reveals the fact that the days of theorising were gone. There was no looking forward. On the contrary the tendency of all the protests, in economic affairs at least, was to turn back the clock. The small farmer resented the encroaching capitalist and fought to retain the medieval common. The dwellers in corn-growing areas protested against the export of their products to other parts of the country where it would command a higher price. The cloth weavers of Worcester and Colchester rioted against the bringing in of non-native workers and foreigners, and for the rigid enforcement of the apprentice system. The silkweavers of London attacked French immigrants and destroyed their machines; the salt-workers of Cheshire sought to protect their industry from expansion by hampering the new method of extraction from rock salt.

It was in this age that smuggling, a lively protest against the imposition of import and export duties, became a recognised profession. Increases in the consumption of luxury goods brought heavy import duties which in turn encouraged the practice of evasion. James I damned tobacco smoking as 'a custom loathsome to the eye, hateful to the nose, harmful to the brain, dangerous to the lungs, and in the black stinking smoke thereof nearest resembling the horrible Stygian smoke of the pit that is bottomless'. But mere words were not enough to stop the import of the weed. Indeed, the trade had to be encouraged, for the fortunes of the newly established settlements in Virginia and the Bermudas depended on a substantial export James raised the duty on tobacco from twopence per pound to seven shillings, and the continuation of the trade showed that it could be borne. By 1614 the smoking habit was well established, for we are told that 'there is not so base a groom that coming into an alehouse to call for his pot, but he must have his pipe of tobacco'. Most of it was smuggled. Lady Earlsfield, who had taken to pipe-smoking, had her supplies from a contraband dealer in Horsham. By 1640 tobacco was the chief item in the smuggler's budget.

Before the end of the century, the avoidance of duty had become a pursuit from which everybody with few exceptions sought to benefit. The justice, the parson, the Lord Mayor of London, the Governor of the Virginia Company, all were deeply involved in it. Ships were specially built for speed to avoid the customs boats, and for every pound invested there were rich returns.

Hardly a spot on the whole coast was exempt. Colliers coming south from Tyneside collected their ankers of brandy, their tea, tobacco and silks and carried them, hidden under their cargo, safely past the London customs. Craft waited offshore by night in the Channel to transfer their goods to the boatmen coming out from the seaboard towns, who ran them into the creeks and dispersed them before dawn. The Isle of Man and the Channel Islands, though British, were constant thorns in the side of the revenue department. Too often posts in the Customs Department were given to royal servants as rewards on retirement.

English wool had always been the best in Europe, and during the Middle Ages its export, mainly to the cloth-manufacturing towns of Flanders, had furnished the money for the wars of the later Plantagenet kings. Edward III realised that the revenue could be greatly increased by having cloth made at home, therefore the export of wool was first forbidden, then controlled through the setting up of export depots, or staples.

In the seventeenth century there was a growing market for

English cloth. It was believed that the export of raw wool would destroy it, and so in 1614 it was forbidden. The result was the rise of another profitable smuggling trade, that of the 'owler' who operated chiefly in south-east England. The centre of the trade was Canterbury; its black spots were the Isle of Thanet, Folkestone, Romney Marsh and Selsey. Cromwell had no more success than the Stuart kings in checking the illicit trade, for justice itself often had an interest in the profits, the gangs were highly organised and the sympathies of the neighbourhood, wherever smuggling went on, were with the lawbreakers, partly because of the rewards, partly out of resentment against the prohibition, while those who were not in sympathy were usually induced through fear of retaliation to keep their mouths tightly shut.

For these reasons, when smugglers were taken red-handed it was hard to obtain convictions. During the following century the trade reached unheard-of proportions, and nothing the government could do at the time could stop it. When, for instance, for every pound of tobacco all but an ounce was smuggled, and when for every pound of tea taken, three hundredweights got away, the loss to the national exchequer can be imagined.

The second effect, even more serious, was to discourage more conventional ways of making a living. The possibility of profits from contraband drew labour away from the fields, and when in agriculture the normal return was marginal, the impact of smuggling was to reduce the production of foodstuffs in the affected districts to subsistence level or even below. Under such conditions it was easy for the farmer and his labourer to convince themselves that without the help of the contraband trade they would not be able to live, therefore that the duties were morally wrong and that their action in running the tea, brandy, silk and other luxury goods was a perfectly justified act of protest. It was not for nothing that the smugglers applied to themselves the name of Fair Traders.

The last and worst effect of all was the dreadful toll of death and injury to many generations of young life caused by the perpetual gang warfare that went on around the coasts. Contrary to the general conception, there was nothing romantic or heroic about smuggling because there was no unjust cause to fight against. And so, though there were many villainous actions, there were no villains. Both sides were in the right, and when in such circumstances one maimed and slew the other only evil could ensue. For two hundred years smuggling was a canker at the heart of English society.

With a little ingenuity it was not difficult to explode the Fair Trader theory. John Harriott, the Wapping magistrate and one of the founders of the Thames River Police, tells in his book *Struggles Through Life* how he did it. In 1786, travelling from Lille to Dunkirk and seeking a passage home, he put up at an inn frequented by Englishmen and fell in with a gang of Kentish smugglers who called on him to join them in a toast of 'Damnation to all Revenue Officers'. His objections were met with furious oaths, but he persisted, and persuaded them to take a bet that he was right in resisting the toast and they wrong in proposing it.

When they noisily accepted the bet he went on to ask them what they would do, and where their livelihood would be if all revenue laws were abolished and all officers dismissed.

'Lost!' said the chairman. 'Lost!' agreed the others and all finally, amid laughter, drank the toast of 'Revenue Officers and Laws for ever'. Harriott returned to England in their craft, better off by several bottles of burgundy. For the professionals, at least, smuggling had become more than mere protest.

The underlying fear and suspicion of this uneasy age is shown by the attitude of the populace, easily led and at the mercy of this and that loud-mouthed agitator. Religious and political animosity produced the most extraordinary scenes, especially in London. In 1678, Titus Oates denounced several prominent Catholics as having joined in a conspiracy to kill the

King and establish Catholicism in England. The effect on the crowd was electric. Effigies of the Pope and the Devil whispering in his ear, with monks, friars and Catholic bishops in all their ceremonial dress, were paraded in procession. Oates, calling himself the Saviour of the Nation, went about in a silk gown and a great hat with a rose on the satin hatband, surrounded by a special bodyguard 'for fear of Papists murdering him'; whoever he denounced was taken and committed for trial.

Anti-Catholicism played a part in the rebellion of the Duke of Monmouth, the last popular rising in England. Though he drew his recruits from the working classes in the depressed mining areas of the Mendips and the unemployed woollen workers of Somerset, at least as important a cause for the choice of the west country for the attempt was its strong protestantism.

The classic protest of the whole period was that of the Seven Bishops. By an order in Council of the 4th May 1688 James II commanded that the Declaration of Indulgence, suspending laws against Catholics and dissenters alike, should be read in all churches. Archbishop Sancroft and six bishops petitioned the King not to insist on their reading it. The King's fury was only matched by that of the crowd when they read the published petition and heard of James' refusal to grant it. In four places only, one of them Westminster Abbey, was the declaration read, and the murmur in the church was so great that it could not be heard. Before the end of the reading the building was empty save for a few prebends in their stalls.

On the 8th June the seven bishops, having refused to appear on a charge of libel in the Court of King's Bench, were arrested, and taken through lines of weeping men and women to a barge which carried them downstream to the Tower, while crowds on the river banks called 'God bless your Lordships'. Even the guards would drink no other health but theirs.

Their trial on 27th June lasted from nine in the morning until six in the evening. What took place in the cross-examinations is immaterial beside the scenes in the streets adjacent to Westminster Hall, thronged with excited crowds, while the jury, held up by the obstinacy of the King's brewer, sat all night long. At ten next morning, when the verdict of Not Guilty was announced, the shouts went from the court to Westminster Hall, from the Hall to the streets and alleys around, and from there out to the suburbs of London. Never since 1666 had the reflection of fire in the sky been so vivid as from the bonfires lit on that June night.

In 1719 the crowds were again whipped up to frenzy, this time when Dr Sacheverell was impeached for preaching a sermon against the Whigs and the Revolution. The prestige both of Marlborough and his party had been shaken by the heavy losses in the war of Spanish Succession, and had been undermined through the intrigues of Harley, St John and Abigail Masham. Noisy crowds surrounded the coaches of the parson and the Queen as they made their way to Westminster Hall where the trial took place. Sacheverell was suspended from preaching for three years. Within as many months the Whig government fell, to be superseded by the Tory alliance. Five years later in the great Jacobite scare the Whigs had their revenge and brought George from Hanover to occupy the throne.

From 1660 to 1760 the history of protest is almost sordid in comparison with the enthusiasm and the vigour of mind of the previous century. The country was governed by an oligarchy for most of the time, and the opposition generally made use of the mob for its own purposes. There is nothing ennobling about the eruption of anti-Jacobite feeling in 1715, in the mass excitement of the South Sea Bubble, in the unscrupulous manipulation of public feeling at the time of Walpole's Excise Bill, a fundamentally wise measure which had to be withdrawn; or in the ridiculous outcry of 'give us back our eleven days' which followed the reform of the calendar in 1752.

The country had to wait many long years before the protests of the individual or the small group could be supported by a discerning and wise body of public opinion.

'Wilkes and Liberty'

IN APRIL 1763, when John Wilkes was in France, he was asked by Madame de Pompadour how far the liberty of the press extended in England.

'I do not know,' he replied. 'I am trying to find out.'

Within a month he had his answer. On the 29th, as he was on his way home he was confronted by the King's messengers with a warrant for the arrest of the authors, printers and publishers of number 45 of the *North Briton*.

The background of the story lies in the political history of Britain. George II had been content to leave the government of the country in the hands of the great Whig families who had held on to power mainly by their handling of crown patronage, buying votes with rewards and places. The system had worked; it had even produced Pitt as Prime Minister, and under his administration France had been defeated, the British colonies in America had been saved, Canada had been won by James Wolfe and the foundations of the British Empire in India had been laid by Robert Clive.

George III, who had succeeded to the throne in 1760, was not content to allow this system to continue. He had been taught from childhood that a king should rule rather than be governed by his ministers. He resented the arrogance of Pitt and he determined to work his downfall, to take into his own hands the power of bribery through pensions and places, to appoint his own ministers and finally to put an end to what he called, in his first speech from the throne, 'this bloody and expensive war'. In 1762 the terms of a treaty were agreed on, and by an enormous campaign of bribery directed by Henry Fox, Parliament was induced to approve it even though public opinion, at least in London, was against it. In February 1763, the Peace of Paris was signed and many of the British gains, especially in the West Indies and Africa, were given back to France. This was the issue which provoked the first open clash between Wilkes and the King.

John Wilkes, born in Clerkenwell, was the son of a wealthy distiller who sought to bring him up as a gentleman. His education in England and Holland gave him the poise and self-confidence which even turned to advantage the ugliness of his person, his bad squint and prominent jaw. While his marriage to an heiress much older than himself was dull, his mode of living as a man about town brought him into contact not only with the rakes and dissolute young men of the day, but also with the Grenville family, who through their alliance with Pitt and Newcastle were still the fount of power and influence. He became the protégé of Richard, Lord Temple, the head of the family, and in 1757 he was Member of Parliament for Aylesbury. In June 1762 with his colleague, the poet John Churchill, he launched the *North Briton*.

Through this journal Wilkes became not only the spokesman of a political faction, but also the mouthpiece of popular discontent. For nine months the King and his Prime Minister were the subjects of every form of attack. Their measures were denounced and their supporters subjected to ridicule in snippets of scandalous gossip and verse. The system of government corruption was mercilessly exposed and the officer distributing the bribes branded as 'a most treacherous, base, selfish, mean, abject, lowlived and dirty fellow that ever wriggled himself into a secretaryship'. What most offended the King was an insinuation that Bute and the Queen Mother were lovers.

In April 1763 the treaty with France had been negotiated, and Bute, stung by his unpopularity, gave in his resignation to the King. Wilkes, through his connections, obtained an advance copy of the King's speech to Parliament defending the terms of the peace, and on the 23rd his leading article appeared in the *North Briton* condemning it.

The main object of attack was not the King but his ministers. George was only considered to be at fault in that he had 'been brought to give the sanction of his sacred name to the most unjustifiable declaration from the throne ever renowned for the truth'. In his speech the King described the peace as honourable to the crown and beneficial to the people, and one from which Britain's allies would derive happy effects. Wilkes denied this, asserting that in making it the King's ministers had deserted England's ally, the King of Prussia, the merchants in Britain had been disappointed, and that the peace itself had only been ratified through extensive bribery. The King was greatly offended, especially by the statement which implied that he was no more than the mouthpiece of his ministers.

The mistakes of the Government in arresting Wilkes and forty-eight other persons concerned with the publication of the journal on a general warrant without naming the individuals, the ransacking of his house by order of the Secretaries of State, the disregard of Wilkes' privilege as a Member of Parliament and his vigorous resistance in challenging the legality of his imprisonment made the trial into the sensation of the day. In his speech before the judge Wilkes related the acts of violence to which he had been subjected and declared that in his case the liberty not only of all peers and gentlemen, but that of all 'the middling and inferior set of people who stand most in need of protection' was at stake, and that the issue of his case would finally decide whether English liberty was to be a reality or a shadow.

He had already attained the stature of a popular hero. When the judge declared that since he was not charged with felony or treason, nor with any breach of the peace, his parliamentary privilege could not be taken away and he must be freed, the audience within the court room set up a shout of joy which was echoed in the street outside. 'Wilkes and Liberty' became for the first time the cry of the people.

The Wilkes affair had through the ineptitude of the Government become more than a quarrel about a peace treaty; it had been magnified into a matter of principle affecting the liberty of the individual. The legality of arrest by a general warrant had been challenged and disproved, the too rapid assumption of the power to arrest by the Secretary of State had been checked.

Wilkes pressed home his victory. Those who had been brought out of bed and whose houses had been searched sued the government officers who were fined heavily. Extra issues of the offending number were printed and put into circulation.

The further adventures of Wilkes, the efforts of the Government to entrap him, the publication of the *Essay on Women*, the duel with Samuel Martin in which he was seriously wounded, his expulsion from Parliament, his exile and outlawry for failing to appear for trial – all these are secondary matters compared with the second great storm which blew up in March 1768. His sources of income had dried up and he was so deeply in debt that Paris was no fit place for him. He decided to risk being taken as an outlaw, to return to London and to announce himself as a candidate for election to Parliament.

He first presented himself for one of London's four seats. He was still the idol of the crowd, but unfortunately for him, the crowd were not the people who had the votes, and he came bottom of the poll. There was still time, however, for him to try for the Middlesex constituency, and with the help of Serjeant Glynn and his friend John Horne (later Horne Tooke), a hasty election campaign was organised, Wilkes himself going through the constituency to canvass the voters. The campaign and the events that followed it seem more like a scene of comic opera than true history. Supporters of Wilkes chalked up the number 45 (the offending issue of *North Briton*) on walls and doors while his opponents went round with wet sponges to clean them off, and his name in large letters swung on the creaking signs of inn and shop.

London inhabitants who were freeholders in Middlesex poured out to the poll at Brentford, and when the result was announced and Wilkes had half as many votes again as the next man, pandemonium broke loose. The trained bands could do naught to check it and in the end it was Wilkes' own followers who patrolled the streets to keep the peace. At that moment, said Benjamin Franklin, if Wilkes had had a good character and George III a bad one, the King would have been turned off his throne. The rejoicing spread to London, with the number 45 marked on houses and coaches, whose occupants paraded anything blue – the Wilkite colours. The Austrian Ambassador was politely invited to dismount from his coach and the number 45 was chalked on the soles of his shoes. At night all the windows were aglow with the light of candles while crowds danced in the streets. It was one of the most good-humoured riots the country had ever known and the damages were negligible.

After it was over Wilkes presented himself, as he had promised to do, at the Court of the King's Bench, but the Attorney-General, Lord Mansfield, refused to have him arrested for fear of the consequences. A week later Wilkes had to send for a sheriff's officer to get himself arrested. On the way to the King's Bench prison the crowd took possession of the coach, removed the horses and dragged Wilkes in triumph through the City. Later, while resting in a tavern, he slipped out in disguise, made his way to the prison in the middle of the night, knocked up the doorkeeper and was quietly let in.

All at once the fields round the prison became a rendezvous for noisy crowds shouting and displaying banners. On 10th May the good humour was broken by tragedy when one of the demonstrators fell foul of the guard. Stones were thrown and the guard fired into the crowd. Not content with a single volley, the soldiers chased the crowd and fired again. Eleven were killed and many others wounded. There was rejoicing in court circles and when the case came before a packed jury they refused to commit.

In June Wilkes was brought up for trial as a returned outlaw. He could have been put in prison for life, but Lord Mansfield, with his wonted caution, discharged the prisoner because of an error in the writ. It was a good excuse to smooth over a situation that could have had ugly consequences. Now Wilkes, no longer an outlaw, had to appear to be tried on the other charges arising out of Number 45 and the *Essay on Woman*. He was fined £1,000, imprisoned for twenty months in all, and bound over for seven years on recognisances totalling £2,000.

On the whole he was satisfied. He was a privileged inhabitant of the King's Bench, in comfortable quarters, well fed, able to read and write and have what visitors he pleased. He had succeeded in making the Government look ridiculous, he was one of the most famous men, not only in England, but also in America where ideas of liberty were already fermenting. In that same month of June 1768, a group of his admirers in Boston addressed a letter to him signed by the Committee of the Sons of Liberty begging for his esteem and assistance, assuring him that he was one of those incorruptibly honest men reserved by heaven to bless and perhaps save a tottering empire . . .

> that majesty can never be secure but in the Arms of a brave, virtuous and united people – that nothing but a common interest, and absolute confidence in an impartial and general protection, can combine so many Millions of Men, born to make laws for themselves; conscious and invincibly tenacious of their Rights.

Wilkes now had the leisure to prepare other stings and barbs. He petitioned Parliament, of which he was now a member, against his treatment, he accused Lord Weymouth, one of the Secretaries of State, of planning a massacre before the affair of St Georges' Fields took place. The Government, urged on by the King, were determined to bring all their power to bear to get him expelled from Parliament, and in February 1769 they succeeded in spite of the warnings of Burke, Grenville and other prominent members, by a majority of eighty-two.

Thus the scene was prepared for another great battle of principle. Wilkes determined to stand for election again. The Commons had put themselves in the wrong. They had bowed to the will of the King and the oligarchy and had slighted the wishes of the people. He stated the principle clearly in his election address:

> If ministers can once usurp the power of declaring who shall not be your representative, the next step is very easy and will follow speedily. It is that of telling you whom you shall send to Parliament and then the boasted constitution of England will be entirely torn up by the roots. The Parliaments of Great Britain will become not only as insignificant as those of France, a mere state engine of government, but a grievous burthen and infinite mischief to the nation.

Though still in prison, he was returned unopposed. On the next day the House of Commons declared the election null and void, and in the hope of forestalling a repeat passed a resolution stating that Wilkes had no right to be elected. There was even talk of trying his supporters and the Sheriffs of Middlesex for contempt. The struggle was clearly between King, Ministry and a corrupt House of Commons on the one hand, and the will of the people of Middlesex on the other. It was obvious that it could only be fought out by a well-organised society with money behind it, and so the most prominent Wilkites founded the Society of the Supporters of the Bill of Rights.

In a third election a candidate was found to oppose Wilkes, but he was so thoroughly abused on the election morning that no person could be found brave enough to nominate him. After this, the third election, Wilkes was again returned unopposed. The very next day Parliament declared the election null and void and ordered another.

This time not one but three opponents appeared. The Government presented Colonel Henry Luttrell, who had already sat in Parliament for a Cornish borough. He was, in a sense, the official candidate. The other two were insignificant. Even Luttrell had to be ushered to the hustings on the election day under the protection of Wilkes' supporters. Wilkes at the end of the poll had 1,143 votes, Luttrell 296, the third candidate 5 and the fourth none. After three rejections by the Commons nobody expected Wilkes to be admitted. Instead, it was ruled that the 1,143 who had voted for the ineligible candidate had thrown away their votes. Luttrell was therefore admitted and duly took his seat.

London was seething with discontent, and when the Common Council refused to consider a petition against the Middlesex election, protests, petitions, manifestoes and pamphlets appeared condemning Parliament as unrepresentative and deploring the use of bribery and force against freely-assembling political gatherings. Not only London but all England bristled with petitions, organised for the most part by Wilkite emissaries who carried out one of the first political campaigns on record. One toured the home counties, another the west country where at that time were the important industries and the main centres of population apart from London. But the north, the growing centres of the ironware, cotton and woollen industries, was not neglected. In the autumn of 1769 the provinces were canvassed for a petition which when complete contained about 60,000 signatures, but it was not even referred to in the King's speech which dealt mainly with the diseases of horned cattle.

London, which the year before had rejected Wilkes, elected two of his most prominent followers as sheriffs and addressed another petition to the King. There was a wave of strikes in the City. The Spitalfields silk weavers rioted, the merchant seamen blocked the port, the coalheavers marched on Westminster. Pitt lent the support of his name to London's campaign, but it was all in vain.

In January 1770 the King, through the appointment of Lord North as Prime Minister, took into his own hands the whole of national policy with results that were to shake the country and the Empire. When Wilkes was released in April he had behind him the solid support of whole centres of population, but was faced by an enemy more determined and perverse than any reformer had confronted. An account of the celebrations in Bradford in that month gives some idea of what must have happened in many other parts of the country:

> . . . the morning was ushered in with the ringing of bells, which continued till ten at night, and in the evening were illuminations, and the following, we hear, was given at the sole expence of Mr Richard Shackleton, at the Bull's Head, *viz*. A bonfire of 45 of coals: a curious representation of the figures 45, composed of 45 candles, under which was wrote in large characters, Wilkes at Liberty: also a supper to the sons of Liberty, which consisted of 45 lbs of roast beef; legs of mutton and tongues 45 lb.; three hams 45 lb.; 45 fowls: a lamb, 45 lb. of bread; 45 lb of vegetables; 45 gallons of ale and 45 bowls of punch.

Wilkes was no sooner out of prison than he was made an alderman of London, and so thrown again into the turmoil of politics. The City aldermen, their petition having been so curtly rejected by the King, determined to follow it up by a remonstrance or protest, claiming, as was their right, the privilege of presenting it to the King in person. After considerable delay, George received the sheriffs and when it had been read he furiously denounced it as 'disrespectful to me, injurious to Parliament and irreconcilable to the principles of the constitution'. London protested with a second remonstrance which the King just as abruptly rejected. Then to the amazement of everybody present the Lord Mayor, Alderman Thomas Beckford, boldly stepped forward and voiced his regret that no promise of redress had been given. To this day the high mark of London's opposition to the King is commemorated in the Guildhall where Beckford's monument stands, the words of his speech engraved on its base.

In his determination to put an end to opposition, George took another foolish step. In spite of a declaration made in 1738 that it was a breach of privilege to publish reports of parliamentary debates, these reports had appeared regularly and were often an embarrassment to the ministers. In 1771 two London printers, having been ordered to attend at the House of Commons to answer charges of breach of privilege, went, on Wilkes' suggestion, into hiding. On hearing of this the Commons offered a reward of £50 for the arrest of either or both these two and several others who were listed. One of them, apprehended by his own servant, was brought to the Guildhall where at the time Wilkes happened to be the presiding justice. Discharging the printer, Wilkes sent off the servant to the Treasury to collect his £50 reward, but at the same time bound him over on a charge of assaulting his master.

Parliament, stung by this rebuff, sent messengers to arrest the printers. One of them, when approached, appealed to a constable who took both printer and messenger to the Guildhall. The printer was freed; the House of Commons messenger, charged with assaulting a freeman of the City of London, was released on bail. On this the Lord Mayor, with Aldermen Oliver and Wilkes, was summoned before the Commons. Wilkes refused to go. The Mayor and Alderman challenged the warrant summoning them as being an illegal act of violence on London's magistrates, and were forthwith thrown into the Tower.

The City was raised to a pitch of fury and excitement. Even to get the coach to the Tower, the Mayor had to pretend to the crowd that he was taking a personal friend, the serjeant-at-arms, for an outing. The Common Council voted to pay for the prisoners' food and lodging out of the funds of the Corporation, and their imprisonment was one continual round of visits, entertainment and festivity. Addresses and messages of congratulation poured in from all parts of the country, besides congratulations from members of the opposition. When the Commons rose, the Mayor and alderman were released, and the printers, in spite of all the threats, were not even arrested. Within three months Wilkes was elected a sheriff of London and in 1773 he was Lord Mayor. In the same year Middlesex electors again sent him, unopposed, to Parliament, and this time he was allowed to take his seat. His last major action had been won.

This was the end of Wilkes' career as an important influence in British politics. In ten years he had made a permanent contribution, but he was not the type of person who could seize on a cause and pursue it to the end. The evils he fought were those which presented themselves to him mainly as a result of the actions of other people. In this sense he was a reformer by chance rather than by design, and when the immediate evils were put right, he went no further. If there was one cause he had at heart it was the reform of Parliament, but after 1769 this was taken up by others and Wilkes had little part in the agitation.

In 1773, however, there were no contradictions in his dual role as Lord Mayor of London and a member of the parliamentary opposition, but the difficulties of holding a post of authority and at the same time being a rebel soon became apparent. At that time, the Government was occupied with the dispute with the American colonies. Both Wilkes and the bulk of public opinion in the City had been against the Government and in favour of the colonists' demands. Wilkites all over the country had sent petitions to both houses declaring their disapproval of the measures the government had taken to subdue the Americans. They deplored the taxes, sympathised with the people of Massachusetts whose charter was taken away, and described the affair not as a rebellion but as a civil war. In this they were in accord both with Chatham and Burke who favoured conciliation. Then in July 1776 came the Declaration of Independence. Wilkes defended it, recognising that the colonies were no more subjects of the British crown, but 'the free and independent states of America'.

Once war between Britain and the colonies had broken out loyalties slowly began to change, first among the middle class and then among the workers. The colonists may have been in the right but when it came to a war, loyalty was stronger than ideals, and Wilkes for the first time in his life found himself at odds with public opinion, so that when in 1776 the office of City Chamberlain fell vacant he was defeated. Success in an election for the same office three years later did not restore his popularity, for in 1780 he was confronted with one of the most violent public outbursts in English history, the Lord George Gordon riots.

The American war was going badly and as the government was badly in need of men to join the army, it was decided to try to attract the enlistment of Catholics, especially in Scotland, by a bill giving them relief from some of their disabilities. There was not much doubt about its passing, as the radicals and most of the Whigs being in favour of toleration would vote for the Government. The bill which became law on 3rd June 1778 did little more than give them permission to inherit land and freed their bishops, priests and schoolmasters from the threat of life imprisonment, provided they had taken the Oath of Allegiance to the Crown. There seemed nothing in the Act that could give offence to anybody, but the hatred of Popery, which had been alive since the days of James I, was still being nurtured by the various Protestant associations which from time to time published inflammatory literature full of the most absurd accusations and incitements to violence. In Scotland chapels and mass-houses were burnt down and the houses of Catholics ransacked by the mobs.

Meanwhile a champion of Protestantism appeared in the person of Lord George Gordon, the twenty-nine-year-old son of the third Duke of Gordon, who became President of the London Protestant Associations. On Friday, the 2nd June 1780, their members proceeded to Parliament to present their petition for the repeal of the Catholic Relief Act. The event stirred up the people of London to unexpected extremes of frenzy, as they crowded round the doors of the two Houses calling on all members who entered to join in the cry of 'No Popery' and assaulting those who offended them, while Lord George, from the head of the gallery stairs, encouraged them and named those, as they passed by, whom he considered were betraying Protestantism. After the mob had been dispersed by the soldiers, they scattered to various parts of London and started the pillaging and burning of houses and chapels. The fury of destruction spread and continued for days, until large parts of London, including most of the prisons, were in flames.

The sympathy of Wilkes, who had always favoured religious toleration, was with the Catholics, and his duty as an alderman was to take measures to help suppress the riots. He could have preserved his popularity, at least temporarily, by inaction, but he realised that to refrain any longer after four days of destruction would bring on London a disaster as great as that of the Fire of 1666. On Wednesday the 7th, he prevailed on the Lord Mayor to call out the *posse comitatus* then, to bring immediate help, got together as many armed men as he could collect and posted them in defence of the Bank of England. The action, in which rioters were killed, was the first serious check the rebels had received. In the days which followed, the fires were mastered, the mobs were dispersed, the refugees returned to the sites of their gutted homes from the parks and open spaces, and London returned to something like normal life.

Wilkes was never forgiven. In this tragic episode he had led men who had shot down his own kind, those who had followed him in the exciting days of the Middlesex elections and the fight for the freedom of the press. Others he had committed to prison for their part in the riots. The wheel had turned full circle, and the arch-protestors had ended by extinguishing protest.

He took no further part in agitation. As political enthusiasms and hatreds cooled he did little more than pass comment and was later to be seen among the supporters of the Pitt government and reconciled with his old enemies, almost even with the King.

There is a story that one day on his way to London from his home on the Isle of Wight, he passed an old woman who, on recognising him, cried out, 'Wilkes and Liberty!'

'Be quiet, you old fool,' he answered. 'That's all over long ago.'

12

Lessons in Organisation

THERE WAS A great expansion of British commerce in the late seventeenth and early eighteenth centuries. First the Dutch, then the French had been overhauled in the race for markets and colonies. Trade with India and the East was growing, and in the American colonies were almost inexhaustible supplies of raw materials such as timber and cotton. This development was followed by changes at home in agriculture and industry which were significant enough to be termed revolutions. With the discovery of iron-smelting by coke, and of steam as a motive power, Britain was no longer bound to depend entirely on its dwindling supply of home-grown timber, either for fuel or for construction, and was able to move forward in advance of all other powers into the new industrial age. A rapidly increasing population stimulated home demand, and this had its effect both on agriculture and industry, encouraging the enclosure of land, increasing the size of farms, giving rise to new and larger-scale methods of production. As with farms, businesses increased in size and complexity, necessitating better methods of organisation.

All these changes had their effects on social life. Towns, which were the natural centres of industry, grew as the workers moved into them from surrounding rural areas, and the balance of population shifted from south to north where swiftly flowing Pennine streams and newly-developing coalfields provided power from water-wheel and steam-engine. With the coming of new trades and industries, the provincial towns rapidly grew into centres of life and culture in their own right. Here, as in London, commercial activity demanded a greater supply of clerks and bookkeepers besides such ancillary services as accountancy and the law, while increased wealth tended to maintain the respectability of specialised handicrafts such as tailoring, the manufacture of hats, shoes, jewellery and certain articles of luxury. All this demanded a certain level of literacy in at least a fair proportion of the population, and there is evidence from parish records that the ability to read was considered a great advantage. Small parochial schools abounded and the reading-master, taking small groups at a few pence a week, was a well-known figure. Provincial newspapers, which had first appeared around the beginning of the century, grew rapidly in number after 1750, and the foundation of societies and clubs for convivial meetings and general discussion stimulated the spirit of enquiry.

One of the main forces influencing the development of the provincial towns was the establishment of a network of good turnpike roads. Places that in the seventeenth century had been reached from London only after days of hazardous travel came in the later eighteenth to be within a few hours' distance. Thus the capital, though it still had pre-eminence over all other parts of the country and a life and atmosphere of its own, came to be bound up more and more with the rest, and was influenced in an ever-increasing degree by the ideas, the needs and especially by the money of the provincials. Moreover, the landed aristocracy was soon to be joined in wealth and challenged in influence by the rising industrialist class which brought with it a new attitude to life and a flood of new ideas. Thus from 1770 onwards we hear much more in national politics of places such as Leeds, Liverpool, Birmingham, Manchester and Sheffield than ever before.

The outburst of loyalty following the outbreak of the War of American Independence made an end of the Wilkite movement as an effective force for reform, but the same war gave rise to a second movement different in character but with similar aims, originating in the provinces.

In 1777 a whole British army was forced to surrender at

Saratoga; in 1778 the French and in 1779 the Spaniards declared war against the British. Hampered by discontent in Ireland and a threatened invasion, with French and Spanish warships cruising freely in the Channel while British admirals and politicians quarrelled among themselves, the North ministry was paralysed into inactivity. Gloom and disappointment spread over the country. Something had gone wrong, and obviously the Government was to blame. It was in this atmosphere that on 30th December 1779 a meeting of Yorkshire freeholders met and drew up a petition urging the Commons to purify the administration by correcting the abuses in the expenditure of public money and the abolition of all sinecure places and unmerited pensions. The originator of the movement was a Yorkshire landowner named Christopher Wyvill.

Wyvill was a Church of England parson who for conscience sake had left his living in Essex, and through his wife's inheritance had become one of the leading gentry in the North Riding. His entry into politics was prompted by the same indignation that many liberal thinkers felt against the corruption of the government and the infringement of the liberty of the subject.

His aim was 'the restoration of national morals . . . and the preservation of our constitution on its genuine principles, then nearly defaced by the wear of passing ages and almost lost under the immense accumulation of abuses'.

The objects were similar to those of the Wilkites, but the appeal was different in spirit. Once again we see in Wyvill's manifesto something of the crusading spirit of the Stuart reformers, with all their idealism if not their religious zeal. It had already appeared in the young republics across the Atlantic whose Declaration of Independence had burst on mankind in an age of cynicism and self-seeking, and reminded men of certain principles which had for many years even in England been conveniently put aside:

We hold these truths to be self-evident, that all men are created equal, that they are endowed by their Creator with certain inalienable Rights, that among these are Life, Liberty, and the Pursuit of Happiness. That to secure these Rights, Governments are instituted among Men, deriving their just powers from the consent of the governed. . . .

Wyvill sought to put the principle in operation in England, to see brought into existence a Parliament representative of the people, and the first step towards this end was to extinguish the bribery and corruption which formed the basis of the government of George III. Once that was done the way would be clear to a radical reform of the electoral and parliamentary systems. With all this in mind he created and built up the Yorkshire County Association. In February 1780 the petition of the Yorkshire freeholders with eight thousand signatures was sent to London, and those of sixteen other counties which also submitted their own petitions and set up committees to correspond with each other.

The importance of this Association Movement lies not so much in its concrete achievements as in the methods it used. Wyvill brought to the movement an untiring and infectious enthusiasm, a capacity for hard and sustained work, an unusual capability for organising and judgment, and a clarity of vision rare in men of his day. His idea was that of a permanent association. If such local associations could exist for commonplace purposes such as the apprehension of felons or the preservation of game, why might not a body of freeholders form one for the checking of corruption and the preservation of the constitution?

This was Wyvill's contribution to politics – a standing extraparliamentary pressure group predominantly middle-class and unattached to any political party. It had a committee of more than a hundred members, a small executive committee of members who lived near its headquarters at York, and a salaried secretary who was a qualified attorney. He, with the Chairman, who was Wyvill himself, collected petitions and made full use of the growing newspaper press for advertising, printing reports and other publicity. Suddenly there had arisen in Yorkshire an extra-parliamentary movement superior to anything London had so far produced, and one which was to be the model of many another in the nineteenth century, so that Charles James Fox could say with truth at one time that Yorkshire and Middlesex made all England.

The campaign never secured the influence Wyvill had hoped it would, partly because the various counties differed in their aims. Wyvill, for instance, was at heart a conservative. He would have been content with household suffrage and economical reform, and regarded a county committee as a body specially organised to push the Government in certain desired directions without presenting detailed schemes, whereas the Westminster Association had a much more radical programme similar to that of the Chartists sixty years later. One of its leading members actually envisaged a country-wide association strong enough to be able to dictate to Parliament and, if necessary, supersede it – a sort of shadow Parliament; again a Chartist conception. After June 1780, the report of the Westminister sub-committee was circulated and members began to fall away. The Gordon Riots in the same month accelerated the process.

Nevertheless, reform was becoming one of the burning questions of the day. In 1780 Burke proposed a measure for a reduction in the number of pensions and places, and this was embodied two years later in an Establishment Act. In the same year Pitt took his first tentative steps in the reform of Parliament with a proposition that a committee be appointed to examine the state of the representation, and his motion was lost by a mere twenty votes. A second proposal of his in the following year was rejected by a heavy majority. In 1793 under dramatic circumstances Pitt was elevated to the premiership and in the following year he consolidated his position by a resounding victory at the polls over the Fox-North coalition. Under him Britain settled down to almost a decade of tranquillity and prosperity.

General satisfaction within the country, the popularity of Pitt whose avowed intention was still to secure a more equitable system of parliamentary representation, plus the dissensions between the various groups of reformers themselves, swept much of the ground from under their feet. Now the reform movement was no longer one of protest since its champion was to be the Prime Minister himself. Wyvill trusted Pitt implicitly and threw himself wholeheartedly into the campaign, stimulating the associations all over the country into action and petition. In April 1785 Pitt disclosed his scheme to Parliament, his bill, which would have set up a fund of £1 million to buy seventy-two seats out of private hands, was coldly received and heavily defeated. Even after this defeat Wyvill made one last effort to gather support for Pitt's plan, but in a meeting of members the current opinion ran against him.

Pitt was not willing to displease the King or to prejudice his position in Parliament by bringing in further measures, and there was no sort of unity among the associations themselves. It was clear to Wyvill that no more could be done, and one by one they passed out of existence. A cause had been lost but, for the agitator and political campaigner, many valuable lessons had been learned.

The lessons were quickly taken to heart, especially in the provinces. As early as 1774 a Manchester Committee for the Protection and Encouragement of Trade had been formed, and this was followed in 1783 by a similar committee in Birmingham whose leading spirits were Josiah Wedgwood and an ironmaster named Samuel Garbett. In 1784 Pitt introduced a scheme for collecting excise duties on dyed cotton stuffs or dyed cotton and linen mixtures known locally as the Fustian Tax. Since Walpole's day, excise, associated as it was with the employment of officers empowered to search, had been a dirty word. The cotton manufacturers of Lancashire and Glasgow remonstrated with the Ministry but to no purpose.

In the following year Pitt presented to Parliament a wise and ambitious scheme for opening up trade in Ireland by admitting that country to all the benefits of trade with England and the colonies. The English manufacturers, fearing that this might undercut their prices, or even cause similar industries to theirs to be set up in competition in Ireland where power was abundant and wages low, were filled with alarm. Within one month of the proposal, at the instigation of Wedgwood, they organised a General Chamber of Manufacturers with a headquarters in London, an executive committee, a permanent secretary and admission to any manufacturer in any of the subsidiary organisations by paying a membership fee.

Success was immediate. When Pitt was forced to cut out the most objectionable features of the Fustian Tax, the Manchester delegates were paraded in joyful procession through the town. The subsequent modification of the Irish proposals which the Dublin Parliament turned down, causing the scheme to collapse, delighted them still more.

The General Chamber of Manufacturers contained features in advance of any previous extra-parliamentary pressure group. One of its most powerful assets was the amount of money and the financial interests backing it. As Garbett explained, it was composed of men many of whom had transactions in every considerable town in Europe and were better informed than any other body on matters of trade. Their meetings were held in private, for they had no need of the support of the noisy crowd. They were an all-England, non-party clique of capitalists who could throw at any time the weight of the whole organisation in support of any one industry or locality. They were an institution, not an agitating body, but they could hardly be expected, as their leaders claimed, to be non-party.

It was, in fact, on matters of an economic policy that the General Chamber, within little more than a year of its founda-

185

tion, came to grief. In 1786 Pitt negotiated a commercial treaty with France which involved a reciprocal lowering of duties on certain articles, and on this question the members of the Chamber were anything but united. The newer industrialists, manufacturers of cotton and woollen goods, ironware and pottery, in which Britain was first in the field, welcomed it, while the older industries, such as silk, ribbons, paper, glassware, clocks and leather, many of which products had been protected by import duties, were strongly in opposition and voted to ask for the postponement of the treaty. The northern manufacturers resented this, regretting that the delegates of such small industries should be allowed voting power equal to those of the northerners, and proposed to found a breakaway organisation. They never did so, and the alliance broke up.

Even Pitt had learned a lesson. Combinations and alliances made up of particular interests were apt to seek their own good, even though it might not be to the general good. Pitt, supremely convinced that he served the community as a whole, was particular never to deal with such groups collectively, but to assemble data and opinions from their various members as private individuals.

The organised group had many long years to wait before it could be recognised officially as a negotiating body.

13

Revolution and Repression

THE EARLY YEARS of the Pitt administration were years of great hopes and lost causes. All chance of parliamentary reform for the time being was extinguished in 1785. The dissenters were bitterly disappointed when in 1789 a motion for the repeal of the Test and Corporation Acts was defeated in the Commons by only twenty votes. The Committee for the Abolition of the Slave Trade, formed in 1787, had had high hopes of achieving its ends, but these were dashed in 1792 after three years of wrangling in Parliament. By that time the energy of Pitt and the British Government was occupied with more immediate matters.

In June 1789 the States-General of France, the first national consultative body to be called for nearly two centuries, in defiance of the King's order to disperse, remained in session and reconstituted itself as the National Assembly. On 14th July the Paris mob stormed the Bastille, the Paris prison and the emblem of royal oppression. The Assembly then set to work systematically to destroy the old order of things and to create a new constitution based on principles set forth in the Declaration of the Rights of Man, the document affirming the belief in the equality of all men, with complete liberty for all to think, say and do anything which did not injure others.

The Revolution was welcomed by many British statesmen who hoped that the setting up of a more liberal government across the Channel might put an end to the traditional enmity between Britain and France. By radicals and dissenters it was enthusiastically received because they thought they saw coming in France a state of things they had striven so long for at home – a country in which all forms of religion were tolerated

187

and in which the people as a whole had the right to elect their own government.

After the rejection of Pitt's propositions in 1789, parliamentary reform no longer appeared to be practical, but liberal thinkers, especially members of dissenting churches, still lived and hoped. As the centenary of 1688 approached, revolution societies were founded in many English towns to keep alive the idea of political liberty as well as to organise celebrations.

Events in France encouraged them, and in November 1789 Dr Richard Price, the Unitarian minister and reformer, friend of Benjamin Franklin, proposed an address of congratulation to the French National Assembly and delivered a sermon on 'the Love of our Country'. He thanked God that thirty million people had been delivered from slavery, and that in France a rule of reason and conscience had been created. This had not even yet been secured in Britain, for two conditions were still lacking: first, the right of the people to choose their own government, and second, freedom of religious belief.

His sermon created in England the most bitter political controversy since Jacobite times, and gave rise to the damning indictment of the Revolution by Burke in his prophetic *Reflections* (November 1790) and to the vigorous and stinging reply of the republican Thomas Paine in his book *The Rights of Man* (March 1791).

Poets, essayists and thinkers entered the lists, the majority of them on the side of the revolutionaries. Controversy boiled up in many provincial towns with constitutional and radical societies on the one side and Church and King clubs on the other. The first tried to persuade by the use of reason; the second did not wait to be persuaded before swinging the club and throwing the fire-brand. In Liverpool the mob tore to pieces an address prepared by the radicals. In Manchester the offices of the radical newspaper were invaded and private dwelling-houses damaged. In Bradford the effigy of Thomas Paine, with cockade in its hat, was put on a sledge drawn by a donkey which was ridden by a sweeping-boy, then hanged by the neck and finally torn to pieces amid great jubilation. In Birmingham three Unitarian chapels and many houses were damaged, among them the home, library and laboratory of the noted natural philosopher and Unitarian divine, Dr Joseph Priestley, which went up in flames.

Radicals and dissenters had long been sources of trouble, so churchmen, aristocrats and extreme Tories were not sorry to see them get what they deserved at the hands of the mob-leaders. Pitt, who had at first looked with sympathy on the rising of the French, could do nothing. King George, though he disapproved of violence, was secretly gratified. 'I cannot feel better pleased,' he wrote to Dundas, 'that Priestley is the sufferer for the doctrines he and his party have instilled.'

Such episodes did not stop the proliferation of revolutionary organisations. The achievements of the National Assembly gripped the imagination, especially of the more literate members, largely self-educated, of the working-class. The apostle of the new kind of group was Thomas Hardy, a Scottish shoe-maker, who had a business in Piccadilly. In January 1792 he founded the London Corresponding Society on a subscription of a penny a week from each member. The money was to be spent on publishing, and on correspondence with other societies of a like nature in the provinces, and in France. Its mentor was Horne Tooke, the 'restless political adventurer' who had been in at the formation of the Wilkite Society of the Supporters of the Bill of Rights in 1769. He brought all his knowledge and contacts into the movement. By the end of the year the Society had hundreds of members in London, divided into groups of thirty, each having a chairman and a delegate to the weekly business meeting, and similar groups had been set up in most of the large towns.

The composition and nomenclature, and even the aims of the scores of societies then existing in England, varied greatly. Some were entirely middle class, survivals in large measure from the old reform agitation, some had middle-class leaders, but to Hardy more than to anybody else is due the credit of bringing the working man of Britain into politics.

Burke's sneer at these working-class politicians as the swinish multitude increased rather than diminished their ardour. Daniel Eaton, a London bookseller, retailed pamphlets and a journal with the defiant title of *Hog's Wash*, while Thomas Spence, once a schoolmaster in Newcastle, then a vendor of saloop and cheap books near Chancery Lane, preached a doctrine of the social ownership of land to be let out at rent to farmers, and hawked a journal called *Pigs' Meat*. The working-men expressed themselves in these cheap periodicals and pamphlets, in a flood of propaganda and doggerel which was eagerly snapped up and read aloud at street corner and beershop.

In 1792, while all this was happening, the second volume of Paine's *Rights of Man* appeared. Its circulation was said to have reached 200,000 within a few months. Its language was violent; it described monarchy as a tyranny, and it prophesied that England would shortly laugh at the idea of sending to Hanover or Holland for kings who were not fit to take on the job of parish constables.

In 1793 many of the dismal prophecies of Burke had come true. The revolution had become blindly aggressive. Terror had gripped Paris, the King had been guillotined, Prussia and Austria had taken up arms, the French declared sympathy with all people who strove to rise against their rulers and had delivered a final affront to Britain by opening Antwerp, a rival port of London, which had been closed by treaty in Britain's interest for more than a century. Threatened by revolutionary doctrine as well as French aggression, the British Government declared war early in 1793. During the succeeding twenty-two years Britain was to be the backbone of resistance against a militant France.

The Government had already taken fright. The enemy, it was

believed, was not only abroad, but within. Fortunately for authority there were more strong arms and cudgels on its side than on that of the revolutionary societies. More Church and King Associations were founded, and their members bombarded the ministers with alarming stories of what was happening in the villages and towns, even among the militiamen, and predicted another Peasants' Revolt since the people were being stirred up by the promise of 'Liberty and absurd Licentiousness'.

In May 1792, a proclamation was issued forbidding seditious meetings and publications. Government intelligence was strengthened by the employment of agents who infiltrated into the ranks of the revolutionary bodies. Reform societies were turned out of their premises by landlords who feared to lose their licences. All this was but a prelude to the great wave of persecutions which took place, first in Scotland, then in England, during the years 1794 and 1795. Thomas Paine, who had left the country, was tried in his absence and outlawed. Horne Tooke, Thomas Hardy and John Thelwall, the Corresponding Society's most powerful orator, were arrested, tried and later acquitted, but the provincial leaders did not fare so well, and many were transported.

The reform movement was choked and most of the societies, starved of members, died. The Corresponding Society became a secret committee of extremists. Francis Place was its chairman until 1796 but left it in the following year. Some of its leaders, implicated in the Irish rebellion of 1798, were tried for treason and one was hanged.

In 1799 the Government completed its programme of repression. By a series of combination acts all associations and trade unions were banned; lecture rooms where payment was made for admission were put in the same category as brothels and disorderly houses; printing presses were registered and rigidly controlled and the sending abroad of English newspapers was forbidden. By that time Pitt had reorganised the army, building barracks for the men instead of dispersing them in civilian billets, so that the soldiery should not be contaminated by revolutionary ideas and would be able to do their work of keeping order the more effectively. The militia, which was raised from the lower classes, was replaced by the enlistment of bodies of volunteers and yeomanry. These, ostensibly recruited for home defence, were mainly composed of young men from the upper and middle classes, sons of farmers and employers, most of them able to fit themselves up with horses and to buy their own uniforms. There were no barriers of sympathy to prevent them from breaking up the mob.

In 1791 the working classes had risen for the first time into the world of politics through seizing on the machinery that Wilkes, Wyvill and the other political reformers had created, and with the help of radical middle-class members, had turned this machinery to their own uses. It was at this point that economic grievances entered again into politics – a thing they had rarely done since the Commonwealth. The grievances had existed throughout the whole of the century, but there had been no way of ventilating them except in riots, which had been numerous. The Militia Acts of 1756 had brought massive protests all over the country. In March 1761 the Yorkshire militia fired on five thousand Northumberland miners who were marching to Hexham to protest against their being balloted for the very same force. Forty-two were killed. Turnpike riots frequently occurred in mid-century, especially in the north and west. In 1757 every toll-gate in the triangle between Leeds, Bradford and Wakefield was torn down and ten persons were killed in the rioting.

Labour disputes, though they find little place in history, abounded. Textile riots were frequent both in London among the silkweavers and in the west country. Marches, violent attacks on suspected persons, machine-breaking and the sacking of buildings took place in almost all industries, but the most common uprisings of all were food riots brought about periodically through the fluctuations in corn prices. These occurred as much in industrial as in agricultural areas. None of these disorders had anything to do with politics, for they were concerned mainly with people who had no share in political life. Most of them were sudden; nearly all were confined to their own particular industries and localities, but they were none the less important for all that, for they betrayed the pent-up dissatisfaction of large sections of the population.

In the mind of Wyvill and his colleagues, reform of the franchise had been connected with nothing more than securing the purity of the constitution, with uprooting privilege, corruption and place-seeking. Among the working men the desire for reform was brought about through a subtle combination of many factors. In the first place there was no hint of treason in their attitude. They may have admired the way the French people had, as they thought, found their way to liberty, but they were none the less patriots and proud of their country. Few of them were republicans and, contrary to the opinion of the English ruling classes, there was little likelihood that Jacobinism would ever take root.

Secondly, most literate working men were proud of their new-found status. Many of them were avid readers, and felt that the right to vote was the qualification of the full citizens they aspired to be. The third factor was economic. The labouring classes had suffered heavily through the centuries partly through economic crises and partly through the injustices of the landed and employing classes, and they dreamed of the days when oppression would be ended. Their fundamental conviction was that this could only be realised when the working man was able to put other working men into Parliament. They were more numerous as a class than all the others put together, and power, they thought, was sure to come into their hands. Once that happened, it would be possible to make laws that would remedy the grievances from which they suffered. This was their hope, expressed in all its visionary grandeur in Daniel Eaton's *Hog's Wash* in November 1793:

> Be ye therefore, unceasingly employed in endeavouring to procure a fair and equal representation, in parliaments of a proper duration. When that is obtained your other grievances may soon be expected to cease. A due equilibrium may be preserved between the respective parts of the constitution – Our gracious Sovereign will be happy in lessening the burthens of his loving subjects – Limitation may take place in the *making* of Lords – Wars may be less frequently necessary – The swarms of pensioners and sinecure placemen may be diminished – Taxes may be lightened – The national debt may be *actually* reduced – The Game laws abolished – The Excise laws rendered less odious – the Statute laws corrected – The partial and oppressive laws against workmen meliorated – The proceedings at Common law rendered more compatible with common sense and equity – The severity of the criminal laws lessened – the Youth may be protected, instead of being dragged into hard and degrading servitude – The aged poor may be maintained – the Clergy more equally and agreeably provided for – The Test acts annihilated – These are some of the many blessings, which most probably would succeed to that Reform of Parliament, which it is your duty to demand, and your right to obtain.

This abiding conviction of the power the working classes could exert once they obtained representation in Parliament was the main factor in bringing about the Chartist agitation in the following century.

The repressive measures of Pitt, in whom before 1793 both reformers and working men had put their faith, destroyed every vestige of hope. Whatever signs of discontent appeared between 1789 and 1815 were the reaction of despair in a population which was still intensely loyal. The outstanding symptom of their reaction was Luddism.

Long before 1811 there had been outbursts of machine-breaking. Arkwright's water frames had been destroyed at Chorley in 1779 as had others at Blackburn and Bolton.

Weavers in Gloucestershire, Somerset and Spitalfields, and miners in Northumberland had destroyed machinery, but none of these sporadic outbursts had been so widespread as the Luddite riots. In 1811 the war with America put about one-fifth of the framework knitters of the East Midlands out of work. Changes in fashion had decreased demand and a series of bad harvests from 1809, which put up the price of grain, had reduced the workers to such a state that Lord Byron in 1812 told the Lords that he had not seen such squalor even in Turkey as was existing in the heart of Christian England.

The name of the mythical Ned, or King Ludd, is said to have originated with a stocking-maker's apprentice who, having been called over the coals by his master, lost his temper and broke up his knitting-frames. In February 1811, the employment of cheap labour and subsequent fruitless negotiations over wage rates brought on the first wave of Luddism, and when at Arnold, near Nottingham, a body of knitters broke up the frames of their employer, the disturbances spread, and the deliberate, careful choosing of targets gave evidence of planning. The calls to action read out to stockingers are reminiscent of the admonitions to the Peasants in Wat Tyler's time.

> Gentlemen all. Ned Ludd's Compliments and hopes you will give a trifle towards supporting his army as he well understands the Art of breaking obnoxious Frames. If you will comply with this it will be well, if not I shall call upon you myself. Edward Ludd.

Troops had to be brought out, the parish constables had to be augmented by the swearing in of assistants, and the fever abated somewhat. In February 1812 a promise of higher wages brought a temporary peace. In the same month the Government passed the Frame-breaking Bill which made the offence punishable with death. This did not prevent much more formidable outbreaks in Lancashire, Cheshire and the West Riding of Yorkshire within a couple of months. They were the most serious in Lancashire where the American war had stopped the importation of raw cotton, and the introduction of the power-loom was threatening the livelihood of the hand-loom weavers. All the paraphernalia of cloak and dagger politics were present, the secret meetings on the wild moor, the soot-blacked faces, the swearing of oaths and the anonymous threatening letters.

The centre of agitation was Stockport where Luddites, dressed as women, led attacks on a mill and on the house of its owner. Others followed in Oldham, Middleton and Holmwood, spreading out to Manchester, Bolton and Rochdale, and even over the county border to Barnsley. The rioters could not, however, stand against the efficient work of the Government spy and *agent provocateur* who infiltrated into the secret meetings and betrayed the leaders. Eight regiments of infantry and three of Horse Guards assisted those parish constables and headboroughs who were brave enough to remain loyal, scouring the moors and moving rapidly among the villages. More than a hundred prisoners were charged at Lancaster and Chester Assizes. There were hangings and transportations before the area was awed into a sullen quiet.

Meanwhile a third outbreak occurred in the Spen Valley around Huddersfield, Liversedge and Dewsbury, penetrating as far as the larger manufacturing towns of Bradford and Leeds. The rising was principally against the introduction of the new shearing machines. There was secret drilling on the moors, mills were set on fire or broken into by gangs of desperadoes armed with hammers.

> *Around and around we all will stand*
> *And eternally swear we will*
> *We'll break the shears and windows too;*
> *And set fire to the tazzling (teazeling) mill.*

One factory was besieged by a body of 150 men but the employer had taken the precaution to set on an armed guard. There were shots and casualties before the raiders were driven off. Threatening letters were received by those who persisted in running the machines, and one, the Chairman of the *ad hoc* Committee of Huddersfield for the Suppression of Outrages, was shot dead on the way home from a meeting. Here, too, spies and the army units did their work. When the chief centres had been 'occupied' by men billeted in the houses, and the malcontents, cowed by the show of force, went into hiding, the hunt for the offenders started. In January 1813, sixty-four of them were tried at York, seventeen were hanged and seven transported.

The forces of law were far too strong for the tactics of the Luddites to be successful. In the Midlands, where the object had been the abolition of cheap labour and the raising of wages, there was some temporary compromise, but in Lancashire and the West Riding where there was no such motive, the introduction of the new machinery proceeded apace. In both cases, though some manifestoes proclaimed the intention of unseating the Government and even mentioned the reform of Parliament, there was no serious political motive behind the risings. They were the reaction of despair to conditions which had become almost unbearable.

Sporadic outbursts of machine-breaking occurred after this time. As a consequence of one of these in Loughborough in 1816, six men were executed and three transported. The long war against France was not over, and the realisation was dawning, even on the working classes, that the economic and social problems of England could not be settled by the machine-breaker's hammer. A more radical approach was needed and that could only be got through the political platform. The only way was to go back to the solution advocated by the leaders of the 'nineties – parliamentary reform.

The idea had been cherished all through the war period by veterans who still lived. In 1811 the London Hampden Club, a body of Whigs and radicals, was founded to keep alive the idea of reform. Its leading figure was Major John Cartwright who in 1776 had written *Take your Choice,* one of the earliest works on parliamentary reform, and who had been a campaigner ever since. Now, though more than seventy-five years old, this Lafayette of the working classes journeyed tirelessly from town to town founding new Hampden Clubs and encouraging them in their correspondence. The new movement was supported by that independent spirit and prince of all protestors, William Cobbett.

Born in 1766, the son of a small farmer, Cobbett was old enough to remember and look back nostalgically on the old days before the 'madness of enclosure' had swept into its orbit the commons and forced thousands of honest labourers into beggary. He had been a sergeant-major in the army, an emigrant bookseller and freelance political writer in the United States of America and a fervent supporter of Church and King after his return to England. At first an ardent admirer of Pitt, he deplored the signing of the Peace of Amiens with Bonaparte, and declined to join in the public rejoicings. For this his windows were smashed by the crowd.

At that time he founded his journal, the *Political Register,* in which he proved himself the enemy of all injustice and corruption – 'The Thing' as he scathingly called the hateful system of patronage. He eventually concluded that the only way to get rid of it was to stop the selling of places in Parliament and bribery of electors by a complete overhaul of the electoral system. Thus, from a high Tory, he turned reformer. In 1809 he wrote a bitter article of protest which brought about his imprisonment. It concerned a mutiny of militiamen which had broken out at Ely over the distribution of knapsacks. It had been put down with the help of four squadrons of German cavalry and the ringleaders had been sentenced to five hundred lashes each.

Cobbett remained in prison from June 1810 until July 1812,

only to return again to the attack. He travelled the length and breadth of the country preaching reform, he reduced the price of the *Political Register* from 1s 0½d to twopence, avoiding the payment of the newspaper tax by omitting all news from it and concentrating mainly on comment. The circulation of the *Register* went up to almost 50,000 a week. He appealed to the machine-breakers to refrain from violence and to consider that the machine was a benefit rather than an impediment to the progress of mankind. In 1817, beset by creditors and assailed on all sides, he left for America, but from there sent regularly his copy to the *Register*. By the time he returned to England in November 1819, bringing with him the bones of Tom Paine, important events had already taken place.

The Hampden Clubs were prospering. Delegate meetings were calling for no taxation without representation, for universal franchise, annual parliaments, equal electoral districts and the abolition of the property qualification for Members of Parliament. Petition after petition was sent to the House and promptly rejected. The Lancashire reformers planned a march on London. On the way they hoped to gather sympathisers and once there to present a petition to the Prince Regent in person. If at first they could not see him, they would camp out round Carlton House, virtually besieging him in his residence, until he was forced to come out and listen to them.

The March of the Blanketeers is important, not merely because it points out the rising influence of the provinces in the working-class movement, but also because it is the first instance of a happening which has been so many times repeated since those days – a protest march on London. The peasants had done it in a rather different way in 1381. In the nineteenth century, London became the Mecca of all organisations which wanted to ventilate a grievance. The Blanketeers had no idea of the kind of obstacle they would have to face. Before they had even left Manchester some of their leaders were arrested. Before they had put many miles behind them they were harried by the yeomanry and hauled away. The great march came to nothing, many of its leaders being imprisoned without benefit of *habeas corpus* which had been suspended in the previous year.

The north was in turmoil. More radical societies, Union Societies and Political Protestants came into being; some, realising that the working class could do little unless its members became able to read, write and cipher, organised classes, entrants paying a penny a week for tuition. They hoped by means of great mass meetings to get their message over to the indifferent multitudes. The great gathering in St Peter's Fields, Manchester, was the climax of a campaign of protest with meetings in London, Birmingham and Leeds. The story of Peterloo and its martyrs is too well known for repetition. The hopes of the reformers were again dashed down by the sabres of the yeomanry.

But it had a deeper significance. The open-air mass meeting which was not a riot had arrived. Though as a result of it the Six Acts were passed putting even more limitations on the power of the working people to express themselves, the lesson of Peterloo was not forgotten. One day, when the shackles were removed from the press and communication had been improved by post, railway and phone, the same method of organised gathering involving thousands of people would be effective, and the provinces would take the lead.

In 1813 Thomas Spence, the London bookseller, died, leaving behind him a small band of enthusiasts for village communities holding land in common. At the same time as Cartwright was travelling the provinces proclaiming the gospel of reform, the Spencean Philanthropists held their own meetings in London. A procession led to a riot, and four of the members of the sect were prosecuted on charges of high treason. One of these, Arthur Thistlewood, released after serving a year of his sentence, organised a conspiracy to murder members of the Cabinet and start a rising. The Cato Street Conspiracy, as it was called, was partly instigated and then betrayed by a Government spy. The plotters were surprised and captured. Thistlewood and others paid with their lives.

The arena of English politics, once the preserve of nobility, landed gentry and privilege, was being invaded by the working classes, though as yet they had not achieved a permanent place.

Protest, moreover, had also passed into other matters besides the strife of sects and classes. Aspects of life which had once been considered right and normal were now coming under question, and the area of protest was widening. Some of these new aspects must be examined.

14

The National Conscience

ON A SUNDAY morning in June 1831, Richard Oastler was visited at his residence at Fixby Hall near Wakefield by six leading members of the local Short Time Committees to ask him if he would join forces with them in demanding a ten-hour working day for children in the factories. After many hours of discussion he consented on condition that both parties should put aside political and sectarian differences. The Fixby Hall Compact, as it was called, was one of the strangest alliances in industrial history.

Oastler was a Tory and a churchman, the six delegates were Radicals, and most of them were Dissenters. Within weeks of the meeting, Oastler the humanitarian was the leader of a great movement which included benevolent manufacturers, politicians, professional men and craftsmen, and which was backed by the demonstrating power of thousands of factory workers in Yorkshire, Lancashire and other industrial districts. In the Fixby Hall Compact, philanthropy and popular unrest joined forces for the first time in the history of industrial England.

There was nothing new about humanitarian protest. Since the decline of organised medieval charity, the plight of the evicted and destitute had called forth bitter comments on the injustices of society by such writers as Sir Thomas More, Robert Crowley, John Moore, Hugh Latimer and Daniel Defoe. In the eighteenth century the growth of towns gave rise to social problems on a scale never before witnessed. The feeding of such large numbers of people thrust into close contact with each other was one of the least of the problems that had to be faced. Already in the previous century, in the parishes outside London the poorer classes had been accommodated in tenements thrown up hastily and without plan by speculative builders. Upper storeys had been built over single-storey cottages and cellars dug out beneath them and in these, many of which had not been touched by the fire of 1666, or in the houses left behind by the rich who had gone away in search of healthier neighbourhoods, large numbers of people lived in squalor and wretchedness. Supplies of pure water were non-existent and there was no drainage save the open ditch or the stinking cesspool in the middle of a courtyard. In many of the rapidly growing towns of the Midlands and the North conditions were even worse. In such breeding-grounds diseases like smallpox, dysentery and typhoid were a constant menace.

Even more serious was the effect on the character and behaviour of the poor who were forced into such dismal surroundings, and into the company of the very worst elements of society. In quarters where the most desperate characters were wont to congregate there was every temptation to laziness and depravity. Drink, especially gin, was cheap and there were no licensing laws. Debauchery and prostitution flourished. The horrors of Hogarth's 'Gin Lane' were no exaggeration, and such conditions could be found in any sizeable town in England.

Life in such surroundings was for the most part short, brutish and insecure. Infant mortality was very high, only one child in five surviving the first few days of life. Many children, especially those born out of wedlock, were abandoned in the streets, either to starve or die of exposure. Those who did not were put out to nurse by the parishes or taken into workhouses where their fate was no better. Jonas Hanway estimated that of these children ninety-nine per cent died before they were twelve months old. To survive was to face new dangers. Some of the parish children were transported to the North to feed the new textile machines, others were apprenticed.

For the child of better-class parents apprenticeship meant learning a trade generally under good conditions, but neither the parish nor the labouring classes could afford to pay the fees demanded by the masters in highly skilled handicrafts. Their children furnished the cheap labour for the lower-class artisans, the smiths, butchers, bakers, chandlers, sweeps, fishermen and publicans, while the girls were bound over to some mistress or other to become domestic slaveys. To this life they were condemned until the age of twenty-four. There is little wonder that the apprentice was one of the most unruly elements in society or that in 1767 the age limit for male apprentices had to be reduced to twenty-one in an attempt to encourage industry, to bring about good relations between master and man, to allow the young to marry and to check rioting in the streets, for which apprentices were notorious.

Yet, even having passed through this stage, life was full of insecurity. The appalling housing shortage drove the poor back into the single room of the tenement house where the awful conditions of the first generation might be repeated in the second. The payment of wages in public houses was an open encouragement to drink and gamble; that and seasonal unemployment drove many into the toils of creditor and tallyman. In such cases the only escape from the dreaded debtor's prison was to flee, leaving behind a destitute family. Once in prison, one's associates were rogues and felons, and because of the fees demanded by gaolers and turnkeys there was no hope of release. Here the unfortunate debtor languished in dirt and misery until released by death from smallpox or gaol fever. In 1716 it was said that there were sixty thousand debtors dying in the prisons of England. In 1719, three hundred died in the Marshalsea prison in three months.

To understand why such evils should be allowed to exist, it is necessary to catch something of the spirit of the time. Since the Middle Ages, poverty and destitution had been accepted as part of life, and in the streets of the medieval or the Elizabethan town the rich had lived cheek by jowl with the poor, and tossed coins to beggars in the streets without any qualm of conscience, unimpelled by any urge to raise them out of their distress. The machinery of parish relief which had been evolved in the last years of the reign of Elizabeth I had, with its elaborations, been sufficient to cope with the worst problems and to salve the conscience of the ruling classes. But, with the uncontrolled growth of towns, the situation got out of hand. If English society was to be saved, the legislators had to be awakened out of their apathy. Where law and justice failed, pity stepped in. This was the humanitarian protest, the source of most of the social reforms of the eighteenth and nineteenth centuries.

It began with individuals. One of the earliest of these reformers was James Oglethorpe, former ensign in the army and aide-de-camp to Prince Eugene. In 1722 he entered Parliament for Haslemere, but he was not by temperament a politician. He was impelled to protest by the plight of a friend of his named Castell who had been imprisoned in the Fleet for debt. The poor man was unable to pay the fees which would have secured him special treatment and was therefore lodged in the cheapest and filthiest part of the prison. There he caught smallpox and died, leaving a wife and several small children.

The fate of his friend inspired Oglethorpe to enquire on his own account into the state of the prisons, and in 1729 he succeeded in obtaining the appointment of a Parliamentary Committee. The results of the enquiry revealed an almost unimaginable state of human degradation and corruption. It described among other things how prison offices were farmed out, often to the most unscrupulous persons who extracted every penny they could not only from prisoners, but from their friends outside; how the prisons were often used as storage-places for goods stolen by prisoners let out for that purpose, and how people, for the mere sake of obtaining money from them and their friends, were taken and put in gaol until the sources of money ran out. Then unable to pay for special accommodation they were thrust down into the 'common side' eventually to pine and die of some foul disease.

There conditions were bad enough almost to shame a Buchenwald or a Belsen – persons suffering from different diseases side by side in filth on the floors, helpless men and women lying in tiers unable to move, unable to eat, simply waiting for death, prisoners crowded for the night into small fetid rooms, tortured by thumbscrew and headcollar, thrust into dungeons and clapped in irons. These were only a few of the scandals brought to light by the Parliamentary Committee of 1729.

What began with protest was continued in action. Oglethorpe, stirred by his experiences in the prisons, resolved to try to give those who had come to grief in England a chance to find a new future in another region, and in 1732, with his board of trustees, he founded in America the colony of Georgia. Here John Wesley, his brother Charles and the great revivalist George Whitefield gained their early experience. Oglethorpe had revealed the shortcoming of the English prison but it was left for another and a greater reformer, John Howard, to provide the ideas which resulted in the introduction of a completely new prison system.

In this sense the philanthropists were protestors, not directly against a government, but against social conditions, and the result of their work was to induce governments to bring in legislation with the object of changing these conditions, and also to alter the point of view of the people as a whole – to persuade them not to accept evil as a necessary part of life, but to fight it.

Thomas Coram, a sea-captain, appalled by the sight of abandoned children lying dead and dying in the streets of London, worked for years to get a hospital established for foundlings. In 1739, with the support of influential people he addressed a memorial to the Government. A charter was granted, subscriptions were received and the Foundling Hospital was the first step towards saving the lives of many unwanted children. At an even earlier date the bookseller, Thomas Guy, had built the first three wards of St Thomas's, had completed and endowed Guy's and had left £400 a year to Christ's Hospital. Other hospitals and medical schools were added during the century.

Another philanthropist, Jonas Hanway, gave the latter part of his life up to the improvement of the conditions of life for children. In the parish workhouses in and around London there was a shocking waste of child lives through lack of care and insufficient food. Hanway sought to remedy this by boarding them out to work in local industries. Child labour was accepted as the rule in the eighteenth century and Defoe writing of his visit to the Yorkshire textile districts, where hardly a child older than four years did not earn a living with its own hands, viewed it with approval. Hanway's act of 1767, while improving the lot of many children boarded out around London, resulted in the sending out of batches of children to the manufacturing districts of the North.

The movement for the protection of the young chimney-sweeps was begun by a letter in the *Public Advertiser* in 1760, probably written by Hanway. It urged the magistrates of London and Westminster to punish any master who allowed his sweeping-boys to go about the streets insufficiently clothed. Public attention was drawn to the plight of the poor wretches, committees set to work collecting information, often from the boys themselves, and publishing it. The work of Hanway was taken up by other individuals and in 1802 a society was formed to supersede the employment of climbing-boys by the use of a machine.

The movement did not lose its identity during the time of national danger, and once the Napoleonic war was over, the voice of protest was again raised. This time it resulted in the appointment of a Select Committee before which the Society produced evidence from masters, visitors, surgeons and from the boys themselves. The most appalling stories were told about boys being stripped naked before climbing, frightened boys forced to go higher by fires being lit below them, boys bought and sold like slaves, beaten to death, suffocated, deformed through carrying heavy bags, crippled through having to crawl through small openings, underfed, overworked, suffering from coughs, scurvy, asthma, cancer and other diseases. Even after the report had been produced the first bill failed to go through for lack of time, and three subsequent bills were thrown out by the Lords. Other bills passed in 1834 and 1840 were not enforced and it was not until 1875 that Lord Shaftesbury secured the effective control of mastersweeps by the issue of licences.

All this agitation, often by individuals and small bodies of well-intentioned men and women, worked as a leaven in a callous and materialistic society and turned the attention of those in power towards rooting out at least some of the worst evils that existed within it. Hogarth's picture of 'Gin Lane' complemented Henry Fielding's *Reasons for the Late Increase of Robbers* to bring forth a general protest in the form of petitions to Parliament from London, from Westminster, from many parishes and provincial towns all warning the Government that the universal drunkenness would if not checked destroy the power and trade of the kingdom.

The Act of 1751 increased the duties on spirits and stopped the sale of gin in the chandlers' shops. Two years later another act brought the public houses under regulation. Though these did not get rid of the evil, they substantially reduced the consumption of spirits. In 1753 Hardwicke's Marriage Act required the calling of banns for all marriages. This put an end to the practice of brokers and crimps who arranged marriages with the sole object of enriching themselves and their clients through robbing and deceiving others. With the passing of this act the scandalous marriages within the precincts of the Fleet Prison were ended, and thousands were saved from family disgrace and lifelong misery.

London was fortunate in having at Bow Street two famous magistrates, the novelist Henry Fielding, from 1749–54 and his younger brother John, from 1754–80. Up to their time the Bow Street magistracy had been an office of profit, and its occupants had been interested only in the amount of money they could extract from trading in fines, a pursuit which resulted rather in increasing than diminishing crime. Henry Fielding, the first non-trading justice, used his office to teach the public how the poor were driven to crime by the terrible conditions under which they lived, and he often discharged offenders when by strict observance of the law he should have sent them to prison.

He was one of the first men to protest against the degrading spectacle of public executions at Tyburn which made punishment not an act of justice as much as a public entertainment. John Fielding continued the same policy of education and prevention. His plan for providing young boys, deserted by their parents, with a seagoing career under good conditions rather than through the questionable methods of impressment led to the foundation of the Marine Society in 1756, and two years later he was the moving spirit in the foundation of the Orphan Asylum for Deserted Girls. His great contribution was the setting up of the first professional police force. With the establishment of the Bow Street Runners (1753) conditions in London rapidly improved. Parishes elsewhere set up their watch committees and the movement for public order resulted in the formation of Peel's Metropolitan Police in 1829 and the later adoption of the new police in all the local government units of England.

In this century, too, arose the protest against slavery and the slave trade. The Quakers had condemned both by a resolution passed as early as 1724, but slavery continued, even in England, almost another fifty years. It was the custom for West Indian planters, when they visited their home country, to bring with them their slaves, some of whom, hoping to find freedom, ran away. The slavemasters appealed to the law officers of the Crown and in 1729 they were confirmed in their property by a pronouncement of the Attorney-General and Solicitor-General.

The capture of runaway slaves became a profitable business and soon any coloured person walking the streets of any English town was in danger of being taken by a gang, sold back into slavery and shipped off to the West Indies. It was estimated that in 1770 there were about fourteen thousand Negroes in England, most of them in the East End of London where slave-catching went on daily, while in Liverpool, the centre of the importation of American cotton, a regular market arose for the auctioning of Negroes.

The sympathy of the populace was generally with the Negroes who were often given help to hide from their pursuers. But, said Sir John Fielding, as a result they tended 'to enter into societies and make it their business to corrupt and dissatisfy the mind of every black servant that comes to England . . . by getting them christened or married which, they inform them, makes them free . . . though it has been decided otherwise by the judges'.

The cause of the Negro slaves was taken up by Granville Sharp, a clerk in the Ordnance department, who rescued and protected a Negro named Jonathan Strong from a man who claimed to be his master. The legal battles which followed resulted in the famous pronouncement by Lord Chief Justice Mansfield in the case of James Somersett (1772) that as soon as any slave set foot on English territory he became free.

This great victory raised the hopes of almost every philanthropist in England that the slave trade and every vestige of slavery within the British dominions might be abolished. Sharp found himself the protector of some hundreds of black citizens, many of them forced by freedom on their own resources and driven into the most abject poverty. A committee for relieving the black poor was founded with Jonas Hanway as its chairman. A scheme was set afoot to settle Negroes from England in some other part of the world, and in 1787 the Sierra Leone

Company was granted a charter and the first colony, with Zachary Macaulay as governor, was set up. Other Negroes were settled in the West Indies as free labourers, but the problem of slavery and the slave trade remained.

Meanwhile England was becoming more and more liberal under the benevolent government of the younger Pitt. In 1787 the opponents of slavery set up the Committee for the Abolition of the Slave Trade with Granville Sharp as its chairman, and within a few months they had enlisted the help of one of Pitt's best friends, the Member for Yorkshire, William Wilberforce. In that year hopes ran high. Wilberforce was encouraged by Pitt to bring in a motion as soon as possible. In May 1789 he did so and was supported by both Burke and Fox. The debates continued into 1790 and by that time the French Revolution was taking precedence in men's minds. The West Indies were threatened and with them the private property and vested interests of British landowners and slave-owners. Wilberforce's motion was rejected by 163 votes to 88. Even had it been accepted by the Commons it would certainly have been thrown out by the Lords.

The abolitionists were dismayed but not defeated, for they still had behind them a large body of public opinion. The Wesleyan Methodists had followed the lead of the Quakers and backed the movement, while within the established Church the new evangelical movement gave its strong support. Already Wedgwood had produced a medal of a slave kneeling in chains, with the inscription AM I NOT A MAN AND A BROTHER. William Cowper's poem *The Negro's Complaint,* printed in leaflet form and set to music, found ready circulation. Nearly five hundred petitions were received in that year by Parliament but there was no hope of legislation.

In April 1792 Wilberforce presented a second motion for immediate abolition, and was supported by Pitt, Fox, Burke and Grenville, but again the opposition was too strong and Dundas carried by a large majority an amendment in favour of gradual abolition. The Lords put off the discussion until the following session. When that time arrived Britain was at war with the French Republic. Abolition of the Slave Trade had to wait until the Fox Ministry of 1806, and total abolition until the Reform Ministry of Lord Grey (1833).

Every evil in time brings its own remedy, and it was probably because of the appalling poverty and wretchedness of the eighteenth century that the humanitarian protest was so strong and so lasting. Though twenty-two years of war muffled its expression, the spirit still remained in the hearts of men and once the fear of political upheaval was ended, it found a stronger voice than ever. Philanthropy had come to stay, and there was hardly an aspect of the life of the poor into which it did not penetrate. Sunday schools, ragged schools, National and British schools spread throughout the country, and temperance societies were founded.

The Wesleys and George Whitefield had spread a new evangel of personal salvation among people hitherto sunk in degradation and brutality, and by the establishment of permanent congregations had leavened the heavy lump of lower-class society. In 1813 Elizabeth Fry commenced her visits to Newgate and later through the association she founded put forward proposals for the classification, instruction and more humane treatment of female prisoners. In 1827 a Select Committee of Parliament reported on the shocking conditions in the private madhouses and this resulted in the passing of the Asylum Act in 1828, bringing all such institutions under the control of the Home Secretary. From 1800 onwards the self-made cotton manufacturer, Robert Owen, was hard at work proving at his mills in New Lanark that the characters of human beings could be moulded and improved by the surroundings into which they were placed. In 1813 he produced his *New View of Society, or Essays on the principle of the Formation of the Human Character*.

For the most part, human beings were not wont to become

restless unless deeply affected by some circumstance which either touched them personally or as groups; and moreover, to be noticed, they had to have the means of expressing that restlessness or dissatisfaction. Most philanthropic efforts, being either on behalf of small minorities or of classes of society whose members were unable to speak for themselves, were not the kind to cause popular unrest. Once, however, that a certain class or large group rose to demand its rights, the movement became political, resulting in a mass protest which could only be dealt with by some action of those in authority. If the Ten Hours agitation had been purely philanthropic it is fairly safe to say that it would, like many other causes, have been kept alive by a small minority of Tory social reformers, but other motives on both sides need to be examined.

In the first place, it is inconceivable that even a majority of the mill-owners were as inhuman as had sometimes been made out. Recent researches have revealed that though there were undoubtedly acts of great cruelty perpetrated on children, these were generally the work of other operatives, and often took place without the knowledge of the masters. It is pointed out that close scrutiny of the Report of the Select Committee and other documents does not support the charge that there was any long-continued and systematic cruelty.

Many people in sympathy with the movement admitted that the evidence brought by Michael Sadler before the Select Committee was one-sided, in that the persons interviewed were chosen purposely to present a picture of cruelty, misery, disease and deformity among the factory children. Out of eighty-nine witnesses, sixty were factory workers and the doctors who were questioned admitted that the physical state of the child factory worker, though bad, was no worse than that of children of the poor in general. In fact, it is believed that in the small factories and workshops which had to face competition from the larger concerns, the conditions under which children worked were by far the worst.

By the time Sadler's Bill was brought up in Parliament (March 1832) the Ten Hours Question had become a political issue with, for the most part, Tories and Radicals on the one side and Whigs on the other. The main issue, and this is certainly true of Oastler and his closest collaborators, was philanthropic, but what about the rest?

The outlook of the manufacturers was purely economic. Industry relied on the labour of children for the performance of both routine work and certain skilled tasks. To lose it would mean a certain loss of productive power. They held that to increase a child's leisure would not be an unmixed blessing. The natural tendency of a child was to be active and it might as well be active doing useful work as getting into mischief. Hence, provided the children were reasonably well treated, factory life would do them no harm. It is as well to realise, however, that the nineteenth-century conception of reasonably good treatment differed considerably from modern standards. The mill-owners were therefore angered by what they considered unjust accusations levelled at them as a class by the philanthropists.

The motives of the workers in supporting the Ten Hours Movement were mixed. One could understand, for instance, the distress of the unemployed parent who had, against all his better feelings, to beat his children into wakefulness at an early hour in the morning so that they could go to the mill to earn the family's daily bread, but this fact in itself raises other arguments which were anything but philanthropic. Children were to a certain extent in competition with their own parents. Moreover, the work older people were doing often depended on the assistance of children, and so it was believed that it would be impossible to reduce the hours of the one without the same reduction being made for the other. The Ten Hours Bill thus became a stage in the fight for shorter hours and, incidentally, higher wages.

The struggle for the passing of the Ten Hours Bill is unique in the story of British protest, not only because of this strange partnership between Tory and Radical, but because of the effective way in which the whole two-year campaign was organised. In this alone it shows a remarkable advance on anything that had gone before. Like most campaigns of its kind, it was fought on both sides with passion and prejudice, and passion was increased by the sometimes sickly sentimentality that accompanied it. Even this, however, gave the occasion for some of the most dramatic interludes ever to take place in the story of the rise of the working classes.

It began, simply enough, with a visit of Richard Oastler, the anti-slaver who had already gained notoriety because of the stand he took for the parishioners of Halifax in a tithe dispute, to John Wood, a Bradford mill-owner who employed some five hundred children in his factory. While talking about Oastler's favourite topic Wood expressed surprise that while he could give so much attention to the condition of the slaves in the West Indies he had not turned his attention to the sad condition of the victims of this other and even more degrading form of slavery – the factory system. His own factory was run on humane lines. The older children worked from five in the morning to seven in the evening with breaks of half-an-hour for breakfast and forty minutes for dinner, but the smaller children worked only ten hours. He had forbidden the use of the strap as a punishment; all those under thirteen years of age had two hours' schooling a day and all had regular medical inspection. He painted a gloomy picture of what went on in other factories and urged Oastler to take the lead in an effort to remove such shameful conditions. Oastler was so profoundly moved by his friend's appeal that early the following morning he promised to do all in his power. That same evening he penned a strong letter to the *Leeds Mercury* entitled 'Yorkshire Slavery'. Though the letter was written on 29th September it was not printed until 16th October accompanied by an editorial which was intended to tone down the severity of its expression.

A winter of fierce newspaper controversy followed, Wood

and Oastler rallying a few of the more humane manufacturers to their side, supported by the Tory *Leeds Intelligencer*. The *Mercury*, which had published the first letter, rapidly took up the cause of the rest of the mill-owners and joined in the attacks on Oastler and his friends.

In that year the atmosphere was charged with political tension. In June George IV died, and the advent of a new monarch caused a general election which brought into power a Whig ministry under Lord Grey, pledged to the reform of the franchise. The working classes imagined that the parliamentary vote, with all that it was believed to imply, was at last within their grasp, and popular feeling ran high. The rejection of the first bill in March 1831 by the Commons resulted in an election and the introduction of a second bill which was thrown out by the Lords in October. Enthusiasm mounted on such a scale that men who had before never been stirred by political issues took part in the riots and demonstrations with the demand, 'The Bill, the whole Bill and nothing but the Bill'. It is doubtful whether, but for the excitement of the reform agitation, the campaign for the Ten Hours Bill would ever have drawn to itself such a volume of popular support.

The Radicals joined in the demand. To them the Bill meant the vote and with it the bettering of working conditions, the shortening of the hours in factories, and the raising of wages. In June 1831 Oastler and the Radical members of the Short Time Committees, though diametrically opposed on this cardinal point of political doctrine, agreed to join forces. While in public all this agitation was going on, both sides of industry – masters and operatives – were engaged in private meetings, planning the campaigns which were sure to follow, and engaging in the prolonged and bitter newspaper controversy.

For this reason the year 1831 was important. Agitation both for the Reform Bill and the reduction of the working hours of children proceeded apace. The masters, too, took up their stand. In March they drew up a list of fourteen resolutions declaring that children of seven to fourteen years of age were capable of long hours of work, that the work in worsted factories was healthy, that the treatment of the children was on the whole humane, and that any attempt to restrict hours would be harmful not only to the families of the workers, whose incomes would be reduced, but also to the country. Legislation to reduce hours or to curtail the freedom of the manufacturer in any way, they maintained, was pernicious and could not be effective.

Meanwhile in all parts of the cotton and woollen districts Short Time Committees were being created. In June the Whig member for Westminster, Sir John Cam Hobhouse, introduced in Parliament a bill to make factory labour for children under nine unlawful, and to restrict the hours of all between nine and eighteen to eleven a day and sixty-six a week. The masters angrily denounced it and were generally very satisfied when through the passing of one amendment after another it was made completely ineffective. Nevertheless, the cause had been brought before Parliament, the newspaper controversy had kept it before the notice of the public and through it the Short Time Committees had gained in numbers and strength. The exasperation of the working classes was increased when in October a second bill for the reform of Parliament, having passed the Commons, was thrown out by the Lords. By this time the Ten Hours Movement had acquired a new champion in Parliament in the Leeds business man, Michael Sadler.

During the winter months England went through a period of great unrest. The Reform Bill which Lord John Russell introduced into Parliament on the 12th December was a great disappointment to the working classes who had campaigned so ceaselessly for it. They regarded the bill, which proposed giving the vote to the propertied classes only, as a betrayal. Many lost heart, taking no more interest in the agitation, others took part in noisy public meetings, and there was rioting in places. But in the North even the cause of Reform did not capture the imagination as did the agitation for the Ten Hours Bill. A great campaign was organised, with pamphlets, broadsides and a succession of public meetings. Trade unions and private individuals subscribed money.

On the day after Christmas Oastler gave his famous 'Strap Speech' at Huddersfield, holding up the leather thong that was laid over the backs of children who were too tired to work. On the next day at Bradford, at a meeting attended by benevolent employers and doctors, he made a second impassioned speech. Suddenly a clergyman stepped forward from the back of the hall and mounted the platform. He was recognised as the Reverend George Stringer Bull, the vicar of the nearby parish of Bierley, who had opened Sunday schools to teach the children of his parishioners to read. He spoke of the bounden duty of a parson to consider the welfare of children, and how even he was ashamed to have to scold children who had been imprisoned in a mill for six days, for coming late to school on a Sunday. From that day the short, burly figure of 'Parson Bruiser, Chaplain to the Ten Hours Bill' was to be seen haranguing meetings and leading processions as Oastler's chief adjutant.

In the spring of 1832 the newspaper campaign rose to a climax. Not only some of the local papers, but *The Times*, the *Standard* and the *Morning Post* all supported Oastler. The organisation expanded and ladies' committees were formed. In April 1832 the Society for Improving the Conditions of Working Children held its first meeting in London. The meetings that were held between January and March at Keighley, Dewsbury and Halifax were, for their missionary fervour and enthusiasm, more like revival gatherings than anything else, but the most impressive event of the whole campaign was the mass march on York on Easter Monday.

The great work of Parson Wyvill had not been forgotten. Some fifty years before he had chosen York as the meeting-place of the county's freeholders to raise their voices for the cause of economic reform. As a county town, with all its historical associations, it was worthy of being the object of a pilgrimage, and well within reach.

For a working-class demonstration this march was supremely well organised. From all the villages the demonstrators came, carrying banners, many of them led by their bands. Most of them wore clogs, few had overcoats and many had no more than a sheet of cloth or blanket to protect them against the cold and rain. The village contingents converged on the larger centres and so the numbers of pilgrims grew as they trudged along the muddy roads in the rain towards their goal, singing hymns and homely dialect songs. As night came on they marched by the light of rough torches. Arriving at the racecourse outside York they found that though the beer supplies had arrived there was no bread. Patiently they waited while parties went off to the townspeople to get food. There was no disorder.

Next day Oastler led them through Micklegate Bar amid cheers. The vanguard of twelve thousand stood in the castle yard to listen to speeches from Oastler, Wood, Sadler and Bull, while another twelve thousand waited patiently outside. All prophecies of trouble were belied. At the end of the meeting the High Sheriff of York, to whom Oastler had given a guarantee of good behaviour, closed the meeting and congratulated the crowd.

That night they set off in the rain on the long march home. Bull and his friends, realising that some of them would never make the journey back, scoured York for covered carts and brought up the rear of the procession picking up the stragglers and caring for them. After a short stop at Tadcaster they reached Leeds, the dispersal point, the next morning. 'I have been at their heels all night myself,' declared Parson Bull, 'and have witnessed such an extent of benevolence and patriotism as I never saw and never heard of in my life.' In the Cloth Hall Yard at Leeds the great company joined in singing the

Doxology then, to the cheering of thousands lining the streets, the men, and the boys with them, made their many ways home. This, the greatest epic of peaceful protest in the nineteenth century, is worthy of a high place in the annals of working-class history.

But it did not get them very far. Michael Sadler had introduced into Parliament a Ten Hours Bill in March, but the matter had been referred to a Select Committee of the Commons which was to collect evidence. The whole summer was occupied in gathering witnesses and taking them to London. For a while the cause was overshadowed by the passing of the Reform Bill which received the royal assent on the 7th June. This alone was a bitter disappointment to the Short Time Committees. In December they received another severe setback when at the Leeds General Election Sadler was defeated by the Whig member Thomas Babington (later Lord) Macaulay. They were encouraged to take on a new campaign when in January the Report of the Select Committee, which revealed the shocking stories of several factory children, was published. But their spokesman in Parliament had gone, and it was time to choose another.

In January 1833 a small committee decided to send Parson Bull to London to find a successor to Sadler. Of the several names suggested to him, not one would consent to take up the cause of the children, but one of them suggested that he might approach Lord Ashley.

'If persuading Ashley to undertake this work had been Bull's only contribution to the social history of this country, he would have deserved to be remembered,' wrote his biographer. The young member for Dorset, as he then was, was appalled at the magnitude of the task that had been put before him, but after long consideration and prayer he accepted it as his duty to God and the poor. For the next few months Bull was constantly in touch with him, always ready with information and guidance.

It was the signal for a resumption of the campaign. On the

5th February Lord Ashley gave notice of a motion to reintroduce Sadler's Bill on the 10th March. On the same day Lord Morpeth followed it with another motion to introduce an Eleven Hours Bill at the end of February. Feelings rose to white heat. Scores of public meetings were held in chapels and schoolrooms, new Short Time Committees sprang up and petitions flooded into the Commons. The violent criticism caused Morpeth to withdraw his motion, leaving the field clear for Ashley, but the Government put back the date for consideration of his motion, and by that time another idea had been put forward and had gained ground. This was that a Royal Commission should visit all the factory districts to make enquiries and present another report. To the chagrin of the Ten Hours Bill supporters, this was agreed on.

The reception of this Commission in the towns of the North was even more thoroughly organised than the protests of the previous year. A larger programme of public meetings was carried out in which leaders put out almost superhuman efforts. Plans were concerted for the Commission to be met at every place they visited by members of the Short Time Committees bringing written protests with them. Wherever they went, the members of the Commission were to be shadowed by 'intelligent discreet and inflexible men of good characters' to find what they did, whom they visited, what they talked about and what pressures were exerted on them by other parties. Every spy was to keep a journal which was later to be forwarded to Oastler. In the evenings, in whatever town they stayed, the factory children were to be marshalled outside their hotel to sing their song and to take part in indignation meetings. Meanwhile protests were to be posted in every village and in every mill with notices calling children to the meetings after working time. The demonstrations rose to a climax on the 6th June when the Yorkshire Central Committee staged a demonstration over the whole factory area. In the days which followed, ragged and maimed children were paraded before the Commission members wherever they went, protests followed them even to the doors of their lodgings and the ubiquitous and silent scouts could not be shaken off.

> *Parliament say what they will,*
> *We will have the Ten Hour Bill!*
> *We want no Commissioners!*
> *We will have the Ten Hour Bill!*

While the commissioners were considering their findings ugly rumours began to gain ground. It was said that the Government was contemplating introducing a shift system for children which might lengthen the hours of adults, and that the proposed fine for masters disregarding the new Act was to be omitted. A last great rally was decided on.

On 1st July 1833, it is estimated that 100,000 people met on Wibsey Low Moor, contingents assembling in their villages, joining together as they had done in the York march, at agreed points, each combination of villages advancing with its band, its banners and slogans, and with horsemen leading it, to the rallying-place. Not a single item had been forgotten. Preliminary hand-outs were even passed on to the press.

The meeting lasted five hours, every leader having the chance to speak. From the point of view of organisation it was a triumph. What its results would be nobody knew, but all hoped. Surely no government could fail to respond to a petition from such a massive gathering.

Events proved them to be wrong. The commissioners produced their report suggesting that thirteen instead of eighteen should be the 'age of discretion', that under that age children should work eight hours a day for a six-day week, that between thirteen and eighteen the weekly hours should be sixty-nine and that those of adults should not be affected. As a humanitarian measure such a bill promised partial success, but politically it did not come near to satisfying the members of the Short Time

Committees. Ashley refused to be responsible for a bill mutilated in this way and a new one on the lines of the commissioners' report was drawn up by Lord Althorp, the leader of the House. Protest meetings were organised in all the industrial areas, but further efforts were in vain. To the great satisfaction of the employers the bill duly became law.

Ground had been gained. The hand of the Government had been forced, and as one reformer said, a bad bill was better than none at all. The cause was by no means lost, for Ashley found in this initial agitation his life's work. As Lord Shaftesbury he continued the task that Oastler had begun. In the story of civil protest the Ten Hours agitation has a special significance, for it showed what could be done by a united body of working-class supporters, backed by a hard core of intelligent, active middle-class enthusiasts. Such a campaign was unequalled in zeal, ingenuity, devotion and organisation by any other movement of the early nineteenth century.

15

The Political Remedy

'PETITION! PETITION! PETITION!' demanded the Radicals when government measures threatened their interests, or when reforms were denied or delayed. Merchants and manufacturers joined them in the public protest against the Corn Laws in 1815, over eighteen thousand signing in Nottingham, nearly fifty thousand in Birmingham and fifty-four thousand from Manchester. In the first three months of 1831 when the first Reform Bill was introduced there were no less than six hundred and fifty petitions from all parts of the country.

The right to petition Parliament had long been considered as one of the fundamental liberties of the constitution, and in the days of the Yorkshire Association the method had been freely used. It served first as a means of expressing the views of the numerous groups within the country and secondly it indicated to the Government the state of public opinion, without any obligation on its part to act on the recommendations of the petitioners if in its opinion they were not in the public interest. Thus radical activity, or for that matter the activity of any other political groups, was tolerated as long as it was useful, and was restrained when it became, in the Government's opinion, dangerous. The extent of that danger could, however, only be measured by reports of what went on in public meetings, by the tone of pamphlets and broadsheets, the language of speakers at processions and demonstrations, the response of the crowds, and what could be found out in secret by Government spies, all of which information was liable to be inaccurate, unreliable and in some cases deliberately fabricated.

When in the opinion of the Government popular fervour had passed the danger point, restrictions could be applied. In 1817, for instance, meetings held within a mile of Westminster Hall for the purpose of considering petitions while Parliament was in session were to be considered as unlawful assemblies. Two years later the Government, ever fearful of violence, passed the Six Acts prohibiting 'every sort of attempt by violent language either spoken or written, or by show of force calculated to produce fear, to affect any public object of an evil character'. This, coupled with the suspension of *habeas corpus,* gave the Government enormous latitude with regard to the arrest and detention of suspected persons.

European upheavals made the dread of revolution a very real thing among the ruling classes in England, but in the sense that revolution meant the introduction of a different political system, the Radicals desired it. The restrictive laws, however, meant that force was out of the question, yet how could a revolution be accomplished without it? James Mill, the liberal political philosopher, had an answer. Firstly the whole population should be united, or should appear to be united, in desiring it. Secondly, the Government should be somehow persuaded that if it did not yield to this unanimous and universal demand, it would risk the outbreak of disorders that could not be controlled.

In 1830 the conditions for this peaceful revolution were fulfilled. The Whigs, returned with a majority to the Commons, believed that the time had come to broaden the basis of Parliament in conformity with the changes that had occurred in British society, which meant to extend the franchise to include representatives from the new industrial classes. Meanwhile in the country at large there had appeared a zeal for reform which could no longer be contained.

The voice of the manufacturing and industrial classes was first raised in the provinces. At the beginning of 1830 a group of business men founded the Birmingham Political Union to exert pressure on the Government through the peaceful expression of public opinion, 'so as to bring it to act upon the legislative functions in a just, legal and effectual way'. In July 1830 it had five thousand members and in January 1831 after the Reform agitation had begun, nine thousand. By that time the idea of political unions, mainly composed of middle-class manufacturers and shopkeepers, was spreading all over the country. Here, at least, was the appearance of unanimity.

In October 1831 a National Political Union was founded under the leadership of Francis Place 'to put the wishes of the people at large in organised array, to give them, by union, so imposing an appearance, that denial of their demands should be hopeless, and direct oppression dangerous'. In other words, this was not a direct threat of action, but rather advice to the Government to yield to the unanimous desire of the people before they became desperate enough to resort to force.

The unanimity of which the political unions boasted did not, however, exist, for the working-class radicals were not content to entrust the sacred cause of universal franchise to groups of manufacturers and shopkeepers. They preferred to set up their own societies to carry on the campaign. Then, when in 1831 it became clear that the new Reform Bill would give the vote only to those who owned or leased a certain amount of property, the zeal of the workers for Reform faded. In October of that year William Lovett, later a foremost Chartist leader, attended a public meeting called by Francis Place, and, given permission to speak, put forward an amendment that the meeting demand universal suffrage, adding that the middle-class National Political Union was trying to make a tool of the working classes to gain its own ends.

From that time onwards the rift between the two classes grew wider. The working classes moved towards Chartism, while the middle classes for the most part joined in the demand for Corn Law Repeal and Free Trade. The political unions held large mass meetings, but could hardly claim that the demand for reform was universal once the terms of the proposed Bill were known. Their warnings of revolution if reform was withheld were unfounded, for though there were riots, they were in no sense a threat to the security of the country.

Violent outbreaks on the Luddite pattern still occurred. In 1830, a year of intense social tension, all the accumulated grievances of the rural labourers – tithe, rents, agricultural depression, low wages and the game laws – combined to produce a revolt. The disorder was sparked off by the introduction of the new threshing machines which were smashed up by the labourers of Kent. The rioting spread rapidly as more machines were introduced, until by the end of November the whole of south-east England was affected.

Local bands went from village to village forcing the labourers to join the army of 'Captain Swing', the mythical leader whose name was derived from the swinging-stick of the hand-flail. Farmers were forced by threats to sign contracts promising higher wages, and made to destroy their own threshing-machines. Those who gave in were for the most part well and courteously treated, but resistance was met not only by the destruction of the machines, but also by the firing of hayricks and corn-stacks. The Ministry acted speedily; the volunteers and the dragoons were brought in. Of the suspects arrested nine were hanged, 464 were transported and some 650 sent to prison.

Eight years later, in 1839, another series of riots started, this time in south-west and south Wales. These, too, expressed the deep dissatisfaction of the farmers and labourers, for much the same causes. Tithe payments played a great part in the discontent, for most of the population were nonconformist and protested against paying for the upkeep of the established Church. The impulse to riot, however, came from a quite different source, the erection of new toll-gates.

The turnpike system had done much for the English roads, but the cost had to be borne by the people who used them, mainly those who lived in the localities through which they ran. New gates meant increased tolls which in turn meant higher costs and more distress. Two of the four gates put up on the Pembroke–Carmarthen border by a local turnpike trust were destroyed at night by men with blackened faces, dressed in women's clothes and following a leader known as 'Rebecca'. The activities of 'Rebecca's Daughters' (*Let thy seed possess the gates of these which hate them—Genesis XXIV, 60*) resulted in a decision of the trustees not to erect any more gates.

In 1842, 'Rebecca' was busy again, this time extending her activities to the neighbouring counties of Cardigan, Radnor, Brecknock and Glamorgan. Operating in small groups, the rioters advanced on the gates, forcing the keepers, and sometimes the constables who were sent to defend them, to tear them down. While toll-gates were the main objectives, some rioters threatened tithe-taking parsons, land-owners and magistrates, destroying fishing preserves and burning ricks. On one occasion a crowd of some two hundred and fifty men and women, some on horseback, marched into Carmarthen and made a tour of the town, leaving a copy of their resolutions at the Guildhall. When an attempt was made to stop them they converged on the workhouse, entered it, broke up the furniture and let out the paupers. In the later stage the movement fell under the command of professional agitators and many of the farmers who had at first supported it joined the yeomanry in helping to crush it. Petitions were sent to the Queen and to Parliament, police were drafted from London and the turmoil died down. A certain amount of success had been achieved, for in time the trusts came to be better organised and later were replaced by County Boards.

These two examples of direct action have certain features in common. Like most others, they were vain efforts to cling to the old order of things, to preserve the old rural ways and handicrafts that, with the coming of capitalism and steam power, were doomed. This feature runs contrary to the spirit of most petitions, which in the main asked for reforms such as Catholic Emancipation, the Ten Hours Bill or the Reform of

Parliament. Secondly, these riots differ in one important feature from the Luddite uprisings of twenty years earlier in that they were joined by many sympathisers who were not directly concerned. Many of these were literate, some well-educated, and a large percentage nonconformist.

The Australian convict records comment on the high moral character of the men transported after the 'Captain Swing' riots. This feature alone helped to put an end to rioting as a means of expressing protest for, with the increase of literacy and better means of preserving public order, the working classes and the farmers came to realise that whatever fears they might have had for the future, it was impossible to bring back the conditions of the past. By this time the general discontent was merging into the greatest petitioning movement of all – Chartism.

A considerable part of the history of the working-class movement is concerned with protest, and most protest takes the form of some kind of political action. Cobbett and the Radicals agitated through the press for parliamentary reform. Others, such as Robert Owen, went further, embracing socialist doctrines and throwing themselves into the organisation of trade unions and co-operative societies. The middle years of the century were therefore taken up by two great movements. The first of these, the working-class movement, was mainly concerned with two aims, to continue the struggle for parliamentary representation through the People's Charter, and to develop the organisation of trade unions and co-operative societies.

The first postwar trade union movement took shape in the north of England where John Doherty, in an attempt to create a united front of all the unions then existing, founded in 1830 the National Association for the Protection of Labour. For a short time it flourished, but when Doherty transferred his headquarters to London the Lancashire section defected and the organisation fell to pieces. Within the next two years the trade union movement turned in the direction of Owenism.

Robert Owen had first approached the social evils resulting

from the factory system entirely from the point of view of the master, and had proved in his New Lanark experiment that it was possible to care for the housing, health and education of his workpeople and at the same time to make a profit. He believed that the way to make machinery serve a social purpose was to replace competition between a class of greedy industrialists by co-operation in which industry was employed for the people's good. This could only be done by the control of industry by the voluntary association of the people themselves. In other words, competition ought to be supplanted by co-operation. He enunciated this principle in his first book, *A New View of Society*.

Later, as a member of a committee set up to raise money for the relief of the poor, he proposed that instead of being squandered on poor relief, it should be used to set up settlements, small model villages in which they could work together to create wealth. As these increased in number they were to be grouped in unions or circles of tens, hundreds and ultimately thousands until the system embraced the whole of society. As a scheme for relieving poverty Owen's proposition found favour, but it was quickly seen that to cover England with a network of socialist village communities would mean the end of the capitalist system. His supporters fell away, his influence in government circles was lost, but the idea of co-operation took root among the working classes.

Owen now devoted himself to the setting up of model communities, first at Orbiston, near Glasgow, and then at New Harmony in Indiana, USA. While he was away other leaders were busy forming co-operative societies in London and other towns, and he returned to England to find himself at the head of a movement. The co-operative societies were small ventures, but Owen had a natural desire to do things on a large scale and embarked on the foundation of labour exchanges. These were centres to which members of co-operative societies could bring the things they had made, and were paid for them not in money but in labour notes based on the cost of production. These they were able to spend on other goods on sale at the exchange. For a while the labour exchanges flourished, but soon became overstocked with goods which they could not sell, and ran into financial difficulties. The last two, in London and Birmingham, had to wind up their affairs in 1834.

By this time Owen had undertaken the leadership of a national trade union movement and had formed the Grand National Consolidated Trades Union. This was to be a huge organisation to which all the unions in the country were to be affiliated and which, he believed, would be able to defeat the employers, to dominate industry and eventually to establish the co-operative society by the sheer weight of numbers. Universal suffrage would then come as a matter of course, for every working man would have his vote in the Union, and the Grand National would

> become a vital and influential member of the state, it instantly erects itself into a House of Trades, which must supply the place of the present House of Commons, and direct the commercial affairs of the country, according to the will of the trades who compose the association of Industry.

This fantastic utopian dream never came within reach of realisation. The four largest unions in the country did not join. Organisation on a limited budget was impossible and the funds were used up in useless strikes. The masters responded by presenting the 'document', forcing their employees to declare that they did not and would not belong to a union, and the Grand National was dissolved in August 1834. In that year trade unionism received another severe setback when the Tolpuddle labourers were condemned to transportation for taking an illegal oath. On the initiative of the Grand National, a London-Dorchester Committee was set up to protest against the sentence pronounced on them but failed to obtain any revision. This was the end of Owenism as a practical solution to the

231

working-class dilemma. What remained was an idea which was to bear fruit in later years.

The problem of the poor still remained. The antiquated system by which each parish took responsibility for its own paupers was totally unsuited to the new developing society. The practice of making up the wages of the labourer out of the parish poor rate in relation to the price of bread and the size of his family had served its purpose in time of war but had been taken advantage of, especially by the farmers, to pay as little as possible. In all parts of England, but especially in the south and south-east, parish poor rates were becoming an almost intolerable burden and something had to be done to ease them.

The Whig Government attacked the problem by appointing a commission on whose report the new Poor Law of 1834 was based. The two main principles were that if the able-bodied pauper wanted relief he should enter a workhouse to get it, but that, to discourage him from doing so, life in the workhouse should be made as grim as possible by the enforcement of strict regulations, low diet, hard work and rigid discipline. Radicals and Tories attacked the measures bitterly. Cobbett condemned it as 'a sort of Austrian project', and prophesied that if it were put into operation it would bring about a revolution. Designed mainly for the agricultural districts, it was put into force in the south and east during the years 1835 and 1836. It was only in and after 1837 when the attempt was made to enforce it in the industrial districts of the north of England that the storm of protest burst in its full intensity. Again Oastler and his lieutenant, Parson Bull, rose to the defence of the impotent poor.

> I tell you deliberately [wrote Oastler], if I have the misfortune to be reduced to poverty, That that man who dares to tear from me the wife whom God has joined to me, shall, if I have it in my power, receive his death at my hands! If I am ever confined in one of those hellish Poor Law Bastiles, and my wife be torn from me, because I am poor, I will, if it be

possible, burn the whole pile down to the ground. This I will do, if my case shall be thus tried, if I have the power; and every man who loves his wife, and who is unstained by crime, will if he can, do the same. . . .

The most violent speeches of all were made by the Reverend J Rayner Stephens, a Methodist minister of Ashton-under-Lyne, who, though a Tory, described himself as 'a revolutionist by fire, a revolutionist by blood, to the knife, to the death'. Strange words indeed for a Tory to speak, but natural considering the bitterness with which the reformer detested the 'cottonocracy' and the 'rule by brass'. It was lawful, he said, to think, to speak and to write against the law. And when that would not do –

> It would be law for every man to have his firelock, his cutlass, his sword, his pair of pistols, or his pike, and for every woman to have her pair of scissors, and for every child to have its paper of pins and its box of needles [*here the orator's voice was drowned in the cheers of the meeting*], and let the men with a torch in one hand and a dagger in the other, put to death any and all who attempted to sever man and wife.

The Times joined issue with the Government in declaring the measure 'the most disgraceful measure that had ever emanated from a Christian legislature'.

> The soup is made weaker, the bread blacker, the cheese harder, offal is given for meat, and the quantity of each is diminished to starving point in order that a few shillings and pence may, for appearance sake, be divided amongst the rate-payers, while many thousands of pounds are distributed to Government hangers-on who are called Commissioners.

John Fielden, the Todmorden manufacturer who had supported Oastler in the Ten Hours campaign, took up the resistance against the election of a board of guardians there and closed his factory in protest. Parson Bull toured the north of England denouncing the act and quoting harassing stories of the plight of poor people who had been mishandled by the new guardians.

These were Tories and benevolent manufacturers. The working-class leaders who had recently been campaigning for the Ten Hours Bill were able to reorganise and form Anti-Poor Law Associations whose members joined in the great mass meetings carrying banners with such inscriptions as 'The Poor have a right to Subsistence in the Land', 'Woe unto him that grindeth the Faces of the Poor', 'The more cruel Tyrants bind us, the more united they shall find us', and here and there the familiar cry, 'Universal Suffrage', and 'Vote by Ballot'.

In every phase of this working-class agitation, even at meetings of the Ten Hours Bill agitators and the Owenite trade unionists, this cry for universal suffrage raised by Wyvill and Cartwright in the previous century had been heard in the odd acclamation or seen on the occasional banner. It had never been completely lost sight of, and the greater the disappointment of the campaigners, the more the conviction gained ground that for all these evils there was still only one all-embracing remedy – the vote. Gradually the protests against the new Poor Law merged into a general demand for reform. The change of direction was guided by two men. The first was Feargus O'Connor, the ex-Member of Parliament for an Irish constituency, and the second William Lovett, cabinet-maker and founder of the London Working Men's Association. It marked the end of the ten-year partnership between Tory and Radical.

With the birth of Chartism, protest gave way to political action on a large scale. There was nothing new in the People's Charter, for its origins can be traced back two hundred years to the theories of John Lilburne the Leveller. Drawn up by William Lovett and the London Working Men's Association, with the help of Francis Place and a number of Members of Parliament, the Charter summarised the demands of the Radicals.

Throughout the whole of Chartist literature the old truth may easily be discerned. The demand was political, the grievances were economic. The test would come, indeed it had already begun to come, as to whether, when economic conditions began to improve, the working classes would lose interest in the oft-repeated demand for reform.

The methods of Chartism were not new. There was the one petition only, signed by workers in their thousands and presented to a government which in the end chose, as many others before it had done, to lay it on one side. There were the same inflammatory speeches, the same division of the movement into moral and physical force sections, the occasional clash with the military, the imprisonments and the defections. As long as the people of England were hungry, Chartism continued to exist. Once the tide had turned and the working-class standard of living had been raised above subsistence level, universal franchise came to be deemed by the majority of the working men as not worth an open clash with the forces of government. For these reasons the movement lost its original verve and ended in fiasco in 1848.

The question before Britain was simple and straightforward. By what measures was the prosperity of the country likely to be best assured? In 1815, when it was predominantly agricultural and only landowners sat in Parliament, the Government had introduced the Corn Laws for the good of the prevailing interest – that of the farmer. All this gradually changed, and after the Reform Bill of 1832 other interests came to be represented on the parliamentary benches. Britain was being given over more and more to manufacture. Industry was capturing world markets, bringing great wealth to the country, and there was as yet no foreign competitor. But industry still had round its neck the millstone of an obsolete fiscal system.

The most obnoxious duty of all in the eyes of the manufacturer was that on corn. Moreover, in spite of the Reform Bill there were more than two hundred Members of Parliament, each representing less than one thousand electors in constituencies in which the agricultural interest was predominant. There was no hope whatever of Parliament repealing the Corn Laws of its own accord. The only way to secure repeal was through a well-organised national agitation designed to go on until its aims were realised. This was the reason for the foundation of the Anti-Corn Law League.

By that time the extra-parliamentary pressure group had taken its place in political life, and much had been learned since the days of Wyvill and the Yorkshire Association. Communications were greatly improved through the coming of the railways and the penny post. The demand for repeal, which had been vociferous in the hard years immediately after the war, had fallen off somewhat after the introduction by Huskisson of the sliding scale of duties in 1828, but after 1835, stimulated by anti-corn law literature, it began to rise again.

Though groups of protestors had been set up in various places, including London, the real home of the movement was the newly-incorporated borough of Manchester where in September 1838 an anti-Corn Law Association was formed, its leading members being some of the local business men. This was followed by other associations in neighbouring towns and resulted within six months in the foundation of the Anti-Corn Law League after a conference in London in March 1839. Subscriptions were collected from firms, individuals and associations, and membership of the League Council was conferred on all who gave £50 or more towards the League funds. By 1845 there were some five hundred council members.

This figure alone shows the difference between the League and all other political associations which had preceded it. For those days it was an enormously wealthy and powerful body. In 1842 it issued an appeal for the raising of £50,000 and in 1843 of £100,000. It had all the advantages of the improvements which had taken place in business organisation. Moreover in Richard Cobden the League found one of the most outstanding leaders for zeal, intelligence and ability of the whole of the nineteenth century.

Cobden, descended from Sussex farming stock, would seem the most unlikely person ever to lead a Free Trade crusade. His education at Midhurst and his early years as a commercial traveller were most unpropitious. Before he was thirty, however, he had entered the business world with two partners as a calico printer in Lancashire and soon became active in public life, especially in the agitation which led to the incorporation of Manchester as a borough. From 1837 onwards he was a dedicated fighter for Free Trade and had the satisfaction of seeing his aims realised in his lifetime. His first signal service was the creation of the Anti-Corn Law League, his last the negotiation of a commercial treaty with France in 1860.

For the organisation of the League Cobden drew on the experience of every former extra-parliamentary group, especially that of the recent Anti-Slavery Society. The League was not a democratic body, for although every £50 subscriber was eligible to serve on the Council, only the few who lived near enough to the League's offices in Manchester were able to do so, and its regular attendance was rarely more than a dozen. Many of the others contented themselves with calling in occasionally. This concentration of power and freedom from control gave Cobden and his lieutenants considerable scope in putting their ideas into practice.

Given enthusiasm and ability, money was the next main necessity, and every means known at the time was employed to get it. Subscriptions over and above the minimum were invited, small Anti-Corn Law groups were encouraged to take collections, run appeals, rallies, tea-parties and bazaars, and help was given in organising fund-raising efforts of every description. The League employed the latest filing system in its offices with differently coloured cards for varying amounts subscribed. It employed a full-time accountant and had a special arrangement with a firm of solicitors. There was a regular business routine for sending out receipts, signing, passing and payment of accounts, and a permanent office staff was employed. Members of the Council who had experience of special branches of the work were often called in for consultation, and the sub-committees were constantly in being to deal with such matters as finance and publicity.

From the beginning the League employed lecturers to tour the country and started a nationwide propaganda campaign with leaflets, pamphlets, and material for newspapers, the object being both to instruct the public as to the benefits of repeal and to work up public opinion in its favour. In 1842 the country was divided into twelve districts, each with a full-time agent. In the following year more than three hundred workers were engaged in the publication of tracts and more than five hundred in their distribution – a packet to every parliamentary elector. More than three and a half tons went through the penny post in a week. The League in 1839 made an annual grant of £500 to the London newspaper the *Sun* in return for its support in the campaign, and helped in the foundation of the *Economist*, besides running its own periodical, *The League*.

Over all these activities was the guiding hand of Cobden. The aim – the complete abolition of all corn duties – was simple to understand. The speakers, Cobden in particular, emphasised not only the practical advantages of cheap bread, but the Christian obligation of those in power to relieve distress at home and, by encouraging trade, to help to make nations dependent one on the other and so further the cause of world peace. The same message was put out with even more force by the League's most prominent orator, John Bright. Repeal was made to seem a Christian duty.

In 1841 a conference of 645 ministers was held in Manchester, all but two nonconformists, and all Repealers. They passed a resolution that the laws were sinful because they violated the paramount law of God and restricted the bounty of providence. The arguments which influenced most of the manufacturers were much less idealistic. To them repeal meant more corn from abroad, cheaper bread, cheap labour and rising profits. These were the objects for which their subscriptions were paid.

At first the League made little progress, and in 1839 its future was very much in the balance. One of the agents wrote that with only three shillings in his pocket he was unable to buy a meal if he was to pay his fare to the office and back. Lectures and tracts turned the tide later, and in 1841 the first parliamentary seat, that of Walsall, was won by a League candidate. It was followed by other victories at Bolton, Bury, Salford, Wolverhampton and Manchester, while Cobden himself was returned for Stockport.

Events did not all move in his favour. There were dissensions inside the League itself, some members wishing to accept a compromise in the shape of a lower fixed duty, while the extreme wing advocated dangerous courses including, for instance, the refusal to pay taxes and the shutting up of factories. In 1842 the inflammatory speeches of some of the lecturers caused the League to be accused of engineering the Plug Plots and machine-breaking of that year. Patiently, Cobden steered a middle course between these factions, always avoiding an open breach and holding on to the idea of a complete repeal. He avoided getting the League mixed up with any other issues such as the Chartist demand for universal franchise and thereby fell foul of the working-class Radicals.

In 1843 the headquarters of the League were transferred to London and 143 meetings were held there in an attempt to win over the capital, while lecturers were sent into the agricultural districts of the south and east to convert the farm workers. Neither of these ventures had much success. Corn Law repeal was essentially a cause of the manufacturer, and its centre was the industrial north.

Mere demonstrations and propaganda were not enough to change the whole economic policy of the country. The remedy was not petition and agitation outside Parliament, but within Parliament itself, and an effort was made to get League members to buy freeholds to qualify as electors. By 1845, £250,000 had been invested in land. All this went on at the same time as the increasing and never-ending campaign to create the national demand for repeal. At the beginning of 1845 Cobden decided on his last significant move – to persuade one member of the ministry at least that early repeal was imperative. He chose Sir Robert Peel.

By this time the country was moving inexorably towards Free Trade. Gladstone, as Chancellor of the Exchequer, had removed many duties on raw materials and Peel himself was convinced that sooner or later they would have to be taken off corn. The wet summer of 1845 which brought the potato blight and the famine to Ireland convinced him that the time had come. At the end of 1845 everything was prepared for the last great effort. Chartism had died down for the time being, and many workers had come out in favour of repeal. Highly successful meetings were held all over the north. In some places the workers even held tea-parties to which they invited their employers, to create and preserve good feeling between masters and men. Peel, returned to power after Melbourne had failed to form a ministry, repealed the duties in June 1846 and split the Tory Party in two.

It was the most significant victory ever gained by protest. At the celebrations meeting in Manchester on 2nd July, John Bright told the assembly that henceforward the great element of power in the country would be found in the cotton and woollen districts of England.

> I don't mean that they must of themselves exert a superiority of other parts of the kingdom, like that which the rural and agricultural counties have asserted over us in time past; but I say that the vast population of those counties, with their interests, their morality, their union, that all these must exercise an immense influence upon all future legislation in this king-

dom, and that the direction of legislation must be in accordance with the prevailing sentiments of the population of those two counties.

Slowly the people, not of the manufacturing counties only, but over the whole of England, were increasing their influence over the Government, as political consciousness spread into the lower ranks of society.

16

The 'Woman Question'

EVER SINCE ADAM'S startled gaze fell on what could be done with a rib, the 'woman question' has existed, but how varied has been its expression, and how different its impact on women's lives! Yet the general belief about the claim of women to the right of citizenship in Great Britain might not unfairly be described as follows: that a tiresome woman called Mary Wollstonecraft started it towards the end of the eighteenth century, that gradually more and more tiresome women took it up, until it developed into a full-blooded political problem involving large numbers of tiresome women, who could roughly be divided into militant and non-militant supporters.[1]

The 'Woman Question' is much older than this. Listen to the schoolmaster's wife, Hannah Woolley, in *The Gentlewoman's Companion*, 1675 – the teacher of domestic arts and good manners to up-and-coming young ladies:

Vain man is apt to think we were merely intended for the world's propagation, and to keep its humane inhabitants sweet and clean, but by their leaves, had we the same literature, they would find our brains as fruitful as our bodies. Hence I am induced to believe that we are debarred from the knowledge of human learning lest our pregnant wit should rival the towering conceits of our insulting Lords and Masters. . . . I must condemn the great negligence of parents in letting the fertile ground of their daughters lie fallow, yet send the barren noddles of their sons to the University, where they stay for no other purpose than to fill their empty sconces with idle notions to make a noise in the county.

[1] *The Pilgrimage of Perseverance*, Ethel M Wood, National Council of Social Service, 1949.

Or Mary Astell, writing in 1697, her *Serious Proposal to Ladies, wherein a Method is offered for the Improvement of their Minds*:

> If from our infancy we are nursed upon ignorance and vanity; are taught to be proud and petulant, delicate and fantastic, humorous and inconstant, 'tis not strange that the effects of this conduct appears in all future actions of our lives. . . . That, therefore, women are unprofitable to most, and a plague and dishonour to some men, is not much to be regretted on account of the men, because 'tis the product of their own folly, in denying them the benefits of an ingenuous and liberal education, the most effectual means to direct them into, and secure their progress in the ways of virtue.

Or Mary Wortley Montagu, writing to her daughter in 1750:

> There is no part of the world where our sex is treated with so much contempt as in England. I do not complain of men for having engrossed the Government . . . but I think it the highest injustice to be debarred the entertainment of my closet, and that the same studies that raise the character of a man, should hurt that of a woman. We are educated in the grossest ignorance, and no art omitted to stifle our natural reason.

This, the rise of female protest, is concerned with education, and there was some justification for it. Mary Astell proposed to found a residential college for ladies where they could study in preparation for teaching others who were not wealthy enough to bring dowries to their prospective husbands.

> . . . it being supposed that prudent men will reckon the endowments they will acquire as a sufficient dowry, and that a discreet and virtuous gentlewoman will make a better wife than she whose mind is empty though her purse be full.

The proposal was nipped in the bud by Bishop Burnet, 'for fear it would be reputed a nunnery'.

Since the end of the Middle Ages England had become a man's world, and this was the substance of the female protest. The women of Hannah Woolley's day must have seen how.

with the decline of domestic and family industry, trades which had once been almost the monopoly of the womenfolk were gradually slipping away from them. The Oxford Polltax returns of 1380 show 37 spinsters, 11 shapesters (tailoresses), 9 tapsters (innkeepers), 3 sutrices (shoemakers), 3 hucksters and 5 washerwomen. The kempster (woolcomber), webster (weaver) and baxter (bakeress) have given us well-known surnames. Men and women worked indiscriminately as innkeepers, listers (dyers), walkers (fullers), even as carpenters and smiths. Brewsters monopolised the brewing industry. Nursing and midwifery were almost exclusively domestic arts. Women leeches were more numerous than men until admission to the profession was narrowed down by the establishment of associations of physicians. Long after that time parishes availed themselves of the services of wise women to cure their paupers of ailments:

July 1st 1753: Paid Mrs Wright for curing Sarah Ironmonger's Brest – 10s 6d. (Upminster, Essex)

As long as domestic industry survived there was a place for a woman at her husband's side as a business partner and, in most cases, she continued her membership of the craft gild after his death. In the city, herb wives, tripe wives, fishwives, oyster wives and numbers of other small traders clogged the streets, while women badgers, pedlars and higglers went from village to village. In the seventeenth century their days were numbered, for the general tendency of capitalism was to destroy their independence, removing the husband to a workplace and driving the wife either into routine domestic work or into a sweatshop.

Hence the resentment of the intelligent woman against men, whom she blamed for creating this state of things. Feminist writers of the nineteenth century dwelt at length on the idyllic stories of heroic Celtic women who were wont to place themselves fearlessly between contending armies, forcing them to make peace, or whom Caesar described as being present in tribal council and camp. Tacitus describes the women of the Saxons witnessing and judging men's conduct in war, of Saxon queens sitting beside their husbands and wearing the crown. Abbesses such as Hild of Whitby and Ethelburga of Barking were as prominent as any men in the religious life of the day, and Ethelflaed, the Lady of Mercia, showed military qualities at least equal to those of her brother, Edward, and her husband, Ethelred, in dealing with the Danish menace in the early tenth century.

Women were every bit as brave as men. Nicolaa de la Haye defended Lincoln Castle for John against both townsmen and barons with twenty thousand besiegers until relief came. Lady Joan Pelham held Pevensey Castle which stood firm for York in the midst of a wasted countryside while her husband, Sir John, was in the north with Henry of Lancaster. The exploits of women in the Civil War were almost legendary; the defence of Lathom House against Fairfax by the Countess of Derby, of Wardour Castle by Lady Blanche Arundel, of Corfe Castle by Lady Mary Bankes, of Nottingham by Mrs Hutchinson who organised a watch of fifty women, the escape of the Duke of York from St James's Palace in 1648 in female costume, contrived by Lady Anne Halkett, and the memorable exploit of Jane Lane after the Battle of Worcester.

The Normans, who were blamed for many social evils, were considered to have debased the status of noble women, since land being held by military tenure exalted the men at their expense. Even then, there were abbesses who held their estates by knight service, women who held manorial courts and views of frankpledge, women who inherited public offices and even knighthoods. Ela of Salisbury (b 1188) was Sheriff of Wiltshire, Anne Clifford (b 1590) Sheriff of Westmorland and Eleanor de Bohun hereditary High Constable of Gloucester. English freewomen could be members of gilds, and could have gilds of their own. Abbesses were qualified by their calling to sit in Parliament, though there is no record that any did. Women who owned pocket boroughs are known to have nominated members and women freeholders may have taken part in elections. At least there was no law barring them from doing so. On a lower level it was by no means an uncommon thing for women to be sextons, overseers of the poor, governors of parish workhouses, parish clerks and even parish constables.

As far as learning was concerned, women were in no way inferior to men. Margaret Beaufort, mother of Henry VII, was a noted woman scholar and patroness of the printer, Wynkyn de Worde. Ladies of the sixteenth century, fascinated by the new renaissance learning, greedily studied classics, divinity, philosophy, modern languages and Hebrew, while their menfolk concerned themselves with affairs of state or war. Describing the home of Sir Anthony Cooke, who had four daughters, Sir William Haddon called it a small university, a Tusculan villa, 'except only that in this Tusculum the industry of the females was in full vigour'. One daughter later became the mother of Lord Robert Cecil and a second the mother of Sir Francis Bacon. Lady Jane Grey at seventeen is described as a woman of singular learning. Mary Sidney, sister of Sir Philip and Countess of Pembroke, wrote a metrical version of the Psalms and was a patron of literary men. Wrote Nicholas Udall:

It was now no news in England to see young damsels in noble houses and in the courts of princes, instead of cards and other instruments of idle trifling, to have continually in their hands . . . some book of scripture matters and as familiarly both to read and reason thereof in Greek, Latin, French or Italian as in English.

Of the women scholars of the sixteenth century Queen Elizabeth herself was the outstanding example. Apart from the queens, very few women played important parts in history or public life. Through the ages, we hear of occasional protests, especially in London. In 1429, shocked by the conduct of

Humphrey, Duke of Gloucester in putting away his wife and taking as his mistress Eleanor Cobham, 'divers stout women of London', led by a Mistress Stokes, 'of good account and well apparelled, came openly to the Upper House and delivered letters to the Duke, to the Archbishop and other lords'. In 1641 a great crowd of women led by Ann Stagg assembled before the House demanding redress of grievances and telling Sergeant Skippon 'that it was as good to die here as at home'. The next day Pym came to the door of the House and promised to attend to their complaints. Two years later when the City of London had petitioned the Commons against the peace offers then being considered by the Lords, a women's demonstration, the very first peace procession England had ever seen, took place. The petitioners, with white ribbons in their hats, delivered their own counter-proposal in favour of peace:

> . . . that your petitioners, although of the weaker sex, do too sensibly perceive the ensuing desolation of this kingdom unless by some timely means Your Honours provide for the speedy recovery thereof. . . . May it therefore please Your Honours that some speedy course may be taken for the settlement of the true Reformed Protestant Religion for the glory of God and the renovation of trade for the benefit of the subject, they being the soul and body of the kingdom . . .

The Commons sent out a deputation of three or four members to appease them and to try to persuade them to go home, but by that time the foremost women, urged on, it was believed, by agitators in women's clothing, rushed the Commons crying 'Peace! Peace!' The disturbance went on for two hours, the soldiers and the trained bands trying in vain to move them, the demonstrators crying out to Parliament to send out the traitors, especially 'that dog, Pym', that they might tear them to pieces. At last when a band of about twelve of Waller's troopers arrived, the women tried to snatch the colours out of their hats. Swords and cudgels were used, and a young girl, having nothing to do with the riot, was shot while crossing the churchyard. The women were finally dispersed by a troop of horse who swung their canes among the remnants of the terrified crowd.

It would have been unthinkable to press for the civil rights of women before the demand had arisen for the rights of man. Hence the first claim of the women of the upper classes was for what their menfolk already had – an education to fit them for life.

The rights of the people as a whole against their rulers became a political issue in the English and American revolutions of 1688 and 1776. The civil rights of men were asserted in the Declaration of Independence but were not respected. The French declaration in August 1789 repeated the assertion and Thomas Paine, in his reply to Burke's *Reflections*, pressed it home in clear, unmistakeable terms. Reformers like Wyvill were shocked at his inflammatory language and feared it would lead to bloody revolution in England, but his book sold in hundreds of thousands. The Rights of Man were on everybody's lips, but what about the Rights of Woman? Even in France, where women had taken part in the Revolution, the new constitution of 1791 denied them the right to civil liberty.

In that year Mary Wollstonecraft published her book, *A Vindication of the Rights of Woman*, dedicating it to Talleyrand, who had been one of the chief framers of the French Constitution.

> Consider – I address you as a legislator – whether, when men contend for their freedom, and to be allowed to judge for themselves respecting their own happiness, it be not inconsistent and unjust to subjugate women, even though you firmly believe you are acting in the manner calculated to promote their happiness? What made man the exclusive judge, if woman partake with him the gift of reason?

This was a new cry. Up to this time there had been several women of rank such as the Duchess of Marlborough and Lady Masham who had taken part in backstairs politics, but the day-to-day government of the country was still in men's hands. In

1739 the Countess of Huntingdon, the Duchess of Queensberry and several other noblewomen stormed the House of Lords and interrupted the debates but this was not a serious protest.

Mary Wollstonecraft's *Vindication* was different; it was a demand for all-out democracy with women as well as men participating, but first of all, it was a call for the re-appraisal of the function of women in society, to liberate them from oppression which caused them to lead useless and often frustrated lives, by giving them opportunities 'to render private virtue a public benefit', by treating them as reasonable and responsible beings.

> From the tyranny of man, I firmly believe, the greater number of female follies proceed; and the cunning, which I allow makes at present a part of their character, I likewise have repeatedly endeavoured to prove, is produced by oppression. . . .
> Asserting the rights which women in common with men ought to contend for, I have not attempted to extenuate their faults; but to prove them to be the natural consequence of their education and station in society. If so, it is reasonable to suppose that they will change their character, and correct their vices and follies, when they are allowed to be free in a physical, moral and civil sense.

What was wanted was not only a revolution in the male attitude to women, but a change in the attitude of the women themselves, and this could only be brought about by education, preferably co-education in day schools.

> If marriage be the cement of society, mankind should all be educated after the same model, or the intercourse of the sexes will never deserve the name of fellowship, nor will women ever fulfil the peculiar duties of their sex, till they become free by being enabled to earn their own subsistence, independent of men; in the same manner, I mean, to prevent misconstruction, as one man is independent of another.

It would be commonplace to describe the ideas of Mary Wollstonecraft as being in advance of the age. They were a presage of the second revolution at a time when the first was only in the making. There is little wonder, when Britain was on the eve of a duel with revolutionary France, that they were received with anger and scorn, yet as often happens with such works the *Vindication* was reprinted again and again.

The early nineteenth century was unpropitious. For the first time, in the Reform Act of 1832, the word 'male' was inserted, specifically excluding women from the franchise, and the same word was included in the Municipal Reform Act of 1835, removing all doubt as to whether or not a woman was qualified for citizenship.

In spite of this apparent setback the first half of the nineteenth century was a period of steady though unspectacular advance. There were many causes for this. It may be that since the Napoleonic war approached nearer to totality than any previous one the need for woman's services enhanced her value to her menfolk and her estimation of herself. It is certain that there was an increase in the number of women, especially of the middle classes, who regarded their sex as more than a mere ornament. Hannah More blazed the trail, and for all her class prejudice and her narrow religious outlook her efforts on behalf of the poor won her universal renown. Elizabeth Fry was moved by pity for the women prisoners in Newgate to spend the whole of her life in the work of prison reform. Mary Carpenter started her ragged school in Bristol and became the leader of the reformatory school movement.

As the century passed on more and more women joined the reforming movements, and every one of them expressed a protest, either against some special injustice or against the exclusion of women from some branch of professional or social life. Every protest was a call to action. Florence Nightingale was the pioneer of nursing as a vocation, Octavia Hill of working-class housing; Baroness Angela Burdett-Coutts extended her philanthropic activities to embrace innumerable causes. Josephine Butler faced with great odds and personal dangers carried on a twenty-year struggle against legalised prostitution in England. An Anti-Contagious Diseases Act Association was organised and a petition presented in 1871 signed by more than 250,000 persons, but it was not until 1886 that the obnoxious acts were repealed. Louisa Twining gave publicity to scandalous conditions in many union workhouses and Margaret Macmillan originated new educational methods in schools for the very young. These were only a few of the many women who changed the face of Victorian England.

Apart from philanthropy, women were advancing on all fronts. Maria Edgeworth, George Eliot, the Brontës, Mrs Gaskell, Christina Rossetti and Elizabeth Barrett were among the foremost novelists and poets of their day. Mary Somerville made observations on the spectral analysis of solar rays and was later made a member of the Royal Astronomical Society. Harriet Martineau wrote tales and essays on political economy.

By the middle of the century women had begun their struggle for better education. A Governesses' Benevolent Institution, having begun to conduct classes, became the nucleus of Queen's College which was opened in 1848 with the encouragement of Queen Victoria. A second group of women took a house in Bedford Square, London, and there founded, in 1900, a school which eventually became Bedford College for Women. Frances Mary Buss, a former pupil of Queen's College, became head of the North London Collegiate School in 1850 and Dorothea Beale, another former pupil, became principal of the newly-opened Cheltenham Ladies' College in 1856.

At that time it was impossible for a girl to enter for the matriculation examination. In 1863 Emily Davies persuaded Cambridge University to permit a number of girls to take a special test. Eighty-three entered and did fairly well. Miss Davies' next idea was to found a college for women and in 1869 Girton College came into being. From these small beginnings, the daughters of the middle classes acquired the kind of education which could lead to professional life if they so desired. For the working classes the Education Act of 1870, though not making education compulsory or free, paved the way for the early introduction of a system of schooling for all.

One by one the barriers were broken down, largely through the efforts of the women themselves. The building of schools increased the demand for trained teachers, especially women, and led to the foundation of training colleges. The medical profession was not long in following suit, though it was only after a struggle that in 1873 Elizabeth Garrett Anderson was elected to membership of the British Medical Association, but a much longer struggle was needed before women were to enjoy the same facilities for study as men. In 1875 Constance Smith entered the postal service, and in the following decade Harriet Mason became an inspector of boarding-out homes for children. Thus, step by step, the civil service was opened to women. As other professional bodies opened their doors, the plea of Mary Wollstonecraft came to be granted in all important aspects save two. The first was the vote and the second the question of equal status.

The Reform Act of 1832 may have given the vote only to the male of the middle class but it made a significant alteration to the position of his womenfolk with regard to politics. They became increasingly useful behind the scenes in electoral campaigns, and in political movements. They played an active part in the anti-Corn Law agitation, helping in the work of distributing circulars, canvassing and obtaining signatures to petitions. While the country gentleman or the industrialist was directly active, his wife often exercised considerable influence in the drawing-room, at the tea-party and as a hostess at his dinner-table. With the appearance of new pastimes in mid-century the young lady was drawn out of her boudoir on to the croquet-lawn and the tennis-court, became a necessary adjunct to the village cricket match and might occasionally be seen riding side-saddle in the hunt.

The second and third Reform Bills of 1867 and 1884–5 considerably increased her social importance, especially in the upper reaches of the working classes. The Ballot Act of 1872 purged the parliamentary elections of the knockabout rowdyism seen at the old hustings and made it possible for women to take at least a minor part in the campaigns. The Primrose League was founded in 1883 'to spread conservative principles amongst the British democracy'. To give it the name of Lord Beacons-field's favourite flower was a happy thought. It perpetuated his memory, but there can be little doubt that the very term 'prim-rose' was a great draw to the feminine sex, whose work in party politics was already important and was destined to be more so. This does not mean that the workers in the League were in favour of women's suffrage. The majority of them would have been shocked to hear it mentioned. All the same, it was a step in that direction.

Other factors, too, brought the 'Woman Question' to the fore during this century. One was the desperate plight of Mrs Caroline Norton, deprived of her children, her property and her earnings by the husband who was separated from her. This resulted in an Infants' Custody Bill in 1839 which allowed women who had not committed adultery to keep their children under the age of seven, and to visit older children. Barbara Bodichon in 1869 published her *Brief Summary in plain Language of the most important Laws concerning Women*, putting before the public all the facts about women's disabilities and indirectly contributing towards the passing of such measures as the Infants' Custody Act of 1873, the Married Women's Property Act of 1882 and the Guardianship of Infants Act of 1886. But on many other questions such as divorce, succession, inheritance, entry into the professions and rates of pay there were many points still to be gained. The most important of these, in the opinion of a number of advanced thinkers, was the vote.

The suffragists of the early nineteenth century were men. The first was William Thompson, an Owenite socialist, the most influential man in the movement next to Owen himself.

253

In 1825 he published his *Appeal of one Half the Human Race, Women, against the Pretensions of the other Half, Men*, in which he examined from both points of view the case for women's franchise and then demolished the arguments against it. In 1832 Henry Hunt, the Orator of Peterloo fame, presented a petition from a Miss Mary Smith, asking for the vote to be given to every unmarried woman who had the necessary property qualifications. Had it been accepted it would have added very few names indeed to the electoral register, but Hunt had not the slightest hope. It was merely a sincere gesture, the speaker realising 'that it might be a subject of mirth to some gentlemen'. This was not to be wondered at, for even some of the most advanced women such as Caroline Norton and Florence Nightingale believed that politics was no fit pursuit for their sex.

The first memorable step after the protest of Mary Wollstonecraft was John Stuart Mill's book, *The Subjection of Women*, published in 1869. This was a closely-reasoned argument based on all the facts available in favour of complete emancipation. Mill argued that in ages long past, human affairs were governed by what he called the law of superior strength, unwilling subjects being overawed by powerful masters. This state of affairs was most evident in the relations between the sexes. In this respect persons did not exercise power according to their worth. The fact that most women accepted their burdens willingly did not invalidate the argument. Ancient custom was admitted to be unjust in essence as in the case of slavery, but the exercise of ancient custom had so distorted the character of women that they had come to accept, and even to enjoy, their inferior standing. It was unlikely, therefore, that women would collectively be rebellious. Thus it was the duty of society to free them of its own accord from all disabilities, so that natural forces would again be given free play in allowing the true character of woman to show itself and her hitherto suppressed capabilities to develop.

The anxiety of mankind to interfere in behalf of nature, for fear lest nature should not succeed in effecting its purpose, is an altogether unnecessary solicitude. What women by nature cannot do it is quite superfluous to forbid them doing. What they can do, but not so well as the men who are their competitors, competition suffices to exclude them from, since nobody asks for protective duties and bounties in favour of women; it is only asked that the present bounties and protective duties in favour of men should be recalled. If women have a greater natural inclination for some things than for others, there is no need of laws or social inculcation to make the majority of them do the former in preference to the latter. Whatever women's services are most wanted for, the free play of competition will hold out the strongest inducements for them to undertake, as the words imply, they are most wanted for the things for which they are most fit; by the apportionment of which to them, the collective faculties of the two sexes can be applied on the whole with the greatest sum of valuable result.

Step by step Mill demolished every argument against equality, so often put forward in his day, and ended by asserting that the admission of women to all the benefits of civilisation, the professions, public office and the franchise, would eventually result in a great liberation of power and talent, and would not fail to confer untold benefits on society.

Women's demand for the vote was a natural consequence of their entry into political life, either as campaigners for a cause or assisting their menfolk. As early as 1847 Anna Knight, a quakeress of Chelmsford and a supporter of the Anti-Corn Law movement, wrote down her beliefs on the question of franchise and circulated them in pamphlet form. In 1851 she helped to organise the Sheffield Female Political Association. Much of the inspiration behind the movement came from the United States where women, who were campaigning energetically in the cause of temperance and the abolition of slavery, also turned their attention to the franchise. In 1850 a great congress was held at Worcester, Massachusetts, to protest against their inferior status and to demand legal and political equality. This was reported with an article in the *Westminster Review* in July 1851 by Mrs Harriet Taylor, who became the wife of John Stuart Mill in the same year.

English women were not long in following the lead of their American sisters, and female suffrage became one of the main subjects of discussion in the eighteen-fifties. In 1858 the *Englishwoman's Journal* was founded to supply exact information on the status of women, their disabilities and the progress of their cause. This was followed by the foundation of suffrage societies in most of the large towns. The Manchester society was supported by a prominent local radical barrister, Dr Richard Marsden Pankhurst, whose family later became the inspiration of the campaign for female suffrage. Slowly the movement was gathering momentum. The first meetings were held in private for it was a thing unknown for women to call together and address large public assemblies. Among the first were Mrs Peter Taylor and Mrs (later Dame) Millicent Fawcett, 'two ladies, wives of Members of this House', said one Member of Parliament, 'who have disgraced themselves – I will not disgrace them further by mentioning their names'.

John Stuart Mill was the most famous of all the suffragists. In 1865 he was elected to Parliament for Westminster on a programme which included the enfranchisement of women. One of the petitions which he presented was taken to Westminster Hall by Emily Davies and Elizabeth Garrett. Mill met them at the door, but they had no petition. Afraid of the gaze of curious members, they had hidden it under the stall of an apple-woman until he arrived. When in 1867 the Second Reform Bill was brought in, Mill moved an amendment to include women among the voters and seventy-six votes were cast in favour of it. Considering the stage of the campaign, this was a great success. From that time one petition followed another, and in 1869 Mill brought the question to the fore by the publication of his *Subjection of Woman* which he had written eight years earlier.

Slowly the doors were opening. In 1869 women house-holders, denied the vote in parliamentary elections, were given the right to vote for town councils, in 1870 were made eligible to vote for and to serve on School Boards, and in 1875 on Boards of Guardians. The vote for County Councils followed in 1888 though women were not allowed to sit on Town Councils until 1899 and not on County Councils until 1907. With the passing of the Local Government Act in 1894 they were made eligible to sit on parish and district councils.

Meanwhile the struggle for the parliamentary vote went on. Public meetings, petitions, and the distribution of leaflets in the streets became commonplace, as the women, often facing hostility and ridicule, fought to persuade the nation that they were more than tea-dispensers for their politically ambitious husbands. In 1870 the *Women's Suffrage Journal* was founded and in the same year Dr Pankhurst drew up a Bill which was introduced into Parliament by Jacob Bright, brother of John, the Anti-Corn Law campaigner. It passed the second reading in the Commons by 124 votes to 91, but when it reached the committee stage, Gladstone, an avowed enemy of women's suffrage, threw the weight of his influence against it and the majority of 33 was transformed into a minority of 136 (94–220).

In 1871 the same bill was reintroduced accompanied by a memorial signed by some of the most emiment women in the country, but this also was defeated by 69 votes (220–151). The suffragists were defeated but not dismayed. They had support in Parliament and an efficient organisation in the country and, above all, a core of enthusiastic and determined leaders. In 1884 when the County Franchise Bill was brought in to extend the vote to admit labourers in rural areas, an amendment was introduced to provide that 'words importing the masculine gender should include women'. Gladstone again spoke strongly against the amendment. 'The cargo which the vessel carries,' he declared, 'is, in my opinion, as large as she can safely carry.' As a result of his opposition, 104 members who had formerly supported the women's vote, turned against them and the amendment was defeated by 271 votes to 135.

Bills and resolutions followed year after year with no apparent progress. Party leaders, hoping to draw the attention of the women from the suffrage question, encouraged them to form women's sections. Increased activity in politics could, however, only lead in the long run to one end – the heightening of the demand for the vote. The repeated rejection of this demand between 1884 and 1906 helped to bring about in Britain an upsurge of unrest such as had never been experienced since the days of the Chartists.

For some years Dr Pankhurst and his young wife, Emmeline, had hoped that the Liberal Party would include women's franchise in its programme, but the attitude of some of the Liberal leaders was against it. In 1894, therefore, they joined the newly-formed Independent Labour Party, one of the main socialist bodies in the country. In 1900 representatives from three of these, the ILP, the Fabian Society and the Social Democratic Federation, met with the object of forming a parliamentary group organised on party lines, to 'promote legislation in favour of labour and to work for the election of labour members'. The result was the formation of the Labour Representation Committee which later became the Labour Party. While the Independent Labour Party members had on the whole been in favour of women's franchise, the new body would give no commitment to support it for, if women were given the vote, it was not in the least likely that they would use it to elect Labour members.

This setback proved to the leaders of the women's movement that they had nobody to rely on but themselves. In October 1903 Mrs Pankhurst, now a widow, invited to her home a number of enthusiasts, mostly wives of Labour Party members, and they formed a society called the Women's Social and Political Union. Its main feature was that it was to be free of all party ties, it was to work for one end only, and it was to pursue the women's cause with all the vigour and ingenuity possible.

It was not long before this new body was making its presence felt. Women speakers appeared at street-corners, in open spaces, in parks, on village greens, wherever an audience, however small, could be gathered together. A band of speakers was enlisted who were on call to go to debating societies, trade union branches, meetings and clubs. Although they often had to stand up to ridicule, sneers and prolonged heckling, the movement gathered momentum as young women recruits came in.

In 1905 a decade of conservative rule seemed to be drawing to a close and a great effort was made by Mrs Pankhurst and others to get the support of members for a bill which was introduced into Parliament. To their dismay it was talked out by its opponents. A body of indignant women gathered by the statue of Richard the Lion Heart outside the Commons to condemn the action of the Government, but they were moved on by the police, to Broad Sanctuary where, after speeches, they were able to pass their resolution of protest.

Now they looked to the future. The Conservative Party seemed doomed to defeat at the coming elections, and so far the Liberal Party had shown no signs of giving way. The supporters of women's suffrage had already begun to separate themselves into two distinct schools of thought. The first, represented by members of the older National Union of Women's Suffrage Societies, believed that members should still concentrate on persuasion, and act through approaches to members, petitions and deputations, while the second, the Women's Social and Political Union, urged more extreme methods. Thus militancy, as it was called, was born. It was not, in the Chartist sense of the word, a physical force movement, but rather a campaign of harassment, political guerrilla warfare in which every woman took part, attending meetings, following Ministers and Members around, heckling, interrupting, using every means possible including disguise to keep the cause always before the eyes of the Government and the public. The new tactics were the same as those used by Oastler and Parson Bull when they dogged the steps of the commissioners with their troops of deformed factory children, but their application was more complex, more ingenious and far more varied. In 1909 two women enthusiasts had the bright idea to post themselves as human express letters to the Prime Minister in Downing Street. They arrived, led by a telegraph boy, only to be returned as 'dead letters' by Mr Asquith's butler.

In 1905 and 1906 the contrast between these two movements showed up very clearly. Before the elections, a group of Mrs Pankhurst's followers gained admission to the Free Trade Hall, Manchester, where the Liberal Party was holding a rally. When all the speakers had finished and question time came, Annie Kenney, a working-class member of the Union, rose and asked if the Liberal Government would give votes to women. When no answer was forthcoming, the visitors unfolded a great banner with the inscription WILL YOU GIVE VOTES TO WOMEN? splashed across it. No answer forthcoming, they repeated their demands. Confusion followed. First the stewards, then the police seized them and dragged them out of the hall, to face the magistrate and a prison sentence. All this was wonderful publicity, and was seized on by newspapers all over the world. It gave them, too, the slogan VOTES FOR WOMEN, the simple but compelling phrase that remained on men's lips for a decade. In the following year the *Daily Mail* made them a present of another word which has passed into history. It called them 'Suffragettes'.

The approach of the National Union of Suffrage Societies was quite different. In 1906 after Sir Henry Campbell-Bannerman had become Prime Minister, he was waited on by a deputation representing 100,000 women including 1,530 women university graduates led by Emily Davies. The Prime Minister told them that although he agreed with their point of view, his Government were divided and therefore he confined himself to giving them advice to have patience, but to go on pestering. This they continued to do, organising meetings, processions and rallies. Though they practised no violence, they were a great asset in showing the volume of support behind the movement.

In the following year a split occurred in the Women's Social and Political Union. Up to that time the normal procedure of democratic election had been in force, but Mrs Pankhurst and her daughter Christabel held that conditions had changed. The Union was at war, and democratic practices in war time lead to differences of opinion and ultimate weakness. On this point a section of the Union under Mrs Despard broke away and founded a second militant organisation, the Women's Freedom League. There was no open rivalry, and both bodies worked together for a common end.

All these organisations employed techniques of protest that had been learned during centuries of struggle. There were the mass meetings, the processions and giant petitions like those of the Chartists, the displays, parades and shadowing of ministers employed by the factory agitators, the elaborate propaganda worked out by the Anti-Corn Law Leaguers and the publication of pamphlets and journals. But the future of the movement lay primarily with the militants for, with remarkable ingenuity, they worked out variations of the physical force motif, adapting and refining them to suit their feminine capabilities. They were ready to make sacrifices equal to anything that political protest movements had before seen. Militancy meant financial loss, working without recompense and, when the time came, suffering imprisonment and physical violence amounting even to torture, with unbelievable fortitude. The years of adventure and trial began in 1906 when the speech from the throne gave no indication that the vote would be given to women. From that day the battle was on.

The militancy was systematic. Ministers and prominent Members were 'shadowed'. Their constituency meetings were

261

interrupted; when they performed ceremonies such as the opening of bazaars they were answered by cries, 'When will you give women the vote?' They were waylaid at the gates of their homes, when they were boarding trains or playing golf. Cars, houses and offices were stoned and windows broken.

The political parties replied by excluding women from their meetings. Some disguised themselves as men and joined the suffragists of the Men's Political Union in asking the oft-repeated question, frequently breaking up the meetings. The revolt was not over even when the offenders had been cast into prison. In 1909 Miss Wallace Dunlop was committed for having stencilled on a wall in the Houses of Parliament the words of the Bill of Rights dealing with the right of petition to the Government. She refused to pay the fine and went to prison for a month. She immediately wrote to the Home Secretary saying that she would eat no food as long as she was in confinement. She fasted for ninety-one hours and was then released. Thus ended the first hunger strike.

By the year 1910 the Liberal Government had clashed with the Lords on the budget, and a new election was fought. This time the Prime Minister could not afford to disregard the women's demands and declared that, should a Reform Bill be brought in, Women's Suffrage would be open to the decision of Parliament. Again the future seemed brighter, the suffragettes called off their militant campaign, the Liberals were returned with a small majority, and an all-party Conciliation Committee was appointed to work out a solution. The Bill which was eventually brought in would have given the vote to about a million women householders but, though it passed its second readings both in the sessions of 1910, and in 1911 after another general election, it got no nearer to becoming law.

The year was one of suspense. It was plain from the many postponements that the Government was unwilling to give way, yet the Commons had indicated by huge majorities the trend of Parliamentary opinion. Moreover, the year of King George V's coronation seemed a fit time for some magnanimous gesture. Throughout the jubilations the lobbying, petitioning and public meetings went on with no disturbances of the peace. At last, in November 1911, the Prime Minister, Mr Asquith, receiving a deputation led by the Labour leader, Arthur Henderson, announced that a Reform Bill would be brought in in the next session extending the vote to men only, but that the House could, if it wished, add an amendment in favour of woman suffrage. A second deputation from nine suffrage societies was received by the Prime Minister and Mr Lloyd George, but could get no further assurance. This procedure of making the women's vote dependent on a general measure did not satisfy them.

The Conciliation Bill was now a dead letter. At a protest meeting at Caxton Hall the suffragists denounced the proposed bill as 'a grave and unpardonable insult to women', firmly refused to allow the political enfranchisement of women to depend on a mere amendment to the Manhood Suffrage Bill, and demanded that the Government introduce and carry in the next session of Parliament a measure giving equal franchise to men and women.

This was the signal for a second outburst of militancy more vigorous than even the first had been. A deputation marching from Caxton Hall to Parliament Square was stopped by a line of police, and after trying to break through, more than two hundred were arrested. That night the windows of government offices, the headquarters of the Liberal Party and some shops were shattered in an orgy of stone-throwing.

'They refuse us the votes,' said Lady Constance Lytton, 'therefore we fall back on riot.' More ingenious ways of causing damage were devised. Fireworks were thrust into pillar-boxes, golf greens were cut up, some museums had to be closed for fear of damage to valuable exhibits. An orchid house at Kew was damaged, the glass covering pictures in an art gallery was shattered, empty houses were demolished, telegraph wires were cut, and the stand at Hurst Park was destroyed.

One suffragette was apprehended carrying housebreaking tools, others chained themselves to the railings in Downing Street, climbed on to roofs to get through skylights into party meetings. On Derby Day, 1913, Emily Wilding Davison threw herself down in front of the King's horse and was mortally injured. A shudder went through the country at this apparent wastage of a useful and promising life.

In these critical years the Government reacted with firmness and even brutality. Suffragettes who went on hunger strike had to submit to the terrors of forcible feeding, but there was no slackening of the campaign. In 1913 the Government sought another alternative in an act commonly known as the Cat and Mouse Act, under which an offender who was on hunger strike could be released on a ticket-of-leave system if her health was in serious danger, and re-arrested when considered physically fit to serve the rest of her sentence. To the inflexible suffragette this was a refined and prolonged torture. Mrs Pankhurst, not content with going hungry when in prison, refused even to sleep or drink. In one year she was arrested no less than twelve times. Militancy, instead of decreasing, went on with even more refinements.

At this time, though the Government was harassed by the Irish question and a wave of industrial unrest, the problem of votes for women was always to the fore. Public opinion was slowly moving in their favour, impelled by the cool reasoning of the non-militants and the sufferings of the rest. Most important, the Labour Party, which had grown in numerical strength, had at last come round to their side. In 1912 a group of Labour sympathisers, including George Lansbury and Harold Laski, attempted to bring about an alliance but failed in face of the Pankhursts' conviction that theirs, unlike socialism, was a purely women's movement. At the same time the Labour Party made women's suffrage a part of its programme, and the more moderate National Union joined in supporting it to the extent of setting up a special fund to help Labour election expenses.

The election never came. On 4th August 1914 war was declared on Germany. Immediately all sections of the women's movement laid their grievances aside with the proviso that they might take them up again once the common peril was over. It soon became clear that this would not be necessary. Women in thousands volunteered for work in every kind of war service, especially in munitions factories which were opened to them through the suspension of trade-union rules. By 1916 popular opinion was definitely in favour of women's suffrage, and in 1917 a committee reported in favour of a franchise limited by age. In March 1917, Mr Asquith brought in a Representation of the People Bill which was adopted by large majorities. After a short fight the Lords too accepted the Bill. It received royal assent in February 1918. The great fight for the rights of women to full citizenship was won in principle. The smaller skirmishes that followed after the war were but the completion of the process.

The agitation of the militant suffragettes, though violent at times, was designed as far as possible not to put private individuals in danger of life or injury. Its importance, however, lay in the ingenuity with which the fighters succeeded in making the most of their nuisance value. Sporadic attempts had been made in this direction before, but the process of harassing the Government had never been elevated into a system capable of such extension in time and elaboration in design and detail. This was a completely new pattern of civil disturbance. In its mildest form it ripened into the phenomenon of civil disobedience; in its most extreme it developed into the terrorism which the modern age knows so well. But the suffragettes were not responsible for that. They fought with one object in view and with the most effective weapons at hand.

17

War and Peace

ON 27TH FEBRUARY 1916, the first Military Service Bill, authorising the call-up of all single men in Great Britain between the ages of eighteen and forty-one, received royal assent. It was followed by a second in May, extending conscription to all married men within the same age limits. Both acts allowed for certain exemptions. One of these was that any certificate, 'in the case of exemption on conscience grounds, may take the form of an exemption from combatant service only'.

Conscientious objection is as old as the Christian faith. In the year 295 Maximilian, a conscript of Thevesta in North Africa, was sentenced to death for refusing to serve in the Roman army on the grounds that Christianity and military service were incompatible. Many ancient writers and medieval religious sects clung to the belief that it was better to let themselves be killed than to kill others. After the Reformation, Quakers, Mennonites and other groups continued the tradition. In 1679 Philip Ford, a Quaker, was fined £14 3s 4d for failing to appear in arms to do duty as a member of a London Trained band. In his defence he urged the examining officer to read the words of Tertullian:

> . . . I think we must first enquire whether warfare is proper at all for Christians. . . . Shall it be held lawful to make an occupation of the sword, when the Lord proclaims that he who uses the sword shall perish by the sword? And shall the son of peace take part in the battle when it does not become him even to sue at law? And shall he apply the chain, and the prison, and the torture, and the punishment, who is not the avenger even of his own wrongs?

The decision for or against bearing arms was, in the Christian sense, a matter for the individual conscience, and the number of men who refused was small.

The states of Europe which emerged after the break-up of the Roman Empire were constantly at war with one another. The ruling caste regarded such actions as the assault and sacking of towns as a normal activity. To the survivor who crept out of hiding to gaze on the smoking ruins of his home, such a calamity had to be suffered with resignation as one of the hazards of daily life.

Yet the question inevitably arose as to whether some way could not be found of avoiding all this suffering. The absolute refusal of a few to bear arms was no solution to the problem as a whole. Some form of collective action on the part of governments was necessary if universal peace was ever to become a reality.

William Penn experienced such action on a small scale in his relations with the American Indians as Governor of Pennsylvania, and put forwards his ideas in his *Essay towards the Present and Future Peace of Europe* (1693). In 1713 the Abbé Charles de Saint-Pierre published his *Projet de Paix Perpetuelle*. These two works with others did much to draw the attention of rulers to the possibility of peace through agreement. The first league of any kind with this avowed object was the Holy Alliance of 1815, but it came to grief partly because it had to function within the framework of power politics, and partly because, in spite of the high-sounding affirmations of its originator, the Emperor Alexander I, it was little more than a tool for the repression of liberal and revolutionary movements in Europe and for forwarding schemes of Russian expansion.

Progress was, however, made in the direction of arbitration, which was resorted to more and more as the nineteenth century progressed. Between 1820 and 1860 thirty-eight disputes were settled in that way, and the classic case was Britain's agreement in 1872 to pay £3 million compensation to the United States for damage done by the British-built cruiser *Alabama* during the

American Civil War. But on questions which a nation regarded as vital to its power and security, arbitration fell far short of being a solution.

In mid-century a third force appeared with the rise of the working-class movement. Marx and Engels, in their Communist Manifesto published in 1847, declared that once the working class had become conscious of its own power, international war would die out and be replaced by the class war. The idea was developed by the International Working Men's Association (later known as the First International) founded by Marx in 1864. The idea was to bring the proletariat of all countries together to hasten the process. Declarations were made denouncing war as a capitalist institution for which the working classes paid with their lives, but the only practical suggestion for ending it was that of the anarchist group which advocated the weapon of the international general strike. Yet when the Franco-Prussian War of 1870 broke out, national solidarity prevailed over international socialist unity. Split by anarchist-Marxist differences, the First International ended in 1876.

The Second International, founded in Paris in 1899, came no nearer to a solution, though the tension was rapidly rising between the two armed groups into which Europe was at that time divided. The idea of a general strike against war was repeatedly defeated, members confining themselves to efforts 'to bring to bear on their governments the most vigorous pressure'. Hence when war came in 1914 the socialist parties of the various countries were in no state to oppose it. Faced by the reality, the mood of most of their members changed. In Germany, in France and in Belgium the socialists, having failed to prevent war, fell back from their position and except for small minorities, pledged themselves to help in national defence. Even in Russia, where 120,000 Petrograd workers were on strike and barricades had been thrown up in the streets, the Bolsheviks could not carry the crowds with them, and the strike collapsed.

Once again the call to arms had proved more stirring than the cold appeal to international brotherhood.

A similar situation existed in Britain. The Independent Labour Party had from the beginning advocated international co-operation of the workers for peace, but this was no part of the programme of the Labour Party which was founded in 1906 and whose small parliamentary representation was based for the most part on pacts with the Liberals. Again the minority, consisting of a few members of both parties, raised their voices against the declaration of war by Britain. On Sunday the 2nd August these advocates of British neutrality addressed mass meetings all over the country. From the plinth of Nelson's column in Trafalgar Square Arthur Henderson moved a resolution protesting against any steps taken by the British Government to support Russia and declaring that Great Britain, having no direct interest in the quarrel between Austria and Serbia, should not enter the war, but should do everything possible in other ways to bring about peace.

On that day the Germans invaded Luxembourg and on the following day Sir Edward Grey, the Foreign Secretary, announced to the Commons that Britain was committed to go to the help of France should that country go to war with Germany. On 4th August King George received a telegram from King Albert of the Belgians announcing that the Germans had demanded passage through that country and he had refused to grant it. The British ultimatum to Germany followed and by midnight of that day Great Britain was at war.

From the point of view of the peace movement everything seemed to have changed overnight. Many of the rank and file, influenced by the argument that national defence now came before every other consideration, changed their point of view. The sentimental picture of 'gallant little Belgium' martyred by the German hordes made neutrality a most unpopular cause, and its advocates, especially Keir Hardie and Ramsay MacDonald, were among the most hated and ridiculed men of the day. Industrial disputes, as well as the campaign of women's suffrage, were laid aside and the Labour Party declared its support for the recruiting drive. The effort of the working-class leaders to prevent war had been no more successful in Great Britain than it had been anywhere else, but it left behind a hard core of objectors, some of them Christian pacifists, others Socialists, who refused to take any part in it.

While over the greater part of the country patriotic fervour was whipped up to a frenzy by stories of gallantry and sacrifice (ours) and hideous atrocities (theirs), the situation on some sectors of the home front was anything but stable. All through 1915 there were strikes and disorders on Clydeside where the more extreme socialist groups held sway. The production of munitions was seriously impeded and the Government had to bring in an act for compulsory arbitration of disputes and, where necessary, for the control of munition works.

Meanwhile events were moving steadily towards conscription. The war, which everybody had hoped would be over by Christmas 1914, promised to be long and hard-fought. In June 1915 a National Registration Act made it compulsory for every person between the ages of sixteen and sixty-five to register, and in October all men between the ages of eighteen and forty-one were invited to 'attest' under a scheme for deferred call-up in various categories. By December it was clear that it was not producing the required number of men, and it was followed by the first Military Service Bill in February 1916.

For this, the anti-war groups had long been preparing. In September 1914, a young Quaker student formed the Friends' Ambulance Unit and in November the first corps arrived at Dunkirk. In the same month the Society of Friends issued its Declaration on the War, affirming the principle that the waging of war was incompatible with Christianity, but at the same time approving the arrangements being made for helping the fight against distress and starvation in the stricken districts of Europe. In December the pacifist sections of the various religious denominations formed a Fellowship of Reconciliation with eight thousand members, which preached the religious basis of pacifism and which spread into many other countries, especially the United States.

The task of co-ordinating the various anti-war groups was undertaken by Fenner Brockway, editor of the *Labour Leader*, who published a request to all men of military age not prepared to take part in the war as a combatant to send up his name and address. The result was the foundation of the No-Conscription Fellowship, an organisation 'for mutual counsel and action'. Of its membership, totalling nearly ten thousand, about three-quarters came from the various socialist organisations, by far the largest number from the Independent Labour Party, and the rest were Quakers and members of other pacifist religious bodies. All refused to fight on conscientious grounds. The reasons for refusing differed widely, as did the point to which the various members pushed their objection. Some, including the Quakers, would do nothing, not even auxiliary service which involved 'becoming part of the military machine'. Others professed themselves willing to accept non-combatant work of various kinds, in hospitals, on roads and railways, even in catering for the comfort of the troops who came out of the line for rest periods. Nothing short of the common resistance against the Military Service Acts would have sufficed to keep these diverse elements together.

In May 1915, Clifford Allen (later Lord Allen of Hurtwood) approached the Quaker organisation which, together with the No-Conscription Fellowship, formed a Joint Advisory Council. The frame-work of resistance was thus complete. When National Registration was introduced, all objectors were recommended to register, but to declare that they could neither take part in military service nor help to produce materials designed to take human life.

In September the Fellowship printed twenty thousand copies of its Manifesto:

The case for and against compulsory military and munition service is being argued by many who, for reasons of age or sex, would not be subject to it. The signatories of this manifesto think it imperative to voice a protest in the name of a large body of men in this country who, though able-bodied and of military age will – in the event of coercive measures – be bound by deep conscientious conviction to decline these services, whatever the consequences of refusal. . . .

We have been brought to this standpoint in many ways. Some of us have reached it through the Christian faith in which we have been reared, and to our interpretation of which we plead the right to stand loyal. Others have found it by association with international movements; we believe in the solidarity of the human race, and we cannot betray the ties of brotherhood which bind us to one another through the nations of the world.

All of us, however we may have come to this conviction, believe in the value and sacredness of human personality, and are prepared to sacrifice as much in the cause of the world's peace as our fellows are sacrificing in the cause of the nation's war.

The Defence of the Realm Act of August 1914 had enacted penalties of up to hard labour for six months or a fine not exceeding £100 or both for anybody found guilty of spreading reports or making statements likely to prejudice the recruiting of persons to serve in any of His Majesty's forces.

Two of the members of the No-Conscription Fellowship were sentenced to six months' imprisonment. Fellowship meetings were broken up by enraged gangs of loyalists in scenes reminiscent of those raised by the Church and King mobs of 1791. Fearing disturbances, authorities refused to let their public halls, and in more than one town soldiers surrounded the meeting-places and prevented the meetings from being held. A London meeting was forcibly taken over by a rival group who ejected the anti-conscription leaders, including Ramsay MacDonald, and turned it into a recruiting meeting.

When, as 1915 drew to a close, the Derby Scheme had failed

to produce the required number of volunteers, it became certain that a conscription act would be introduced, and the main object of the moderate anti-conscriptionists became the insertion in it of some provision for recognising the all-out conscientious objection as well as that made to combatant service. This was put forward in Parliament by Quaker members, but met with no success. The Bill became law in February and was followed by the first arrests. On the 8th and 9th April the No-Conscription Fellowship held its second national convention in London. Amid threats from the noisy crowd outside to burst open the gates of the hall where they met, the delegates heard the speakers in silence, waving their papers as a sign of approval. Before the meeting ended, the names of the first objectors to be arrested were read out by Fenner Brockway and the two thousand delegates stood to listen to the pledge that all agreed to keep.

> We, representing thousands of men who cannot participate in warfare, and are subject to the terms of the Military Service Act, unite in comradeship with those of our number who are already suffering for conscience sake in prison or in the hands of the military. We appreciate the spirit of sacrifice which actuates those who are suffering on the battlefield, and in that spirit we renew our determination, whatever the penalties awaiting us, to undertake no service which for us is wrong. We are confident that in this we are advancing the cause of peace and so rendering such service to our fellow men in all nations as will contribute to the healing of the wounds inflicted by war.

In proclaiming its own gospel of peace, the Fellowship had entered on a different kind of war, the war for the respect due to the individual conscience.

The call-up of conscripts for the military service began in the first week of February 1916, and the forms were sent out in due course to all men of military age whose names were on the national register. Claims for exemption were judged by tribunals appointed from among the most prominent citizens, generally of non-military age, by the local authority. It could hardly be expected that these people, who sat for the most part because of their zeal for recruiting and furthering the war effort, would be capable of unbiased judgment, especially in matters affecting the individual conscience. From the beginning, therefore, the conscientious objector had the scales weighted against him.

In a circular of 3rd February the Local Government Board emphasised that, whatever the view of the members of tribunals, they must endeavour to interpret the Act 'in an impartial and tolerant spirit', so that conscientious objectors should feel that their cases were being fairly tried. While it was relatively easy, however, to grant or withhold exemption to a man whose employer needed him, the judging of matters of conscience was admittedly most difficult, and very few absolute exemptions were given.

One other glaring defect in the tribunal system was the lack of any sort of uniformity of treatment. While the members of some tribunals honestly attempted to exercise the tolerance recommended in the circular, others made a virtue of harassing and bullying any objector who came before them. The man who objected on religious grounds and could prove that he had held such opinions for a considerable time was much more fortunate than the socialist, for many tribunals did not consider political objections to be matters of conscience. The young, especially the inarticulate, were at a great disadvantage, for many tribunals held that a person of nineteen was not old enough to be able to make a judgment on such matters. Every tribunal was attended by a military representative who made it his business to oppose almost every claim to exemption, whether conscientious or not. The result of all this was the emergence of a number of grave scandals, many of which were ventilated by Philip Snowden in the House of Commons. That, however, was the last that was heard of most of them, for there was little sympathy for the objector from people whose sons and brothers were in the firing line.

The fact that there was no unanimity among the various groups of conscientious objectors made it possible for the Government to deal piecemeal with the problem. For those who objected to combatant service only, the War Office organised a non-combatant corps whose members would be employed in ancillary services behind the lines. More than three thousand allowed themselves to be drafted into it. The Board of Trade also brought out a scheme by which tribunals could grant exemption on condition that applicants would undertake work such as agriculture, forestry, transport, food supply, mining, teaching, work in hospitals and asylums and other public service classed as being 'of national importance'. Some five thousand accepted this, and other forms of national service. Nearly four thousand were later released from prison to work under a special Home Office Committee. They were to perform tasks of national importance and, though classified as a section of the Army Reserve, were not subject to military discipline. This left a hard core of objectors who refused either themselves to take human life or to perform such services as would release other men to take it. Some even objected to appearing before the tribunals on the grounds that no tribunal was the valid judge of matters appertaining to the individual conscience.

All appeals having been rejected, the conscientious objector received his call-up notice. If he did not report to the place appointed for his enlistment he was forthwith classed as a deserter, arrested, taken to the police station and duly brought before a magistrate. After being fined for not reporting he was handed over to a military escort and taken to the barracks. On his refusal to change into uniform he was placed in the guardroom, eventually brought before a court-martial, and sentenced to a period of hard labour, usually in an army detention camp.

Here many objectors were exposed to long periods of systematic persecution and brutality by the commanding officers, a fact which brought from the War Office in September 1916 a circular stating that a conscientious objector should be treated no differently from any other soldier who was guilty of acts of insubordination, and threatening camp commandants who disobeyed the order with the possible loss of their commands. This, however, did not stop the brutality. Some groups of objectors were shipped off to France, where, they were told, they would be shot.

By diverse means the outer world got to know what was happening and the matter was brought before Parliament. That the sentence on thirty-four men had been commuted on the field to penal servitude for ten years did not lessen the scandal and Prime Minister Asquith had to assure the House that such a thing would not happen again. More objectors were, however, sent to France in 1917 and the brutal treatment by army prison officers by no means ceased.

While all this was going on the No-Conscription Fellowship developed into a highly efficient service for the benefit of conscientious objectors and their families. Because of the fear of prosecution under the Defence of the Realm Act, much of its work had to be done in secret. Records were kept of all known objectors and their movements, representatives attended the various courts-martial, and an underground communications system kept many of the prisoners in touch with their families. In May 1916, an Army order decreed that in future conscientious objectors should be committed to the nearest civil prisons. While this did not concern those who had already been sentenced, it was welcomed as a step towards more humane treatment.

From then on, increasing numbers of men arrived to serve time at places such as Dartmoor and Wormwood Scrubs. Where there was ill-treatment, the news was smuggled out of camp and prison, and a special department communicated the details to such newspapers as would publish them, while the organisation also produced its own small closely printed weekly journal, the *Tribunal*. The Political Department supplied information to sympathetic Members of Parliament and organised deputations and lobbying. The offices in Fleet Street were repeatedly raided by the police and its meetings were broken up, but through the keeping of duplicate papers the records were kept intact. Prosecution of members only increased the publicity the Fellowship acquired.

From the beginning there was the conviction among the 'absolutists' of the No-Conscription Fellowship that the forming of non-combatant corps, and the launching of other government schemes, would split the movement, as indeed they did. The degree to which a man would express his conscientious objection depended on the strength of his convictions and whether he was prepared to face the hardships and degradation of prison life, social ostracism and an uncertain future even after the war was over. It was commonplace at the time that there were more conscientious objectors in the conscript army than outside it, but most of them were willing to face the enemy rather than the disapproval of the people at home. As ing of non-combatant corps, and the launching of other government had everything in its favour. Having arranged for alternative service, it could well afford to refuse to recognise the absolute objectors, and David Lloyd George could say of them (26th July 1916):

> With that kind of man I personally have no sympathy whatsoever. I do not think that they deserve the slightest consideration. With regard to those who object to shedding blood, it is the traditional policy of this country to respect that view, and we do not propose to depart from it; but in the other case, I shall only consider the best means of making the path of that class as hard as possible.

Thus the two main groups of conscientious objectors, the alternativists and the absolutists, were split off from one another. The former were concentrated in Home Office centres at various places in England and Scotland and including the prisons at Knutsford, Wakefield and Warwick. The population around many of the centres was often hostile and there were scenes in which working parties going out or returning to the centres were attacked by roughs and beaten up. Later, Dartmoor was cleared of convicts, and organised as a working centre accommodating fifteen hundred men, employed in such tasks as stone-breaking and the sewing of mailbags.

For the absolutists there was nothing but the prison sentence. They were at first sentenced to 112 days, then released under the same kind of cat-and-mouse procedure as had been formerly applied to the suffragettes, taken before the magistrate and sentenced to serve the next 112 days. There was remission for good conduct, but since the first month after arrest was a period of extra hardship, few tried to gain remission. Later the sentence of hard labour was extended to two years. Bad conditions and insufficient diet told on the health of the prisoners, so that before the war was over and in the influenza epidemic of 1918 more than seventy died, and some thirty lost their reason. As the last months of the war dragged out, several went on hunger strike and had to be forcibly fed. Others, including Clifford Allen, refused to work. By the beginning almost all the leaders of the No-Conscription Fellowship, except women and men over military age, were in prison. In February Bertrand Russell was sentenced to six months for attacking the rejection by the allies of the German peace offer in the previous December. Yet, in spite of reverses and the fall in circulation of the *Tribunal* from 100,000 to 6,000 and, after February 1918, to 2,000, the fight still went on.

On the 11th November 1918, the armistice was signed and shortly afterwards the demobilisation of the armed forces began. It was April 1919, however, before the first conscientious objectors were released, and August before the rest were out of prison and the Home Office centres were done away with. The British people were glad enough to forget about the war

278

though they still remembered the men who had refused to take part in it. Meanwhile, among the members of the No-Conscription Fellowship acute dissension arose. Some members wanted all-out condemnation of war as an institution, while the socialist wing saw in it a weapon in the fight against international capitalism. There could be no permanent co-operation among people expressing these two points of view, and at the end of November the No-Conscription Fellowship voted the abolition of the main organisation, leaving only three committees to maintain its work against conscription and to carry on peace propaganda. Though pacifism was cherished by the small minority as a faith, it almost ceased for more than ten years to have great public significance. In those ten years when Britain had to struggle through a series of economic and financial crises, the animosity against war-time 'conchies' was forgotten by most people.

During this period the international outlook was brighter. The League of Nations was functioning and had not yet faced its gravest tests. In Germany and France, Stresemann and Briand were speaking peace to each other while other powers approvingly looked on. Optimists were coming to believe that the last war of all had really been fought. *Journey's End, All Quiet on the Western Front, Farewell to Arms* and other works reminded them of an age that was lately past and which, if man were a sensible being, he would never allow to come again.

They had to be reminded by the more realistic thinkers that not far away an upstart named Mussolini was preaching Italian greatness and the manly virtues of war, that in the Far East Japan was thrusting her claws into China and in Germany a new militant party was rising under an ex-corporal named Adolf Hitler. The world trade depression of the early 'thirties turned hope to despair as the malcontents rose up in strength. Japan began the conquest of Manchuria in October 1932. Three months later Hitler became Chancellor of Germany.

Few English people saw these steps as the first of a sequence

279

towards a Second World War. Most believed that it could be avoided by the collective security machinery elaborated under the League of Nations. In intellectual circles, however, a more absolute form of pacifism was arising, stimulated partly by political feeling, partly by religious belief. In February 1933 the Oxford Union Society passed by 275 votes to 153 the resolution 'that this House will in no circumstances fight for its King and Country'. In October 1934 the famous radio preacher Dick Sheppard founded the Peace Pledge Union which launched an appeal for signatories of the pledge, 'We renounce war and never again directly or indirectly will we support or sanction another'. The Union was supported by some of the most influential public figures in Britain, including the Leader of the Labour Party, George Lansbury.

In a Peace Ballot conducted in 1934–5 under the auspices of the League of Nations twenty per cent of the $11\frac{1}{2}$ million voters rejected the use of arms against an aggressor. Absolutism as a doctrine was not dead. The Spanish Civil War and the rising threat from Germany sufficed to separate the religious from the political objector. Many socialists who had refused to take up arms in 1916 joined in the fight against Franco and others supported rearmament against Hitler.

For these reasons the No-Conscription League of 1939 had nothing like the success of its predecessor of 1916. The majority of the objectors in the Second World War were absolutists. Their convictions were respected for the most part by tribunals that were more tolerant, and there was no need for underground activities by the Central Board for Conscientious Objectors. In this war, in which the civilian was as much exposed to terror as the man in uniform, many an objector served heroically in fire prevention and rescue.

The reaction to the horrors of the German concentration camps and death chambers, the dropping of atom bombs on Hiroshima and Nagasaki, and the disillusionment in discovering that after four years of military co-operation the heroic

Russian ally had suddenly become the arch-enemy, knocked away most of the props from the peace movement in Britain. The efforts of a Labour Government, the first to have an absolute majority, involved the country in the complex tasks of healing the wounds of war, promoting nationalisation, and creating the welfare state, and the energies of many an erstwhile pacifist were wholly absorbed in other activities. During the four years after the war, the peace movement, led by a small body of devoted enthusiasts, kept up its activities and the publication of its organ, *Peace News*.

Late in 1946 the first revelations of the destruction wrought by the atomic bomb appeared in John Hersey's *Hiroshima*, and doubts were raised by prominent scientists as to whether Britain would be able to survive atomic assault. Professor Kathleen Lonsdale, a nuclear scientist and future Nobel prizewinner, accused the Government of using the Civil Defence organisation to create a false feeling of security. In 1948 a decision was taken by the defence sub-committee of the Cabinet to begin work on a British atom bomb, and this was tested four years later. Meanwhile the Russians had announced that Russia was a nuclear power (1949), and the first open clash had occurred between east and west in Korea (1950).

In November 1952 the Americans exploded their first hydrogen bomb and in August of the following year the Russians followed suit. Ten years after the end of the Second World War, the leaders of the great powers were talking in terms of megatons. From events such as these the British peace protest drew new life.

Assuming that no possible method of defence could save Britain if atomic weapons were used against her, it was clear in the minds of the protestors that armaments would be of little use. Their policy was therefore to urge the Government to disband armed forces, to stop the British manufacture of atomic weapons, to withdraw from the North Atlantic Treaty Organisation, and to leave no excuse for a Communist power to attack by ordering the withdrawal of all American forces from Britain. In other words, the only possible hope of saving the British from annihilation was to reduce the country to complete military impotence. In 1949 the Peace Pledge Union set up a non-violence commission to discuss all aspects of the question and to consider how a non-violent policy for Britain could be brought into effect.

In 1950 the peace movement began to gather momentum. The Government received a petition from a group of Cambridge scientists asking for a pledge not to manufacture the hydrogen bomb. Hiroshima Day was commemorated in Trafalgar Square with an attendance of three thousand. Dr Donald Soper, one of the speakers, had already created a sensation by declaring that, rather than see the world at war for a third time, he would prefer even a Communist Britain. Other new names rose to prominence including those of Canon John Collins, Dr Alex Comfort and the publisher, Victor Gollancz.

January 11th 1952, when eleven people sat down outside the War Office, marks a new stage in the history of civil protest in Britain. The procedure was aptly called Operation Gandhi, for the Mahatma had already shown what could be done in India by non-violent methods of resistance and civil disobedience, though the idea of a sit-down was not new in England. In December 1938 when Oxford Street was crowded with Christmas shoppers, a body of about two hundred unemployed men had suddenly lain down in the middle of the road, spreading over themselves posters carrying the slogan, 'Work or Bread'. What was new about the 1952 sit-down was that the police were notified beforehand of what was to happen. Inexperienced at the time in such matters, they twice dragged the silent protestors to their feet before carrying them off to Cannon Row police station. They were subsequently fined thirty shillings each at Bow Street. Though comparatively insignificant in itself, this event attracted the public attention the movement needed. In 1953 a national campaign against the hydrogen bomb was mounted with the object of getting a disarmament conference convened, but this, though supported by many pacifists and some Labour MPs, was neither clear nor specific enough for the advocates of direct action.

Between 1953 and 1957 the public was brought by the press to realise the dangers to life and health through atomic fall-out, and the number of small societies campaigning for the abolition of nuclear tests grew. Earl Russell collected support from scientists for a resolution against the bomb, and at Christmas 1954 issued his solemn broadcast warning on the possible extinction of human life on earth if an atomic war should break out. In 1957 the National Committee for the Abolition of Nuclear Weapon Tests was formed, and operated from an office in Fleet Street lent to it by the National Peace Council. In the same year a Quaker couple, Harold and Sheila Steele, volunteered to sail into the area around Christmas Island where the British hydrogen bomb was to be tested, and they were supported by another newly-formed Committee for Direct Action against Nuclear War. Though the test had already taken place before they could reach the prohibited area, the projected journey did what was needed in bringing the question of nuclear tests before the public.

By this time the movement was taking shape. The Direct Action Committee, first formed to gain financial support for the journey of the Steeles to the Pacific, now became a permanent body and began to work out the next stage in the campaign, which was to be a protest march to the atomic weapon establishment at Aldermaston. Early in 1958 massive support was added by the foundation of another movement, the Campaign for Nuclear Disarmament (CND). Its chairman and moving spirit was the Reverend John Collins, Canon of St Paul's, ex-chaplain of Bomber Command and a devoted campaigner for humanitarian causes. If evidence was needed of the immense support of Britain's brains and talent for the cause of nuclear disarmament, it was here, for among the committee and

283

sponsors were several of the most distinguished names in the country including its president, Earl Russell, J B Priestley, Kingsley Martin, Michael Foot, E M Forster, the Reverend Trevor Huddleston, Sir Julian Huxley, Sir Compton Mackenzie, historian A J P Taylor, publisher Victor Gollancz, sculptor Henry Moore, actress Flora Robson and many others. The new committee took over the funds and most of the personnel of the old National Committee for the Abolition of Nuclear Tests.

In February 1958 the Central Hall, Westminster, had to be supplemented by two overflow meetings to accommodate the thousands who came to hear speeches from the campaign leaders. The platform called for moderation, but after the meeting closed a crowd of about a thousand went to Downing Street, where the cry 'Ban the Bomb' was raised. Part of the crowd started a sit-down, and there were some arrests. The Westminster meeting was followed by others all over the country. The scene was set for the first march to Aldermaston.

There was nothing new about the idea of a march. The Blanketeers of 1817 had set off to march to London, as had the hunger marchers of the nineteen-thirties and the unemployed Welsh miners. Suffragette processions had converged on Hyde Park in 1908 attracting an enormous crowd, and the supporters of the Ten Hours Bill had marched to York on the Easter Monday morning in 1832. This was somewhat different. It was a march from London on Aldermaston, and the marchers were out for a novel purpose – to try to stop the development of nuclear weapons. It was something, too, which they had little hope of achieving in a country whose Government was committed, but though, as one leader said, there might be little chance of winning, one had to try.

Thus, four thousand demonstrators set off on the morning of Good Friday 1958 from Trafalgar Square. They were mostly serious-minded middle-class and professional people, quietly intent on registering their protest, with a good sprinkling of earnest young people, many of them students. Everybody in sympathy with the aims of the movement was welcomed; some marched all the way, others only a few miles, and when the procession reached Aldermaston its numbers had swollen to between five and ten thousand.

The 'overnighters' had slept in schools and church halls, helped by sympathisers who supplied food and bedding. There were speeches at the halting points, appositely worded marching songs and parodies on the way, while people lined the streets of towns and villages through which the protestors passed.

Great Britain, as a member of the North Atlantic Treaty Organisation, was completely involved in the joint defence system. In 1957 it was decided to install ballistic missile sites in East Anglia, and in 1960 an American tender, the *Proteus*, was stationed at Holy Loch at the mouth of the Clyde to support the submarines which carried the Polaris missile. Grave fears as to what might happen to a small, densely populated country in case of atomic assault or an accident to a bomb-carrying plane stiffened the objections to nuclear bases, and helped to make nuclear disarmament into a political question, especially in the Labour Party which for a time was split from top to bottom.

Such conditions gave the members of the Direct Action Committee an increased sense of urgency, and of the importance of their mission. In April 1958 they held vigil for a week outside the Aldermaston Research Station, and picketed it again in the summer. In the autumn they intensified their campaign by appearing at the nuclear weapon bases in East Anglia, lobbying workers and holding public meetings. On one occasion, at Swaffham, they gained entry, took possession of a cement mixer and were only evicted after having been drenched with water from hoses and dragged through the mud. Another detachment sat down a fortnight later in the way of lorries, and forty-five demonstrators had to be carried away by the police. Thirty-seven of them spent Christmas in gaol.

By this time the cleavage between the moderate and extreme sections of the movement were becoming more marked. CND was composed mainly of older people with more political experience and therefore more cautious. The activists were in general younger, more uncompromising and idealistic, and most of them were up to that time unknown. Canon Collins and the CND executive refused to accept civil disobedience as an essential part of the campaign and the two sections fell wider apart. In 1959 Direct Action concentrated on civil disobedience acts at rocket bases, the issuing of leaflets (for which they were imprisoned), and attempts to persuade workers not to take part in the production of nuclear weapons. The breach between the two sections was made absolute when Earl Russell, President of CND, was elected President of a new group calling itself the Committee of 100, which eventually took over the functions of the old Direct Action Committee. After some wrangling he resigned the presidency of CND.

From that time on, although CND organised Aldermaston marches and carried out other projects of non-violent demonstration, the more sensational and newsworthy events were those on which Direct Action prevailed. In February 1961 a body of some thousands marched quietly down Whitehall to the Ministry of Defence where Earl Russell and the Rev Michael Scott fastened to the door a demand for nuclear disarmament and the abolition of the Holy Loch base. In April another march down Whitehall took place. When surrounded by police specially drafted there to deal with it, they sat down in the road. Eight hundred and twenty-six demonstrators were carried bodily to black marias.

The demonstrations went on all summer and everybody knew what to expect with the approach of Battle of Britain Week in September. The police, hoping to forestall the troublemakers, summoned Earl and Lady Russell together with thirty-four other members of the Committee of 100 to bind themselves over to keep the peace. Those who refused were sentenced to two months' imprisonment, of which Earl Russell, on account of his age and health, served only one week.

Battle of Britain Sunday 1961 marked the very highest point of the Direct Action Campaign. The four thousand police on duty in and around Trafalgar Square arrested 1,314 people between six in the evening and one the next morning, while 351 were arrested at Holy Loch. There was no lack of newsprint and pictures following these momentous happenings. The last protest of the year was a December march on the American Wethersfield Air Base. The news had leaked out, a fence had been erected round it and three thousand police had been alerted. The homes of members organising the march were searched and they were arrested for offences under the Official Secrets Act. In spite of all this, about five thousand people demonstrated and eight hundred and fifty were arrested.

Protest can only be successful if authority is convinced that it is justified, and takes measures to remedy the evils complained of, but this does not always happen quickly. In this respect the Corn Law League and the Ten Hours campaigners had been lucky. Few of the early reformers were alive when the first steps were taken to extend the franchise, and none when complete manhood suffrage was achieved. Wilberforce died the month before the Act was passed abolishing slavery. It took a war to convince government and people that women deserved to have the vote. Other movements failed through internal dissension and lack of outside support. All these causes had something to do with the decline of the influence of the Campaign for Nuclear Disarmament.

The most obvious was the clash between CND and the Direct Action Group, and this was further widened in 1962 and 1963 by the incursion of foreign elements into the latter. In the Aldermaston march of 1962 the front and rear of the procession were brought up by Communist youth. On May Day, meetings of the Labour Party in London and Glasgow were broken up by mixed groups, but not before they had been violently denounced by Hugh Gaitskell at the latter meeting. The Cuba crisis in October did more to assist the process of disintegration. There were sit-downs, meetings and processions in which banners with 'Hands off Cuba' were prominent, but the older people, faced with the possible annihilation of themselves and families, remained at home. From that time the movement never got them back.

> CND, up until Cuba, had lived on demonstration: the mass assembly was the fibre of its being. After Cuba, demonstrations began to be left to the people who enjoyed them.[1]

The Aldermaston march of 1963 forwarded the process. The numbers were smaller and one-third, mostly young people, were newcomers. It was interrupted by members of the Committee of 100 who called themselves 'Spies for Peace', distributing a pamphlet giving particulars of fourteen seats of government, each one planned to govern its region of the country in case of atomic war. Members of the Committee offered to lead demonstrators to one of these; some six hundred followed, and squatted on the site. The march ended with disturbances in London, in the course of which many were arrested.

The newspapers made great capital out of the events, and accompanied their accounts with references to rebellious irresponsibility, juvenile carousal, dishevelled exhibitionists, the end of moderation and the growing influence of Communism, trotskyism and anarchism. The public image of 'respectable' CND was badly damaged by the 1963 march.

The Campaign for Nuclear Disarmament, though it will not figure in history as of equal importance with some others which had gone before, was in many ways of greater significance. Firstly, it was the first movement for world peace which succeeded in stirring youth to active participation. More young people debated and demonstrated than had ever done before,

[1] *The Disarmers*, Christopher Driver, Hodder & Stoughton, 1964.

and large numbers of these took up the standpoint of the absolutist conscientious objector, that not only nuclear war but all war was evil, and that Great Britain should bear witness to this belief whatever the consequences not only by scrapping nuclear weapons, but by total disarmament.

The infiltration into the movement of extreme political elements and eccentrics did not diminish its influence in forcing the people of Britain to think seriously about the two alternatives, either of possessing or rejecting the independent deterrent. Meanwhile the world situation changed rapidly with the detonation of nuclear devices by France and China, the emergence of West Germany, India and Israel as possible nuclear powers, the development by General de Gaulle of the *force de frappe* and the expulsion from French soil of NATO forces, together with the enormous technical advances of the 'sixties. The situation was infinitely more complicated than it had been when the first small groups of demonstrators had sat down outside the War Office more than a decade before. The cry 'Ban the Bomb' was no longer realistic with the ever-increasing prospect of proliferation. When the tumult and the shouting had died down, however, there still remained the hard core of absolute objectors, remnants of a once large army.

18

The Fragmentation of Protest

PROTEST CANNOT EXIST unless the individual or the group is conscious of limitation, and has the desire to put an end to it. These two factors do not necessarily go together. Many a slave must have considered his security under the protection of a benevolent master infinitely preferable to the risks of injury, unemployment or destitution run by the free labourer. The medieval serf did not normally contemplate escape from the toils of manorial thraldom, and medieval man in general was content to hand over the care of his conscience to the Church Universal. Whoever at that time tried to free himself from the fetters of tradition did so at his peril.

Yet even in those days, when the affairs of men were conducted within a rigid social system, the seeds of popular discontent were present and must have sprung to life in odd places about the country long before any evidence of disturbances appears in surviving documents.

With the sense of limitation and the desire to end it comes another factor – the possibility of success. It is reasonable for a man to consider carefully the obstacles which stand in his way and it is human to minimise them. The peasants who thronged to London in the June days of 1381 were confident that the young King had both the will and the power to put an end to their grievances, a misjudgment that was repeated more than once in centuries to come. The Levellers must have believed that they would be able to win over the army and its commanders, and the Diggers that they would be left in peace to cultivate their commons. While such as Wilkes acted in response to stimulus and achieved almost immediate results, others had to persist in the struggle for years. Badly organised and sporadic local protest such as those of the Luddites, the plug plotters, the rick burners and the 'Sons of Rebecca' arose out of desperation and had no real hope of success, doing little more than to draw attention to the plight of certain sections of society. They were incidents in the longer story of improving social conditions.

Protest is first expressed in words, but it is born and nurtured in the brain. Freedom of thought is the parent of freedom of expression, as is borne out by the so-called brainwashing techniques practised by governments in certain parts of the world. The twentieth-century 'Big Brother' has at last found limited means of penetrating the undergrowth of the human mind and taking it up by the roots. His forbears had to rely on the soldiery, the government spy and the police.

Hence the power to protest has been limited by the field of man's vision which in its turn was limited by many other factors. Twentieth-century man sees the whole world moving through the medium of the newspaper, the radio set or the television screen. The antipodes are nearer to him than the next village was to medieval man, and his mental outlook is such that what happens in Korea, in the Congo, in Vietnam or Israel is capable of causing him much more concern. Any event in any part of the world may send him marching down Whitehall, besieging a foreign embassy, lobbying Members of Parliament or, if he does none of these things, brooding in his armchair at home, ventilating his feelings in the pub or writing to his newspaper. The whole world has become his field of protest, whether his own country happens to be involved or not. Lloyd George and many more Britishers denounced the Boer War as unrighteous and protested against the conduct of British generals towards the enemy in its latter stages. In the nineteen-sixties an equal or greater volume of protest arose in Britain against the attitude of the Government in a war in which this country was taking no active part – the struggle in Vietnam.

Knowledge, especially of political matters, may be prevented by a government from reaching the community in order to prevent protest from being aroused. Gagging of the press was common in Lilburne's day. But, as the publication of facts and the expression of opinion on the facts became freer, the field of protest widened in proportion. In Britain the main incidents in the struggle for freedom of expression took place in the eighteenth century, and these were followed by far-reaching reforms in national and local government in the nineteenth and twentieth. The citizen became an elector, the education acts added to him the attribute of literacy, the growth of a popular press provided him with a vast store of information and comment enough to enable him to make up his own mind about any subject under the sun. He was thus given the power and even invited to pass judgment on everything, including his rulers and his Church, and to take part in political activity on all levels without fear.

Authority in Britain is stratified, with one layer over another in such a way that protest may exist between layers. In one part of the country, a large industrial concern applies for planning permission to erect a large plant. Individuals who object to this form an *ad hoc* association and make their protest. Local authorities decide one way or the other, as does the county, and the matter is finally settled after a public enquiry and/or the report of a commission. The parents of children in a certain district object to changes being made in the organisation of the school system and begin a fight against the local education committee, or, on another level, the Government lays down a policy which in turn calls forth protests from local authorities. A borough council decides to raise the rent of its houses and brings forth a movement of protest from the occupiers. One class of workers in a trade union objects to its treatment by the parent body and takes action, possibly in an unofficial strike. Examples of this kind of sectional and local protest are reported almost daily in the newspapers.

In the medieval state life was simple, and the social group

was small. The peasant's lot was hard and he had neither the time nor the energy to occupy his mind with many concerns other than his own or those of his immediate neighbours. Even the largest town was a close, compact society made up of a few thousand people, only a fraction of whom were freemen. Its walls stood as a barrier against the world outside and its gates were closed at curfew. Its privileged burghers were protected just as efficiently by trade laws against the 'foreigner' who came in from the countryside or from another town. Over the whole country, communities such as the manor, the parish and the gild were intricately fashioned of interdependent units, and they made up a society in which man was, in fact, his brother's keeper. Wider functions within this society, such as the building of roads and bridges, education and charity, were catered for in great measure by the Church and out of private benefactions. There were few causes which even a rich man could do much to help except by good works when living and legacies for the benefit of his fellow man after his death.

Private benevolence was extensive but its sphere was severely limited. Much of it went into clerical hands, some to the establishment of chantries and their schools. Whittington, one of the great benefactors of his day, who died in 1423, included a library, a prison, a college, a hospital and London's water supply among the good causes to which he left money. There is all the difference in the world between him and Jonas Hanway who more than three centuries later gave not merely his money but also his energy to the cause of the parish children and the young sweeps. The gifts of the benefactor had become supplemented by the efforts of the protestor.

The contrast between these two forms of philanthropy illustrates one phase of the transition from medieval to modern England. In the first, group protest arose mainly on account of the needs of the members of that particular group, a fact which holds good in the case of the peasants, the Lollards and the various religious sects. Poverty and suffering were relieved by institutions characteristic of the Middle Ages. When, however, these institutions disappeared, as the monasteries did in 1536–40, the chantries a few years later, when the flood of private benefactions dried up and at the same time an economic revolution deprived a great section of the English people of their employment and even of their homes, new developments occurred. In such works as More's *Utopia*, Crowley's *Way to Wealth*, Latimer's *Sermons* and John Hales' *Commonweal* we have the plea of one section of society on behalf of another less fortunate. This persisted throughout the seventeenth century until in the eighteenth and nineteenth a wave of humanitarian protest swept the country, laying bare injustices, evangelising, educating and finally persuading governments to bring in reforms.

The radical change not only in English life but in the Englishman's view of life is no better shown than by considering one question alone, that of crime and punishment. In modern England the punishment of an offender is strictly private. He is withdrawn from the public gaze the moment sentence is pronounced, and he serves his time within the walls of a prison so that the public forgets about him and only notices his case again when two or three lines in a newspaper column mention his release. In the Middle Ages it was different. The grimmer realities of life were much nearer the surface than they are today. Poverty, disease, hardship and famine were the constant companions of medieval man, torture and death did not dismay him, and from birth he was inured to sights in the street and public square such as modern man has only witnessed on the battlefield or in the concentration camp.

Crime being considered an offence against the community, the punishment was generally carried out in public where, as was considered just, the public could witness it. Fraudulent bakers were drawn through the streets on hurdles, then stood in the pillory with the loaves hung from their necks, and brewers who suffered the same fate were made to drink their own bad beer. Public hanging was a common enough occurrence, and after 1284 traitors were hanged, drawn and quartered. In 1400 the burning of heretics at the stake was made legal by the statute *de heretico comburendo* and went on until 1610.

In the eighteenth century the old arguments for punishment in public no longer held good, for in the swiftly growing cities there was not the same close community spirit. Slum areas had become the resorts of criminals, and the opening of turnpike roads had made highway robbery profitable and frequent. Public execution, which had once been a warning to the crowd, now became a degrading public show, and the highwayman was regarded as a popular hero. Henry Fielding, among others, was the first to protest, but the practice of hanging criminals in public went on. In 1849 Charles Dickens was among the crowd who witnessed such an execution. His forthright letters to *The Times* gave rise to a nationwide controversy, but opposition was so great that it was not until 1868 that public hanging was abolished.

For more than half a century after this, public opinion was satisfied with things as they were, and the only changes in the law were the abolition of the death penalty for persons under sixteen (Children's Act, 1908) and the Infanticide Act of 1922 which reduced the crime for mothers who killed their children, within a certain time of birth, from murder to manslaughter.

The protest against the larger issue of capital punishment had been kept up by small groups all through this period but with no success. Hopes rose, however, in the 'twenties with the formation of the Howard League for Penal Reform (1921) and the National Council for the Abolition of the Death Penalty (1925), which was a body set up to co-ordinate the work of the various abolitionist groups. The progress of the movement, which resembled in the nature of its activities most other propagandist bodies, need not be described in detail. Though it had many supporters in Parliament, was encouraged by the advent of Labour governments, and after the war its chief spokesman, Sydney Silverman, proposed an amendment to the Criminal Justice Bill of 1947 to suspend the death penalty for an experimental period of five years, this was heavily defeated in the Lords.

From that time the agitation against capital punishment mounted. A series of controversial cases, all involving the death penalty, increased the sense of urgency. In 1955 the cause was taken up by Victor Gollancz who, with Canon Collins and the writer Arthur Koestler, mounted a national campaign. Since the non-abolitionist side also had its propagandists, the movement now passed into the stage of debate and controversy. Voting statistics showed that in Parliament the main opponents of capital punishment were on the Labour benches, while its supporters were mainly Conservatives and members of the House of Lords.

In the work of twentieth-century organisations, protest, though still the main element, was supplemented by many other activities. The following account of the work of the Howard League in 1958 shows, for instance, how these had developed since the time of the Anti-Corn Law movement.

> The activities of the League include the education of public opinion by close contact with newspapers, radio and television; the provision of public lectures, summer schools and conferences; the publication of an annual Journal and occasional pamphlets; the provision of speakers to other organisations; and the supply of information to a large number of enquirers, many of them from overseas. Parliamentary work consists of the briefing of Members of both Houses of Parliament, and the promotion of Bills. Consultations with, and recommendations to, the Home Office and the Prison Commission, and the presentation of evidence to Departmental Committees and Royal Commissions, are other major activities.
>
> All this work is maintained by the subscriptions of people who feel that as citizens they have a responsibility for the rational treatment of crime and criminals.

In England, and indeed in all parts of the world where a person is allowed to speak his mind freely, societies of all kinds have proliferated, and in all of these protest, or the power to protest, has its place. Some, such as industrial, distributive and financial groups, organisations of employers, employees, property owners, taxpayers, ex-service men, pensioners and minority ethnic groups exist to watch over the interests of their own members. Others, known as promotional groups, are made up of people having similar attitudes towards a particular question or questions. Of these the Howard League is an example. Their aims are to promote their respective causes by the methods available under modern conditions. One needs only to mention any human activity or cause – education, religion, psychical research, cycling, physical culture, peace, family planning, abortion, clean air, road safety, antiquities, animal welfare, the blind and physically handicapped, among hundreds of others – to perceive how every one of these is in a position to protest if its interests are threatened. In some groups such as those for animal welfare and anti-vivisection, protest plays a greater part than in others. In groups where the stress is on such matters as art, science and education generally, it does not figure so prominently.

In considering the activities of groups, it is difficult to draw a rigid distinction between protest and dispute. A strike, in so far as it involves direct action by a group or groups of employees to obtain or to resist changes in their conditions of employment, has in it the elements of protest, though it is normally considered a dispute.

In 1926 a situation of this kind arose which attained national importance. Since the end of the First World War, the industrial struggle in Britain had been largely concerned with the working conditions of the coalminers. In 1921 a strike had been defeated by the Government's emergency measures, and in 1925 the mineowners gave notice of the termination of a national wages agreement that had been made in the previous year. The cause of the miners was fought by the Trades Union

Congress, and Prime Minister Baldwin eventually reached a temporary solution by the granting of a government subsidy. In May 1926 when the term for which it was granted was due to expire, the mineowners demanded wage cuts which were rejected by the mineworkers and the TUC. The result was the imposition of the fiercest pressure tactics any government had ever had to face, when the TUC decided on 'co-ordinated action' to support the miners. Such co-ordinated action, in which transport, steel, building, gas, electricity and printing operatives joined, matured on 3rd May as the General Strike, and for nine days the industrial life of Britain was paralysed. What had begun with sectional protest ended in industrial civil war.

Between the fourteenth and the twentieth centuries Britain was transformed from an agricultural to an industrial country and, just as our account begins with the agricultural unrest culminating in the Peasants' Revolt, it is fitting that it should end with the most impressive protest of the present century – the Hunger Marches of the 'thirties.

In 1930 Great Britain, already unfit to face an economic crisis, was caught in the backwash of the great world trade depression, from which it never fully recovered before the outbreak of war. In the winter of 1932–3 unemployment rose to the unprecedented figure of three millions and, though it slowly declined in the following years, large pockets of distress and poverty existed, especially in the shipbuilding areas of the north-east and the mining districts of South Wales.

Discontent was first aroused by the drastic pay cuts made in the great economy drive of 1931. Postal workers, teachers and other government employees marched through the streets of London with bands and banners. In protest against reductions of up to twenty-five per cent in their pay, twelve thousand sailors of the British Atlantic Fleet at Invergordon refused to muster for sailing. There was no disorder, and the normal manning of the ships was kept up. The men won their point when the Government announced that no reductions would be more than ten per cent. There were no courts-martial and only thirty-six men were dismissed the service with no charges brought against them.

Even ten per cent, however, was more than an unemployed man, already living on the verge of starvation, could bear without reacting. The reduction in unemployment benefit produced the most extraordinary organisation Britain had so far seen. This was the National Unemployed Workers' Movement, founded by a young communist named Wal Hannington. In October 1931, fifty thousand unemployed marched through Glasgow. There were demonstrations in London and repeated brushes with the police in Whitehall. The banning of demonstrations outside labour exchanges by Lord Trenchard, Chief Commissioner of the Metropolitan Police, was considered an attack on free speech and the right of public assembly reminiscent of Castlereagh's Six Acts. With a bare minimum of funds and few assets, save the energy of the unemployed leaders, the agitation was kept up.

In May 1932 the NUWM held a two-day conference in London at which a great campaign was launched to get a million signatures for a monster petition to Whitehall in favour of the abolition of the Means Test, the restoration of the ten per cent cut in unemployment benefit and the cuts in the social services. This coincided with the preparations for the first great Hunger March.

The pattern had been laid down by the Ten Hours Marchers a century earlier when they had assembled in their contingents for the march on York but, compared with Oastler's achievement, this was a demonstration of gigantic proportions, and much more difficult to plan and organise. Routes, meeting points and timing had all to be worked out with precision, reception by special committees in the towns through which the marchers were to pass, and demonstrations along the route had to be arranged. Apart from what would be given to them, the marchers would have no means of subsistence, and the goodwill of thousands of people all along the proposed routes was necessary to provide them with food and sleeping quarters. Above all, previous medical examination was necessary to make sure that every man of the two thousand five hundred in the proposed expedition should be physically fit. In communities of deprived and ill-nourished people this was no easy task and many an eager would-be marcher had to be sent ruefully home.

From the point of view of organisation the march was a tremendous success, and on Saturday, 27th October 1932 an estimated 100,000 workers flocked to Hyde Park to greet the marchers. On the Sunday a second great demonstration was held in Trafalgar Square. On both occasions there were sundry clashes with the police. On the following Tuesday the great petition with its million signatures was being borne towards Westminster when the police seized it at Charing Cross. The crowd objected, the police charged, and this led to a three-hour battle which overflowed in minor skirmishes into the Strand, the Embankment and even as far away as the Haymarket and Piccadilly. Heads were broken, arrests were made and the marchers did not succeed in presenting their petition. They were not therefore granted the privileges that their forerunners the Chartists had had in 1848.

For many years the leaders of the NUWM carried on a well-organised campaign in which the main feature was the march. In 1933, amid a series of local demonstrations, two county hunger marches took place in Scotland on Edinburgh, and in Lancashire on Preston. The introduction of a new Unemployment Bill which would provide for the establishment of a National Assistance Board was the occasion of a second great Hunger March on London and a request that the marchers' spokesmen should be heard at the bar of the House. Among others, Mr Attlee, then Leader of the Labour Party, spoke up for them:

The marchers are fair representatives of the great masses of unemployed. The injustice from which these men and women are suffering is very widely known in all parts of the House, and the feeling in the country is now tremendous. There is an ever-increasing volume of opinion that the unemployment problem should be grappled with. There is no reason why these men should be refused a hearing by the Cabinet.

The rejection of the petition brought forth an outburst of sympathy from all quarters, and members of the Government had to face hostility almost everywhere they went. All through 1934 and 1935 the marches and demonstrations continued, and thousands flocked to the great protest meetings. In the latter year the National Union succeeded in getting some slight relaxation in the severity of the cuts, and conditions were quieter as the time for a General Election approached.

When the revised scales of unemployed pay due to come into force in November 1936 were published by the Government in July, they showed very slight advances on the former ones, the maximum increases being only two shillings a week, no change in pay for married couples, single male householders, young men of eighteen to twenty-one or in allowances for dependent children. The NUWM immediately resolved on another national Hunger March to London. This almost coincided with a resolution of the Town Council of Jarrow to organise a march of two hundred men to appeal to the Government to re-open the shipyards there.

In 1935 Jarrow had elected a Labour member, Miss Ellen Wilkinson, a lifelong fighter for the cause of the depressed worker. Though she consulted Hannington, an expert in the organisation of marches, her chosen band of 'Jarrow Crusaders' was composed of men of many political convictions. The Conservative marchers made it their business to call at the Conservative headquarters at every halt to put forward the case of their stricken community.

The 1936 Hunger March, whose members arrived in Lon-

301

don after the Jarrow Crusaders had left for home, was an altogether more ambitious venture, and was joined by hundreds of trade union and co-operative branches. Fearing that disorders would break out if the marchers entered the metropolis, the Prime Minister spoke over the radio strongly advising them to return home, but his words only had the effect of stiffening their resolution to go on. They reached London on the 8th November when a crowd estimated at some 250,000 assembled to receive them in Hyde Park. The demonstration, at which leading Labour Party members spoke, was one of the most orderly ever staged there. On the following day the spokesmen of the Union met some two hundred Members of Parliament at the House of Commons and a deputation was appointed to wait on the Minister of Labour. This time they were successful in obtaining a promise of concessions.

Though in 1937 the unemployment figures went down, the distress in many areas still continued. The rises in the cost of living brought a demand for larger allowances, and especially for increased amounts for extra expenses in winter. In the last year before the outbreak of war, many groups of unemployed workers, weary of peaceful demonstrations, adopted tactics reminiscent of the old suffragette days. They prostrated themselves in front of the Oxford Street traffic, they invaded the Grill Room of the Ritz and sat down at tables all laid ready for the evening guests and startled the waiters by proffering two-pence each for tea. Another group hung a twenty-foot banner from the top of Wren's Monument inscribed 'For a Happy New Year the Unemployed Must not Starve', while another held a mock funeral following a black coffin on which were the words, 'He did not get Winter Relief'. Surprising the police, they got the coffin to the very door of Number 10 Downing Street before the driver was arrested and the van with the coffin driven away.

No quantity of medical evidence, no profusion of commission reports, statistics on income, diet surveys, cost of living figures, no amount of argument on one side or the other could alter the fact that roughly half the population of Britain were living below the level necessary to maintain proper health. Sir John Boyd Orr, the expert on nutrition, affirmed it in his report *Food, Health and Income* in 1935 and declared it again and again in the following years.

> The majority of well-to-do people do not realise what a large proportion of the population falls below the poverty line, nor what a low standard the poverty line represents. Unless we have a clear idea of what the present standard of living is and of what it might be if we utilised the resources we have, we cannot appreciate the importance of the problems of health and agriculture. . . .
>
> There is no longer any doubt about the effect of bad feeding due to poverty on health. . . . Our own health statistics show that the incidence of many diseases, such as rickets, tuberculosis and bronchitis, is from two to three times as high among the poor as among the well-to-do. Probably the best indication of the health and vigour of the community is the ability of women to rear children. Infant mortality among the well-to-do is just over 30 per 1,000; among the working class it is over 70; among the unemployed it is over 100. There is reason to believe that if the poorer families were supplied with sufficient of all the necessities of life, their infant mortality rate would be reduced to about the level of the rate amongst the well-to-do. There are thus many people suffering from ill-health who need not suffer from ill-health and many children die who need not die. (1939.)

There was little need of statistics. The threadbare clothing and blank grey faces seen in the depressed areas were proof enough. What the country needed was full employment. It came suddenly, thanks to the impulse provided by Hitler and Mussolini late in 1939.

Public protest may alter the course of governments, but man is an individual, and what affects him most is often the private, insignificant and often chance incident neither intended nor taken at the time as an act of protest. Hardly anybody who lived through the years of dearth could fail to have been touched by one or other of these.

Consider: on a winter Sunday afternoon you sit in a deep armchair before a blazing coal fire, the occasional table laid for tea and the smell of toasting muffins floating out of the kitchen. It is falling dark outside and the sleet drives in from the north-west. As you rise to draw the curtains you hear a faint singing voice in the distance, which comes nearer, and presently a man's figure appears in the street. He is tall, greying, wears a threadbare undersize raincoat and walks slowly along the middle of the street, cap in hand, turning to right and left. The reedy voice grows louder and then tails off to the end of a popular chorus.

> ... *Might have been a big name,*
> *But there are millions just the same*
> *Who are dreaming of what they might have been.*

Pity? Conscience? Christian charity? You forget to draw the curtains and thrust your hand into your pocket, hurrying out to catch him. Eyes averted, you thrust the coin into his cold, lean hand.

Before he can thank you, you are away again towards your still open door and the warmth of your big coal fire.

That is, unless the cold, lean hand happens to be your own.

Authorities and Bibliography

Chapters 1–4

MEDIEVAL ENGLAND

Apart from the works in single volumes (Feiling, Trevelyan etc.) on general and social history, the following may be found useful for establishing the atmosphere of the period.

R W Southern, *The Making of the Middle Ages*, Hutchinson, 1953.
J Huizinga, *The Waning of the Middle Ages*, Edward Arnold, 1924.
G G Coulton, *The Medieval Scene* (and other works), Cambridge University Press, paperback edition, 1961.
Frederick Harrison, *Medieval Man*, Murray, 1947.
Marion Gibbs, *Feudal Order*, Cobbett Press, 1949.

Articles about peasant conditions and disturbances in medieval England may be found in:

Carus Wilson (ed), *Essays in Economic History*, Edward Arnold, 1962:
  by R H Hilton – 'Peasant Movements in England before 1381'
  by E A Kosminsky – 'Services and Money Rents in the Thirteenth Century'
  by Nora Ritchie – 'Labour Conditions in Essex in the Reign of Richard II'.

The complaints of the peasants quoted in this book may be found in:

G W Owst, *Literature and the Pulpit in Medieval England*, Cambridge University Press, 1933.
Nevill Coghill (ed), *Visions from Piers Plowman*, taken from the poem of William Langland and translated into modern English, Phoenix, 1949.
J H Dixon (ed), *Ancient Poems of the Peasantry of England*, Percy Society, no 62, 1846.
Thomas Wright, *The Political Songs of England*, Camden Society, 1839.

The Rising of Jack Cade (1450) is dealt with in:

G Kriehn, *The English Rising of 1450*, Strasbourg, 1892.

Economic problems:

R H Tawney, *The Agrarian Problem in the Sixteenth Century,* Longmans, 1912.

R H Tawney, *Religion and the Rise of Capitalism,* John Murray, 1922.

R H Tawney and E Power, *Tudor Economic Documents, Volume III,* Longmans, 1924.

Hugh Latimer, *Sermons before Edward VI:* 'The Voyce of the Last Trumpet', 1550, 'Of Pleasure and Payne', 1551. English Reprints ed E Arber, 1869.

Robert Crowley, *The Way to Wealth.* (Select Works, ed J M Cowper, E E T S, 1872).

Thomas Becon, *The Jewel of Joy,* 1553.

General:

J O W Haweis, *Sketches of the Reformation,* 1844 (works of minor preachers).

C M Gray, *Hugh Latimer and the Sixteenth Century,* Cambridge, Mass, 1950.

John Hales, *The Commonweal of this Realm of England,* 1549.

The Pilgrimage of Grace:

Gasquet, *Henry VIII and the English Monasteries,* G Bell, 1920.

Ket's Rebellion:

F W Russell, *Ket's Rebellion in Norfolk,* 1859.

Joseph Clayton, *Robert Ket and the Norfolk Rising,* Secker & Warburg, 1912.

Elizabethan England:

A L Rowse, *The England of Elizabeth,* Macmillan, 1950.

J Dover Wilson, *Life in Shakespeare's England,* Cambridge University Press, 1911 gives accounts from temporary writers on every phase of English life. Protests against manners and customs, innovations, accounts of vagabonds, etc.

The Essex Recusant and other local history periodicals supply many accounts of conduct towards the Catholic minority.

Simonds d'Ewes – journal of all the Parliaments during the reign of Queen Elizabeth, 1682, gives notes of Parliamentary debates in which Wentworth took part.

Historical Review, 1924 – article by J E Neale on Peter Wentworth.

Chapters 8–10

THE SEVENTEENTH CENTURY

G M Trevelyan, *England under the Stuarts,* Methuen, 1904 etc.

G P Gooch, *English Democratic ideas in the Seventeenth Century,* Cambridge University Press, 2nd ed, 1927.

Alan French, *Charles I and the Puritan Upheaval,* Allen and Unwin, 1955.

C H Firth, *Oliver Cromwell and the Rule of Parliament in England,* Putnam, 3rd ed, 1924.

C Brinton, *The Anatomy of Revolution,* Cape, revised edition, 1953. A comparative study of the three revolutions—English, French and Russian. Very valuable.

Christopher Hill, *Puritanism and Revolution,* Secker and Warburg, 1958.

Margaret James, *Social Problems and Policy During the Puritan Revolution, 1640–1660,* Routledge, 1930.

The Levellers:

T C Pease, *The Leveller Movement,* American Historical Association, 1916.

H N Brailsford, *The Levellers and the English Revolution,* Cassell, 1961.

Pauline Gregg, *Freeborn John,* Harrap, 1961.

M A Gibb, *John Lilburne the Leveller,* Lindsay Drummond, 1947.

W Haller and G Davies, *The Leveller Tracts, 1647–53.*

D M Wolfe, *Leveller Manifestoes of the Puritan Revolution,* Nelson (New York), 1944.

The Diggers:

E Bernstein, *Cromwell and Communism, Socialism and Democracy in the Great English Revolution,* F Cass, translated H J Stenning, 1930.

L Berens, *The Digger Movement as Revealed in the Writings of Gerrard Winstanley,* Simpkin Marshall, 1906.

G H Sabine (ed), *The Works of Gerrard Winstanley,* Cornell University Press, 1941.

L Hamilton, *Gerrard Winstanley: Selections from his Works,* Cresset, 1944.

Fifth Monarchy:

P G Rogers, *The Fifth Monarchy Men*, Oxford, 1966.

Restoration to 1714:

Max Beloff, *Public Order and Popular Disturbances, 1660–1714*, Oxford, 1938.

G R Cragg, *Puritanism in the Period of the Great Persecution, 1660–1688*, Cambridge, 1957.

John Moore, *The Crying Sin of England in Not Caring For the Poor*, 1653.

Arnold Lloyd, *Quaker Social History, 1669–1738*, Longmans Green, 1950.

Chapters 11–12

THE EIGHTEENTH CENTURY

George Rudé, *The Crowd in History*, Wiley, New York, 1964. A very valuable account of the features of crowd action covering the movements of the eighteenth and early nineteenth centuries in England. Includes eighteenth-century agricultural disturbances, Church and King, Luddism Rebecca riots, etc.

L Namier, *England in the Age of the American Revolution*, Macmillan, 1961.

George Rudé, *Wilkes and Liberty: A social study*, Clarendon, 1962.

R Postgate, *That Devil Wilkes*, Dennis Dobson, 1930.

O A Sherrard, *Life of John Wilkes*, Allen & Unwin, 1930.

S MacCoby, *English Radicalism, 1762–1785*, Allen & Unwin, 1955.

Christopher Hibbert , *King Mob*, Longmans, 1958. An account of the Lord George Gordon Riots.

Lessons in Organisation:

H Butterfield, *George III, Lord North and the People, 1779–1780*, Bell, 1949.

D Read, *The English Provinces*, Edward Arnold, 1964. A valuable account of the influence of the provinces on political and social life up to the present day.

E C Black, *The Association:* British Extra-Parliamentary associations, 1769–93, Harvard University Press, 1963.

Ian R Christie, *Wilkes, Wyvill and Reform*, Macmillan, 1962.

A Cobban, *Burke and the Revolt Against the Eighteenth Century*, Allen & Unwin, 1929.

Chapter 13

REVOLUTION AND REPRESSION

P A Brown, *The French Revolution in English History*, Allen & Unwin, 1918, etc.

Thomas Paine, *The Rights of Man*, 1791 and 1792.

M E Woodward, *Thomas Paine, America's Godfather*, Secker & Warburg, 1946.

John dos Passos, *The Living Thoughts of Tom Paine*, Cassell, 1940.

S MacCoby, *English Radicalism, 1786–1832*, Allen & Unwin, 1955.

J Royston Pike, *Human Documents of the Industrial Revolution*, Allen & Unwin, 1966.

L G Johnson, *The Social Evolution of Industrial Britain*, Liverpool University Press, 1959.

E Halévy, *History of the English People in the Nineteenth Century*, Benn, 1923.

G D H Cole and A W Filson, *British Working-class Movements*, select documents, Macmillan, 1965 edition.

R J White, *Life in Regency England*, Batsford, 1963.

F O Darvall, *Popular Disturbances and Public Order in Regency England*, Oxford University Press, 1934.

R J White, *Waterloo to Peterloo*, Heinemann, 1957.

John Stanhope, *The Cato Street Conspiracy*, Cape, 1962.

D Read, *Peterloo*, Manchester University Press, 1958.

Olive D Rudkin, *Thomas Spence and his Connections*, Allen & Unwin, 1927.

G D H Cole, *William Cobbett*, Collins, 1924.

M L Pearl, *William Cobbett*, Oxford University Press, 1953.

Dona Torr, *History in the Making* – Cobbett to the Chartists documents, 1815–48 (ed) Max Morris, Lawrence & Wishart, 1948.

R F Wearmouth, *Some Working-class Movements of the Nineteenth Century*, Epworth Press, 1948.

Chapter 14

THE NATIONAL CONSCIENCE

For nonconformity and humanitarianism:

R G Cowherd, *The Politics of English Dissent*. The religious aspects of the liberal and humanitarian movements from 1815 to 1848, Epworth, 1950.

K S Inglis, *Churches and the Working Classes in Victorian England*, Routledge, 1963.

For the Poor Laws:
Mary Hopkirk, *Nobody Wanted Sam*, John Murray, 1949.

For the work of Select Committees of Parliament:
S Gordon and T B Cocks, *A People's Conscience*, Constable, 1952.

For the anti-slavery movement:
Sir R Copeland, *The British Anti-Slavery Movement*, Cassell, 1964.
Oliver Warner, *William Wilberforce*, Batsford, 1962.

For the history of the Ten Hours Bill:
F D Hayek (ed), *Capitalism and the Historians, Part II*, Routledge, 1964:
  by T S Ashton – 'The Standard of Life of the Workers in England, 1790–1830',
  by W H Hutt – 'The Factory System of the Early Nineteenth Century'.
C Driver, *Tory Radical: The Life of Richard Oastler*, Oxford, 1946.
J C Gill, *The Ten Hour Parson. Christian Social Action in the Eighteen-Thirties*, Epworth, 1959.
'The Labour of Children in Factories', report of a Parliamentary Committee, 1832.
The Oastler Papers, London University, 1830–33.
G F A Best, *Shaftesbury*, Batsford, 1964.

Chapter 15

THE POLITICAL REMEDY

J L and B Hammond, *The Bleak Age*, Pelican, 1947
Dona Torr, *History in the Making*, Labour's Formative Years, ed B Jeffreys, Lawrence & Wishart, 1948.
G D H Cole, *William Cobbett*, Collins, 1924.
Wiliam Cobbett, *Autobiography*, Faber, 1947.

Owenism:
G D H Cole, *Life of Robert Owen*, Macmillan, Revised Ed. 1930.
A L Morton, *The Life and Ideas of Robert Owen*, Lawrence & Wishart, 1962.
M J Cole, *Owen of New Lanark, 1771–1858*, Batchworth, 1953.
Robert Owen, *A New View of Society*, Dent, 1927.

The Poor Law:

S E Finer, *The Life and Times of Edwin Chadwick*, Methuen, 1952.

Political methods:

Joseph Hamburger, *James Mill and the Art of Revolution*, Yale University Press, 1963.

Social conditions in the towns:

G Mayer, *Friedrich Engels: A biography*, Chapman & Hall, 1936.

Chartism:

J L and M Hammond, *The Age of the Chartists, 1832–54*, Longmans, 1930.

R G Gammage, *History of Chartism*, Browne & Browne, 1894.

Mark Hovell, *The Chartist Movement*, ed T F Tout, Manchester University Press, 1966.

A Briggs, *Chartist Studies*, Macmillan, 1959.

Y V Kovalev, *Anthology of Chartist Literature*, Central Books, 1956.

F C Mather, *Public Order in the Age of the Chartists*, Manchester University Press, 1959.

Other books on Chartism include Cole's *Chartist Portraits*, and biographies of chartist leaders – Lovett, O'Connor, Jones and Harney.

The repeal of the Corn Laws:

N McCord, *The Anti-Corn Law League, 1838–46*, Allen & Unwin, 1958.

J Hobson, *Richard Cobden, The International Man*, T F Unwin, 1919.

G M Trevelyan, *Life of John Bright*, Constable, 1913.

Chapter 16

THE 'WOMAN QUESTION'

M Phillips and S Tomkinson, *English Women in Life and Letters*, Oxford University Press, 1927.

Alicia C Percival, *The English Miss, Today and Yesterday*, Harrap, 1939.

G M Cuddeford, *Woman and Society*, Hamish Hamilton, 1967. A good brief account of the progress of women through the ages.

Janet Dunbar, *The Early Victorian Woman*, Harrap, 1953.

The early days:

B Wardle, *Mary Wollstonecraft*, Richards Press, 1952.

Mary Wollstonecraft, *The Rights of Women*, Dent, 1929.

John Stuart Mill, *The Subjection of Woman*, Dent, 1965.

Books on the history of women's rights and other questions:

G. W. Johnson, *The Evolution of Woman*, Robert Holden, 1926.

R J Blackham, *Woman in Honour and Dishonour*, Sampson Low, 1936.

Georgiana Hill, *Women in English Life* (two vols), Bentley, London, 1896.

Charlotte M Stopes, *British Freewomen: Their Historical Privilege*, Swan Sonnenschein, 1894.

Ethel M Wood, *The Pilgrimage of Perseverance*, National Council of Social Service, 1949.

Lady Stenton, *The English Woman in History*, Allen & Unwin, 1957.

D L Hobman, *Go Spin, You Jade*, Watts, 1957.

David Staars, *The English Woman*, Smith Elder, 1909.

Nellie Alden Franz, *English Women and the Professions*, printed for the author, Cincinnati, 1965.

Maud I Crofts, *Women Under English Law*, Butterworth, 1928.

E Moberly Bell, *Storming the Citadel: The Rise of the Woman Doctor*, Constable, 1953.

The Franchise:

Ray Strachey, *The Cause*, G Bell, 1958.

Roger Fulford, *Votes For Women: The Story of a Struggle*, Faber, 1957.

Christabel Pankhurst, *Unshackled,* ed Ld. Pethick Lawrence, Hutchinson, 1959.

David Mitchell, *The Fighting Pankhursts*, Cape, 1967.

See also biographical lists for such names as Harriet Martineau, Florence Nightingale, Elizabeth Garrett Anderson, Josephine Butler, Caroline Norton, Barbara Bodichon, Elizabeth Fry, Lady Mary Wortley Montagu, etc.

Chapter 17

WAR AND PEACE

David Boulton, *Objection Overruled*, MacGibbon and Kee, 1967. The story of the conscientious objectors, 1914–19.

J Ferguson (ed), *Studies in Christian Social Commitment: A Christian Pacifist Symposium,* Independent Press, 1954.

Christopher Driver, *The Disarmers: A Study in Protest,* Hodder & Stoughton, 1964.
Peter Mayer (ed), *The Pacifist Conscience: An Anthology of Pacifist Writing,* Hart-Davis, 1966.
H Clavier, *The Duty and Right of Resistance According to the Bible and the Church,* Blackwell, Oxford, 1956.
W M Miller, *Non-Violence: A Christian Interpretation,* Allen & Unwin, 1964.
David Boulton (ed), *Voices From the Crowd Against the H-bomb,* Peter Owen, 1964.
E G Rupp, *Principalities and Powers: Studies in the Christian Conflict in History,* Epworth, 1952.
G F Nuttal, *Christian Pacifism in History,* Blackwell, 1958.

Chapter *18*

THE FRAGMENTATION OF PROTEST

B Magee, *The New Radicals,* Secker & Warburg, 1962.
S MacCoby, *English Radicalism, 1886–1914,* Allen & Unwin, 1953, and *English Radicalism, 1914–1959,* Allen & Unwin, 1961.
H Ausubel, *In Hard Times: Reformers Among the Late Victorians,* New York, 1960.
F Owen, *Tempestuous Journey: Lloyd George, His Life and Times,* Hutchinson, 1954.
R J Symons, *The General Strike: A Historical Portrait,* Cresset, 1957.
A M Potter, *Organised Groups in British National Politics,* Faber, 1961.
James Christoph, *Capital Punishment and British Politics,* Allen & Unwin, 1962.
Wal Hannington, *Ten Lean Years,* Gollancz, 1940.
Wal Hannington, *The Problem of the Distressed Areas,* Gollancz, 1937.
Jose Ortega y Gasset, *The Revolt of the Masses,* Allen & Unwin, 1961.

Index

315

317